During these times of turbulence, the management of change, and the role of leadership within this, is of crucial importance. This book has the strapline of authentic leadership-surely the only thing that will mobilize war-weary employees and organizations. It deals with the question of authenticity by lacing the book with pragmatic advice from senior leaders but linking these evident leadership skills to the complex problems that we all know sit beneath the challenge of leadership. A clear view of the ways in which leaders can work their way through the challenges they face inside their organizations.

Professor Paul Sparrow, Director, Centre for Performance-led HR, Lancaster University

The book genuinely fills a void. There are many practitioner based recipe books and articles, and at the other end of the spectrum academic research treatise on the subject. There are however relatively few options for those looking for an end to end text on the subject, moving from soft leadership skills, through process and on to evaluation. I can see potential for this book for executives leading change and for students of change on postgraduate programmes.

Professor Robert Galavan, Head of School, School of Business, National University of Ireland

In this important and timely book, Johan Coetsee and Patrick Flood provide a lucid, readable and unprejudiced account of what organisational leaders need to do make to change longstanding – to make it authentic! With great clarity, reason and empathy, the authors guide the reader through the complexity of authentic organizational leadership and change. A must read for managers and practitioners.

Professor Paul Teague, Queens University, Belfast

This book identifies how change can be managed in an authentic manner and in doing so promises huge benefits to organizations, leaders and managers at all levels, and to students of change overall.

Dr. Phillip Stiles, Judge Institute Cambridge

This book firmly endorses an authentic approach and the importance of self-knowledge and awareness in leading change.

Paul Neville, Managing Director, Data Displays Limited

About the Authors

Dr Johan Coetsee is an expert on leadership, change management and the evaluation of the effectiveness of interventions. He received his DPhil from the Rand Afrikaans University and his MBA from the University of Pretoria. He is an executive consultant with over 20 years of leadership and change management experience in private and public sectors. This includes organisations in manufacturing, healthcare, government and service industries located in South Africa, Ireland and the United Kingdom. Prior to joining academia, Johan was in senior management positions for 10 years. As a published author, he has significant experience in presenting at industry conferences, workshops and seminars. In his academic role he teaches on leading and managing change in senior executive programmes to a range of organizations.

Johan has proven results helping organisations improve their leadership and change capability. He has led the design, development and delivery of various cross-functional solutions and programmes to clients. Blending solid industry experience with a deep theoretical understanding of the dynamics of leadership and change, Johan creates unique methodologies enabling clients to implement sustainable solutions. His passion lies in working with organisations to ensure that through the use of customised models and approaches, employee commitment towards the change is enhanced and that they become ambassadors of the change.

Patrick Flood is Professor of Organizational Behaviour at Dublin City University Business School. He is an expert on leadership, change management and the impact of management practice on business performance. HR magazine has ranked Patrick #8 in the top ten 2012 Influential International Thinkers category.

He teaches on leading and managing change in senior executive programmes worldwide and has addressed many industry conferences. An alumnus of the London Business School International Teachers Programme (ITP-1998) he has won teaching awards for both MBA teaching. His previous book, Persuasive Leadership: Lessons from the Arts (with Professor Steve Carroll) was published by Josssey Bass in 2010. He currently holds visiting professorships and fellowships at Cambridge Judge Business School, Northeastern University, China and Capital University of Economics in Beijing. He has also worked at IMI, London Business School, University of Maryland and the AGSM.

His publications for managers include 14 books and monographs including, Change Lessons from the CEO (Josssey Bass, 2013); Persuasive Leadership: Lessons from the Arts (Josssey Bass, 2010), Leadership in Ireland (Blackhall, 2010); Strategy Implementation (Blackwell, 2000), Effective Top Management Teams (Blackhall, 2000) and Managing without Traditional Methods (Addison Wesley, 1996).

Change Lessons from the CEO

Real People, Real Change

Johan Coetsee
Patrick C. Flood

JB JOSSEY-BASS™
A Wiley Brand

This edition first published 2013

Under the Jossey-Bass imprint, Jossey-Bass, 989 Market Street, San Francisco CA 94103-1741, USA
www.josseybass.com

Registered office
John Wiley & Sons Ltd, The Atrium, Southern Gate, Chichester, West Sussex, PO19 8SQ, United Kingdom

For details of our global editorial offices, for customer services and for information about how to apply for permission to reuse the copyright material in this book please see our website at www.wiley.com.

Library of Congress Cataloging-in-Publication Data

A catalogue record for this book is available from the British Library.

ISBN 978-1-119-94314-3 (paperback) ISBN 978-1-118-74176-4 (ebk)
ISBN 978-1-118-74181-8 (ebk)

Cover design: Dan Jubb

Set in 9/13 pt Trump Mediäval LT Std by Toppan Best-set Premedia Limited

Printed in Great Britain by TJ International Ltd, Padstow, Cornwall

Thanks to my wife, Rene, for her love, support and encouragement. I also would like to include my children, Tiaan and Izanne: although separated by distance, you were never far from my heart!
Johan Coetsee

Dedicated with love and thanks to the change agents in my life including Patricia, Chris and Patrick Ellis; my mother, Catherine and my late father, Bartholomew.
Patrick Flood

Contents

Preface

Who is this Book for?

Our aim is to provide a book that offers senior managers, managers, change practitioners and students a user-friendly guide which highlights the latest approaches, issues and pitfalls of change management in a contemporary managerial environment.

Purpose of the Book

Between 60–70% of all organizational change efforts fail to meet their initial objectives or are unsuccessful. This is astounding given all the change models and textbooks we have at our disposal. Our inspiration to write this book comes from our combined 50 years of experience working with senior organizational leaders in the field of change management and leadership. This includes lecturing and working with MBA and Masters students on five continents. Each of them has taught us much about the process and experience of change. We thank them for their generosity of spirit.

Our book moves beyond the standard theoretical approaches toward managing change and provides an integrated perspective of relevant change theory and application of the theory in practice. Linking and integrating real-world CEO experiences with current theoretical perspectives of managing change, facilitates theoretical depth and insight into the complexities of managing change. It therefore addresses the most fundamental question in change management, that is, *how do I lead and implement change in the workplace in an authentic manner?*

Features

A unique feature of each chapter is that it is based on real Chief Executive Officers' (CEOs) experiences of leading change: the 'lived experience of change'. This approach not only contextualizes change but empowers the change leader to build his/her own model or approach to change. This is made possible by the carefully selected examples of change approaches used by CEOs, practical exercises and key lessons extracted from practice. This is illustrated in the example.

When leading change . . .

Authentic behaviour creates trust

Congruence between actions and words is crucial

You cannot declare yourself as authentic – it is ascribed to you by your followers

Being authentic means also a willingness to share your emotions

'I think it's very easy to say things but people will see you doing things, hear you saying things that they then will look at your body language, will look at what actions you then take, will look at your history and question whether, in their minds, it all adds up to genuineness and whether you really are a leader that does exactly what you say you're going to do and the minute you cross that line, and don't, I think people then question how authentic you are. I think – there's a great programme The Office *which I think is the classic of when people are sort of challenging authentic leaders because* The Office *is a great example of a leader who nobody believes is authentic, who has picked up all the right phrases to say, all the right ways of leading that you're meant to do, but in practice doesn't do it and doesn't believe it and you can see through that. So I think for me authentic leadership is about probably what comes from the heart, what you genuinely stand for and particularly when things are tough, whether you're true to everything you talk about and say is important to you. So I think it's very much about the emotions that you share, that you show, the vision that you have, the values that you have and then what people actually see you doing and then they will make judgements based on that.'*

We have ensured that the design of the book is engaging and interesting by including life experiences of CEOs, their perspectives on how to lead change successfully as well as the pitfalls to look out for. These perspectives are linked to theoretical perspectives and this makes leading and implementing change easy to understand.

How is this Book Organized?

The book is divided into seven chapters. Each chapter begins with an introduction that provides a brief overview of the chapter content. This is followed by beginning cases which create the context for each chapter. A typical chapter explores relevant theoretical concepts and this is explained through examples and lessons learned from practice. Several exercises are included in each chapter and these provide further opportunities for contextual application. The chapters are:

Chapter 1: Your journey to leading change authentically
Chapter 2: Change readiness: are you ready for leading change?
Chapter 3: Leading change: winning hearts and minds
Chapter 4: Getting employees ready for change
Chapter 5: Understanding how people change
Chapter 6: Coaching for change success
Chapter 7: Change politics and change levers

Acknowledgements

The writing of this book would not have been possible without the support of many people. We are particularly grateful to the 25 CEOs for dedicating their time and sharing their experiences with us. We would also like to express our gratitude to our university colleagues and the many people who saw us through this book, all those who provided support, read and offered comments. A big 'thank you' to Niall Saul, Professor Noel Whelan, John McMackin and Joanne James for their input and support.

CHAPTER 1

Your Journey to Leading Change Authentically

Chapter at a Glance

In this chapter you will learn the fundamentals of leading change in an authentic manner together with some self-assessments to enable you to gauge your capacity to do this right now. It further aims to give you an understanding of *what does it mean to be an authentic leader* and *leading change in an authentic manner?* This chapter, based on the real experiences of CEOs we interviewed, will illustrate the importance of aligning your values and beliefs with your actions when leading change. Real change starts with you – it stems from your willingness to own your weaknesses, confess your failures, and recognize that many life stories do not have a happy ending (Block, 1997). However, while many of our life stories are turbulent, we do not have to remain prisoners of our past. We have the power to influence our future and therefore can still create a bright and optimistic future for the people we lead through difficult times. Being authentic is a choice you have to make; nobody can do it for you. Leadership which is authentic is central to effective change leadership and the chapter consists of two major components. In the first part, authentic leadership is discussed and an opportunity is provided for you, the leader, to explore the influence of personal life events on your authenticity. In the second part of the chapter, authenticity is linked to leading change. Complete the various exercises in the chapter, as this will provide you with powerful personal insights that are needed for leading change in an authentic manner.

Beginning Cases: Preparation

What does it mean to be authentic? The following quotations provide some perspectives of authenticity in practice. It seems an understanding of *who you are* and the *willingness to be true to yourself*, irrespective of the context, manifests in behaviour that is experienced by others as genuine and worth emulating.

Be true to yourself

'Well when you're running a big business, there are times when you cannot be nice, there's times when you have to make very tough decisions, there's times when you have to be very hard and tough and that is all part of one's character. But you also know when to smile and you also need to have a little twinkle in your eye, you need to know how to manage people. But it's only when you're really your own man can you really be yourself because the moment you're having to please other people and think, am I going to get the promotion, am I now going to be able to move from this company to that company because I want them to recommend me, think I'm a nice person – no different than in your activity in a university, you don't want to go around being right or being confrontational by saying well that's not right and this and that . . . they'll say, well he's a difficult bloke we don't want to work with him. People used to think I was difficult – not difficult – people used to think I was very aggressive when I was younger – I was, so what?'

Be authentic

'Well the way I've always thought about authentic leadership is exactly what it says in the description, it's the authenticity of an individual and whether people really believe that what they see versus what they hear a leader saying they believe in and what they're going to do and how closely those two correlate.'

Understand who you are and why

'My mum probably is very important in that. She's not the only one but she's important at two different bits of my life because she and I had a very feisty, very argumentative relationship, not very comfortable, not very happy when I was very small, not very happy at all and she asked a lot of me, she asked me to be very adult very early on and the older I got the more I resented that. We were rather alike temperamentally, so quick to temper and yet like my father, I don't like being angry but my mum rather relished it. So I got caught between these two personality types that I wanted – what my father seemed to be able to model which was a rather calm existence, a patient existence but in fact I was very easily wound up. And I think that battle has been very instructive in how I try to conduct myself and the sort of places that I've wanted to work in, the sort of roles I've wanted to take on. But also she and my father were ambitious for me and there was certainly a sense that nothing was quite good enough which again, when I was much younger I resented hugely – I don't anymore. But I listened none-the-less, the sense that praise didn't come very easily. The interesting question was why you didn't do better – always. So that drives me too, it also can be debilitating sometimes but it drives me for sure, always asking could it have been done better, could I have done it better? And the reason I say – there's a lot in between of course – but my mum passed away when I was 33 which is nearly eight years ago and that time in my life was quite a difficult one professionally which I might say a bit more about in a second, but having actually a very powerful experience (she was ill for a year, very ill) and so I had this extraordinary – I think in a way almost fortunate experience of having a very close relationship with her in that time which wasn't something that I think my mum and I thought we would have in our lifetimes and whilst I wouldn't have wished it on her, I think I have a much happier memory of her than perhaps I would've had if things had been different. And so it was very powerful – in a way, getting to know her, I think that's what I'm

saying – getting to know her and getting to know myself through that relationship at a time when I was having quite a complex professional struggle. And then a great loss which is very – "levelling" might be the word I'd use, that although it's a bit of a cliché, it does actually put things in perspective and I think I am a happier, calmer (?) more strategic leader now and I think some of that is about losing my mum; that moment of crisis. The professional struggle at that time which I do think has shaped me before.'

Chapter Introduction

Some 500 years ago Machiavelli, in his book *The Prince*, highlighted problems we can expect when implementing change. He stated

> . . . there is no more delicate matter to take in hand, nor more dangerous to conduct, nor more doubtful in success, than to set up as a leader in the introduction of changes. For he who innovates will have for his enemies all those who are well off under the existing order of things, and only lukewarm supporters in those who might be better off under the new (Machiavelli, 1992).

This is still true today. It is estimated that between 70–80% of all change initiatives fail to reach their objectives or achieve only partial success, or in the worst-case scenario, make the situation worse. In fact, some managers are actually surprised that so many change initiatives are successful! Either way, there is a great deal of opportunity for improvement. It seems that, despite the numerous change models, approaches and methodologies available in the literature, leaders do not fully appreciate what is required in guiding their organizations through change. Putting it differently, leaders continue to lack a clear understanding of change, its antecedents, its processes or the ability to engage employees in change initiatives (Armenakis and Harris, 2002).

Organizational leaders are responsible for developing the change strategy, strategy implementation and monitoring. They also act as change agents in the organization. While the execution of organizational change must be well-managed, fundamentally it requires effective leadership. There is growing evidence that leadership characteristics and behaviours influence the success or failure of organizational change. But change leadership is more than a skill, more than the knowledge of change theories and requires more than just the effective use of cognitive abilities. It is the ability to act with purpose and ethically while constantly adjusting as the change situation requires. A successful change leader requires moral character, a strong concern for self, others and ethical values. Why is this important? As change leader you need to influence employees and they will only follow you if they trust you. This means you need to lead and act in a specific manner. George et al. (2007, p. 2) argue in this regard that,

> . . . the essence of leadership is not trying to emulate someone else, no matter how brilliant they are. Nor is it having the ideal leadership style, achieving competencies or fixing your weaknesses. In fact, you don't need power or titles to lead. You only have to be authentic.

This is also true for the leadership of change.

What is Authentic Leadership and What is it Not?

In order to understand 'what does it mean to lead change in an authentic manner?', the starting point is to understand what we mean by the term *authentic*. Authenticity, the idea of being oneself or being true to oneself has been described in many different ways and there is no agreed definition for authentic leadership. Indeed the terms vary across culture. In Israel the term *mensch* is used to describe a fully rounded 'juicy' person of integrity and goodness. Kernis (2003, p. 13) describes authenticity as 'the unobstructed operation of one's true, or core self in one's daily enterprise' consisting of four components: awareness, unbiased processing, authentic action and relational authenticity. Walumbwa et al. (2008, p. 94) building on this definition regard authentic leadership as,

> . . . a pattern of leader behaviour that draws upon and promotes both psychological capacities and a positive ethical climate, to foster greater self-awareness, an internalised moral perspective, balanced processing of information, relational transparency on the part of the leaders working with followers, fostering positive self development.

Despite the different ways the concept is described, it is possible to identify themes from the literature. Authenticity is to be informed by the 'true' self, authentic leaders demonstrate high levels of self-awareness, have clarity about personal values and convictions and the connection between authentic leadership and moral leadership, are highlighted (Ladkin and Taylor, 2010; Cooper, et al., 2005; Shamir and Eilam, 2005).

Therefore, the core of authenticity can be regarded as 'to know, accept, and remain true to oneself' (Avolio et al., 2004, p. 402) and authentic leaders are not only aware of their personal values but act accordingly. Organizational change is inherently chaotic and puts enormous pressure on the change leader. Having a clear understanding of what your values are all about and acting according to your values, provides you with guidelines on how to act and behave during organizational change. Defining authentic leadership and identifying antecedents for authentic leadership, Gardner et al. (2005a) and Avolio, et al. (2009) argue that key variables such as *self-awareness* (which include the leader's values, identity, emotions and goals) and *self-regulation* (which consists of balanced processing of information, internalized regulation, authentic behaviour and relational transparency) can be regarded as two important building blocks of authentic leadership. This means that authentic leaders are motivated from their values and convictions to act and are not obsessed or driven by prestige, status and organizational position. They are clear on what is important to them, how they feel and what their needs are. Putting it differently, change leaders who act in an authentic manner exhibit qualities such as honesty, integrity, credibility; they are straightforward and dependable. Our CEOs describe this as follows:

When leading change . . .
Authentic behaviour creates trust

Congruence between actions and words is crucial

You cannot declare yourself as authentic – It is ascribed to you by your followers

'I think it's very easy to say things but people will see you doing things, hear you saying things that they then will look at your body language, will look at what actions you then take, will look at your history and question whether, in their minds, it all adds up to genuineness and whether you really are a leader that does exactly what you say you're going to do and the minute you cross that line and don't, I think people then question how authentic you are. I think – there's a great programme, The Office, *which I think is the classic of when people are sort of challenging authentic leaders.* The Office *is a great example of a leader who nobody believes is authentic, who has picked up all the right phrases to say, all the right ways of leading that you're meant to do, but in practice doesn't do it and doesn't believe it and you can see through that. So I think for me, authentic leadership is about probably what comes from the heart, what you genuinely stand for and particularly when things are tough, whether you're true to everything you talk about. So I think it's very much about the emotions that you share, that you show, the*

vision that you have, the values that you have and then what people actually see you doing and then they will make judgements based on that.'

Being authentic means also a willingness to share your emotions

Be willing to be open and honest about the 'self'

Being authentic is being consistently genuine and true to yourself

Authentic behaviour leads to identification with the leader

Authentic leaders do not hide behind masks

'Authenticity for me – very simply – is you've got to be you. Don't be anybody else, therefore what that means is be prepared to self-disclose, be prepared to talk to people about your strengths, but absolutely in equal measure be very prepared to talk to people about your limitations and where you need their help because the more that you do that, as a leader, the more they will identify with you as a human being and the more they'll be likely to help you when they realize you're in trouble because you're in an area you know nothing about or that you're weak at. It also means only promising what you can deliver and not falling into the trap of over-promising – people hate that, they hate it. It means – for me, it means being utterly true to your own sense of purpose and belief and value. So I suppose the old beliefs and behaviours thing – if your behaviours, as a leader, are in sync with your beliefs as a person, you're going to be authentic and you can see my behaviours because they're manifest, but you can't see my beliefs. So it follows: If my beliefs are somewhere else and my behaviours are still what they are today I am a fraud and you'll probably be able to detect that even though you don't know what my particular belief sets are, it will become very clear to you because human beings are not stupid, unless I am the world's greatest actor, that my behaviour is not a reflection of my true beliefs and in that sense I am inauthentic and as an inauthentic leader I don't command any respect because you can't identify with me as a human being, you can't identify with me as somebody who would be a role model, for you to follow, if I don't set an example, you know I fail, on the rudimentary basics of being a leader. So for me, authenticity is critical and it's amazing to me, how many people get up in the morning with their partner or spouse or whatever and have breakfast with the family and they're themselves and they get in the car

or on the bus or the tube or whatever it is to go to work and they're all themselves and they get out of the car or off the bus or whatever and they come up to the front doors of the office and as they hit the front doors of the office they change and they start using language that they don't use at home and adopt a suddenly managerial tone of talking and think that they can get away with it! And of course everybody sees them for the sucker that they are. But they're there, they exist, they're all over the place, we see them all the time and they're not leaders, they're fakes.'

However, in an attempt to live up to organizational expectations and norms, managers do not always act authentically or act in accordance with their own values, that is, being able to be true to oneself. In some organizational contexts it may be dangerous to be yourself: perhaps in inauthentic organizations. However, too many managers believe that the road to success needs to be hidden in deception and they wear a mask of inauthenticity. This façade is used to manipulate and they are hardly ever able to reveal the true self. Exploring the dark side of leadership, Kets de Vries (1993) argues that narcissistic leaders need power, prestige, drama and enjoy the manipulation of others. He describes narcissistic leaders as follows: 'They do not tolerate criticism, are reluctant to exhibit give and take behaviour and surround themselves with sycophants' (p. 46). Some leaders are unable to express emotion and lack the ability to empathize, encourage creativity and respond appropriately to conflict. Palmer (1994, pp. 25–26) argues in this regard that,

> . . . a leader must take special responsibility for what is going inside his or her own self, inside his or her consciousness, lest the act of leadership create more harm than good . . . I suggest that the challenge is to examine our consciousness for those ways in which we leaders may project more shadow than light . . . The problem is that people rise to leadership in our society by a tendency towards extraversion, which too often means ignoring what's going on inside themselves.

George, et al. (2007, p. 1) summarize the characteristics of authentic leaders as follows:

Passion
Value-driven

Authentic leaders demonstrate a passion for their purpose, practice their values consistently, and lead with their hearts as well as their heads. They

Meaningful relationships Results establish long-term, meaningful relationships and have the self-discipline to get results. They know who they are.

Leaders need to explore their inner world and must be able to look inside themselves. This is important as who we are (and how much we understand about ourselves) determines how we lead change. You cannot become authentic by imitating someone else – you have to be yourself. Understanding and developing this capacity is important to successful leading change. However, authenticity is not defined by you; that is, 'I am authentic', but it is defined by what other people see in you. Putting it differently, *it is a quality that others must attribute to you*. Expressing and demonstrating your authentic self is a choice that you have to make (Goffee and Jones, 2000; 2007; Nicholson, 2013) and these authors ask a very pertinent question: *Why should anyone want to be led by you?* What does it take to lead change effectively, to engage people and revive their commitment to organizational change? The starting point on the journey of becoming a great leader is the expression of the authentic self and in the next section this will be explored in more detail. Dee Hock, founder of Visa put it like this:

Leadership starts with you *'Control is not leadership; management is not leadership; leadership is leadership. If you seek to lead, invest at least 50% of your time in leading yourself – your own purpose, ethics, principles, motivation, conduct. Invest at least 20% leading those with authority over you and 15% leading your peers.'*

Becoming Authentic

The question then becomes, *are authentic leaders born or raised*? From previous research on how people can become and remain authentic, it seems that 'an individual does not have to born with any universal characteristics or traits' (George et al., 2007, p. 1), but it is possible to discover your potential and develop authentic leadership. Authentic leaders are defined by their unique life stories, and the way they frame and understand those life stories to discover their passions and the purpose of their leadership. Authentic leaders display different type of behaviours and in the next section this is discussed in more detail.

Understanding and making sense of the past

The personal history of the leader, that is, family, role models, early life challenges, educational and work experiences, can be regarded as key trigger events which shape the individual in that they 'constitute dramatic and sometimes subtle changes in the individual's circumstances that facilitate personal growth and development' (Gardner et al., 2005b, p. 347). It is these *significant events* (e.g. personal struggles; extreme challenges; failures; triumphs; people) and how they made sense of these experiences *that have shaped them as leaders*. These significant events can take many forms and influence how we view and lead change. The loss of one or both parents or adversity associated with family poverty has a formative influence on (1) how change is viewed, (2) the capacity to lead, and (3) how change is managed. Fundamental life goals are formed by these experiences. The key to understanding the relevance and impact of the past is finding answers to two fundamental questions: what is going on here? and, what do I do next? (Weick et al., 2005). Some of these group sensing skills are learned at a very early age in either the family or amongst peer groups of friends. The role of early life challenges and making sense of these events can be explained as follows:

Awareness of challenge

'My own upbringing got a rude shock when I went into the Military. There, I learnt to do what I was told, to start off with, but about two-thirds of the way through it I became aware of my political side and I became aware that everything that I'd been fighting for was flawed – deeply flawed, and that's not a great place for a soldier to be. It's not a great place for a leader to be and I was a leader in the

Sense-making of the situation

National Service, even though it was only a small stick or platoon of troops, it was nevertheless a position of leadership but a position of leadership in a war environment. When you have deep concerns about what the hell you're doing, I just thought this is nonsense, the vision that I'm fighting for is madness, it's never going to work – ever – EVER. So what the hell are we going to do about that? But I'm just one tiny little cog, so what do you do if you don't believe in the strategy of the company? If you don't believe in the strategy of the organization? You've got to get out. But I think that experience and my incredulity at the fact that my parents – who of course until then I had loved unquestioningly – clearly endorsed the wrong that was the white minority regime, was a massive problem for me,

Taking action

personally, at the time. So all of a sudden all of my benchmarks of solidity were shattered. So, my parents were wrong, I was right but I was on my own and I had to get out and so I came to Europe as a pretty vulnerable, mixed up but very resilient – I mean I had to be, to get through that – young man.'

The experiences of the military leader provide a set of circumstances, that is, his leadership role in a military context and his disillusionment with the purpose and objectives of the war he was involved in. This highlights a process in which Weick et al. (2005) suggested that sense-making starts with noticing and bracketing; that is, inventing new meaning as well as labelling ('everything that I'd been fighting for was flawed'). Making sense of the past also has an action component: *what do I do next?*, that is, choosing and commitment to act, developing the commitment to act. Sense-making therefore involves placing the life experience into a framework, deriving new self-relevant information from social experiences and imposing meaning on the information to inform one's understanding (Roberts, et al., 2005, p. 716). It is through life stories or self-narratives that the leader achieves self-concept clarity. It provides him or her with a meaning system 'from which to feel, think and act' (Shamir and Eilam, 2005, p. 402) and provide answers to questions such as, *how and why have I become a leader?*; making sense of the past and present. Two other processes can be used in the sense-making process: reflection and feedback. *Reflection* can be regarded as the process of analysing, reconsidering and questioning experiences within a broad context of issues (Murray and Kujundzic, 2005). This means we ask ourselves questions around strategic direction and relationships, for example: (1) Are we pursuing the right strategy before we implement it? (2) Do we relate well enough to each other to effectively co-ordinate our actions for goal achievement? An example of reflection is as follows:

Reflection	*'So I've spent a lot of time understanding what happened – what's happened in my career that shaped the person that I am and why I do things the way that I do.'*
Reflexive assessment	*'Constantly saying "Hang on, are we going in the right direction, let's just reassess, let's revalidate, let's reflect, let's bear in mind what's going on outside ourselves" and let's bring that knowledge back in and inform our behaviour as leaders.'*

It involves challenging our own assumptions; thinking in such a manner that it challenges our beliefs, values and our way of seeing reality in order to assess their impact on our lives. A further process used in synthesis and making sense of history and trigger events is the use of feedback. Such feedback often has to be elicited to create self-awareness. The following narrative explains how feedback can be used as a sense-making tool:

Use measuring instruments to obtain feedback

Engage in dialogue about your strengths and weaknesses

Be open and honest in receiving feedback

Do not be defensive

'We are rigorous with 360°s and one-to-ones and feedback sessions and we use those as tools to ensure that we have the right dialogue, so I will always have brutal open dialogue with my people about my leadership style, their leadership style, how we're working together, areas where I can improve. And, everyone is flawed – everyone is flawed, we're all making mistakes all the time and so a massive part of the job of being a leader is to be self-aware enough to know when something's not quite right and then to seek guidance and counsel as to what it is that may be wrong behaviourally and then to act on it. But you can't do it without dialogue, you've got to have the tough conversations, the open, honest, mutually respectful conversations with your people because if they're frightened of you or if they think you're an idiot, you're not going to get those conversations but if you've got the balance right, if they do get inspired by you – in fact, if they get inspired by you, and then that very same person is asking them for advice that's doubly inspirational because you think 'Wow! Somebody who I'm inspired by is actually asking me for help and advice.' So it actually works – it's a double whammy if you like. So we identify – or I identify – my development needs through a mix of using tools like the 360° but overwhelmingly more importantly, through dialogue, through deep-rooted, open, honest, transparent dialogue. That's how you find out how you're doing.'

Getting *feedback*, as many of the CEOs interviewed have done, is an important mechanism that can be used in the sense-making process as it assists in understanding your own strengths and possible areas for improvement as well as identifying actions. The story about 360 also emphasizes the use of helping relationships, that is, being open and trusting about problems, and sharing them with subordinates. This also highlights the fact that sense-making does not take place in isolation but various social factors, for example dialogue and communication, assist in the sense-making process. What is important is that the leader must not deny or distort or ignore feedback but uses the feedback to understand the relevance and importance of events. Leaders who do not encourage and support feedback during the change process weaken their positions considerably. Mechanisms to elicit feedback include asking employees how the change is going using 'barometer surveys' to gauge reactions; observation; and establishing 'ginger groups'. A *ginger group* is a representative cross-sectional group of employees who provide feedback on the plan itself, its communication and its implementation. This may allow groups who are not part of the executive team to input in important ways and it is a way to respect the minority voice in the organization.

The quotations that follow highlight specific trigger events and express the storytellers' identities, 'which are products of the relationship between life-stories and the organized stories of these experiences' (Shamir and Eilam, 2005, p. 402). Gardner et al. (2005a) suggest that trigger events serve as positive forces in developing leader self-awareness. It seems that it is predominantly significant life events (in contrast with routine life experiences) that trigger changes in the self-knowledge structures of leaders. Roberts, et al. (2005) suggest in this regard that revisions in self-knowledge structures occur when 'individuals undergo an "aha" experience or jolt – a discrepant or surprising event that causes people to pause and reflect on their experience' (p. 716). It is not only the positive experiences that we can learn from but also from our negative life experiences or life events. These 'crucibles' of leadership, a transformative experience which forces you to examine your values, question assumptions and your purpose (Bennis and Thomas, 2002), and your ability to overcome adversity, distinguishes good from extraordinary leaders. A crucible refers to the vessel in which alchemists, during medieval times, attempted to turn base metals into gold. In other words, a crucible is a transformational experience which toughens and changes people and gives them a new sense of identity, motivation and purpose. A crucible is not the same as a life stage or transition, like moving from adolescence to adulthood, but is more like a test that corners individuals and forces them to answer questions about who they are and what is really important to them. It can be explained as follows:

Example of a crucible

'I'm one of seven children and my parents were divorced when I was 11. Both of my parents were alcoholics, my mother from the age of seven was prescription drug dependent and she was drug dependent until she died. She had two nervous breakdowns after my father left and she was in and out of mental hospitals. My – I'm the third in the seven – my two elder sisters left home as soon as they possibly could, they both left at the age of 16.

Sense-making of the situation

Assuming responsibility in the family

At the age of 14, I was the mother to my four younger sisters and brothers because my mother just wasn't capable of looking after us. We lived on benefits and we – I cannot remember my teenage years being anything other than daily struggle. That's not an exaggeration, some days you got home from school and there was nothing to eat and you had to try and pacify four younger children who weren't going to get any tea before they went to bed. So that's what it was like and what that did – well there was a number of things that did for me – I am hugely independent and one of the things that I've had to deal with whilst being in this role is making sure I have a coach and a mentor myself. I needed a support structure because I couldn't do what I needed to do without it, but I very, very rarely asked for help. In fact I never asked for help before I came into this job because I'm hugely independent because I had to make sure that my brothers and sisters were OK, they were all looking to me to make sure they were OK. So I couldn't fall apart because I had a mother that was falling apart and I had a father that wasn't there so I was 'it.' So that sort of shapes your – well, definitely shaped my approach to life and change. The other thing it did was drive me to ensure that I was never ever, ever in that situation again.'

Learning to make decisions without support structures

Resolving never to be in such a situation again . . . ever

Understanding or making sense of your history and meaningful moments of your life is a key building block on the journey of becoming an authentic leader. The following exercise will assist you in this regard:

The first step in becoming authentic is by constructing and understanding your life story. Life stories provide you with a meaning system from which you can act authentically, i.e. interpret reality and act in a way that gives your interpretations and actions personal meaning (Kegan, 1983, p. 220).

Constructing your life story

Think of your life as it were a novel. Divide your life novel into the following chapters:
Chapter 1: Early childhood (6–12 years)
Chapter 2: Adolescence (13–18 years)

Chapter 3: Young adulthood (19–35)
Chapter 4: Middle adulthood (36–55)
Chapter 5: Late adulthood (56+)

For each chapter identify and describe critical events in your life – incidences/challenges/key turning points in your life; disappointments; 'crucibles'. Also describe the feelings you experienced, the people involved or who impacted on your life. (The analysis of your life story will take place in a later exercise.)

Being self-aware

Self-awareness refers to the extent the leader understands his/her own strengths, weaknesses, motives, how they are perceived by their followers and know what is important to them. Self-awareness refers to the extent to which the leader is aware of various aspects of the self and 'to which their self-perceptions are internally integrated and congruent with the ways others perceive them' (Klenke, 2007, p. 78). Sense-making can be regarded as the precursor to achieve self-awareness and it is through the use of different sense making processes that the leader gains insight and understanding of his/her values, identity, and emotions (Kernis, 2003). Avolio and Gardner (2005) as well as Walumbwa et al. (2008) argue in this regard that the starting point of authentic leadership is self-awareness which implies that a leader knows what he or she regards as important (May et al., 2003). Learning from the past can be explained as follows:

Self-awareness move beyond surface level thinking

'And I think it taught me resilience. So frankly, after the horror of the war that I fought in, like any war, business issues are a walk in the park. I mean you know, stuff that goes wrong is just easy in comparison, you know, it's not life and death and people take themselves far too seriously in business I always find. And I think that's been a rock for me to depend on, that history.'

Self-awareness is making sense of events and interpreting your circumstances

'I learnt that I shouldn't be ashamed or embarrassed about the things that I'm good at and I also shouldn't stress too much over the things that I'm not very good at. Perfection is one of my weaknesses and I continually strive for the perfect solution to

everything and actually you know, if it's 80% good enough, it's good enough but I beat myself up – I go home – and I say this to my team now – I go home some days and I stand in front of the bathroom mirror and I say "that was crap, you did a crap job today, you did this and you said this and that was completely and utterly the wrong thing to do, you stupid woman." And I do that, I am my biggest critic of myself and what that tends to do is, it overshadows the things that I'm damn good at and what I think I've learnt in previous roles.'

Self-awareness is obtained through self-observation and reflection

'You've got to have that belief in yourself, I mean I'm right but you know, at my age, I don't have to worry whether I'm right or whether I'm wrong because I'm quite contented with my life, I've been through all the problems, I've been through more nonsense than 99.9% of people that would've – survived, built an empire, nearly lost it, lost a fortune, hanging over the side of the cliff with my fingernails and fighting back and building another empire.'

Self-awareness can be regarded not as an end in itself but a continuous process where the leader develops self-knowledge through understanding the meaning of their life-stories. Shamir and Eilam (2005, p. 402) state in this regard 'this creates self-concept clarity because it organises life-events into gestalt structures that establishes connections between those events so that the person's life is experienced as a coherent unfolding process'. Self-awareness helps a leader to understand his/her unique capabilities, knowledge and experiences and is achieved through self-reflection and feedback. It is through self-awareness that a leader understands their own biases, mental models and the impact these may have on their ability to lead change effectively.

Understanding your values

Values are learned through socialization processes, are formed by life experiences, are internalized and then become key components of the self (Gardner et al., 2005a). The importance of values is highlighted by authors such as Allport (1955) and Swartz (1994) and it is argued that values 'direct behaviour, serve as standards and once internalised, become an integral part of the self' (Gardner et al., 2005, p. 350b). A key dimension of authentic leadership is a clear understanding of one's values, and is regarded as a prerequisite for authenticity and authentic leadership (George, 2003). This can be explained as follows:

There needs to be congruence between organizational and individual level values

Demonstrate your values through behaviours

Early life-experiences, parents, role models play an important role in value formation

'Well we have our values at Organization X and of course when I was being selected to come as a Chief Executive of Organization X from outside the business, one of the most important things was to ensure that my own values were very aligned to "Organization X" values because if there was a misalignment there I think it would cause real problems; to have a Chief Exec whose values were different from the values of the company. If you go through the Organization X values, it's about being enthusiastic and supportive in everything that we do – well that's very much how I think I am as an individual, it is very much about treating everyone with consideration and respect which are very much the values I was taught probably as a child by my parents. That what was expected of me as an individual and of everyone in society; that you should treat people with consideration and respect no matter who they were. And then the last one I suppose is about being open and honest and that is very much me, sometimes I would say possibly to a fault, I'll always be open and honest and – except that sometimes it doesn't make it an easy path for you to follow if you're being open and honest when you're being asked your views about things or when you need to give your view about things. So those values that I've just described are what would be written down that you would see written down for Organization X and I think they're very much the values that I would have. I suppose I'm very much someone who – the values that I was taught to stick up for the underdog, to stick up for those who can't really fend for themselves. I come very much from a working class background where, you know, times were tough when I was growing up, there wasn't a lot of money around and therefore I think you were taught the value of anything from clothing to treats to food on the table that, you know, you mustn't really take too much for granted in life because you never know when you're

personally not going to have much. So I think they're quite deep rooted ingrained values around respecting others, appreciating what you have and trying to do as much as you can to help those who are in a less fortunate position than you.'

Values develop through social interactions with role models for example parents, are learned and may result from personal introspection and reflection. The core characteristic of authenticity can be regarded as 'to know, accept, and remain true to oneself' (Avolio et al., 2004, p. 402) or as Shakespeare puts it 'This above all: to thine own self be true, And it must follow, as the night the day, Thou canst not then be false to any man'. Authentic leaders are not only aware of their personal values (Avolio et al., 2004) but act accordingly (Ilies, et al., 2005). Values guide behaviour and the following serve as examples in this regard:

Understanding your own values takes a conscious effort on your part

'So I understand now what my values are and why they are that, why they are as strong as they are, because I've gone through this period of understanding of why I do things and why I think in certain ways and why I believe in certain things and not others. I wouldn't have had that understanding if I hadn't invested the time in understanding myself.'

Act according to your own values system – irrespective of the circumstances

'I'm a very straightforward honest person; what you see is that you get. That appeals to some people; it's not quite the English psyche because English people are very good sometimes at putting a smile on their face and not telling you what they really think. I tell you exactly what I think, if I don't like it, I'll tell you. I believe in what I believe in, I don't affiliate myself politically with different parties, I'm happy to work with all good politicians, whether they're left, right or centre, providing they're good people and sincere and what I think they're doing is good for the country and that's where I sit. So different leaders of different political parties ask my opinion on things from time to time – am I flattered about it? I'm one of the few people who'll give them a straight answer and if they don't want my opinion, don't ask me, it's quite simple but you know, I'm not here to be a sycophant, I'm not looking, either, to make too many new friends in my life.'

Authentic leaders are specific and clear about their personal values, understand how their values influence their behaviour and live their life according to these understood values (Ilies, et al., 2005). Not only is it important for the leader to act according to his/her own values and be authentic in their interaction with others, but the leader should also be resistant to social or situational pressures and not compromise those values. The following exercise will help you to identify and articulate your values:

	My core values . . .
What are your values?	What in life is most important to me? From the things you liked, can you identify any core principles or values? What are your Top 5 values and when did they become important to you? How do your values influence your behaviour? (Examples of values: dependable; reliable; loyal; committed; open-minded consistent; honest; efficient; innovative; creative; humorous; motivated; positive; optimistic; inspiring; passionate; respectful.)

It is relatively easy to live according to your values when things are going well. The test, however, is the ability to act according to your values when you are under pressure. Martin Luther King summarized this succinctly by stating: 'the ultimate measure of a man is not where he stands in moments of comfort and convenience, but where he stands at times of challenge and controversy.' A core set of values enable you to develop leadership principles, that is, values translated into action. Principles are guidelines and act as a compass to help us determine how to act in certain circumstances. Authentic leadership theory proposes that the authentic leader's values guide his/her behaviour, possesses self-knowledge which reflects clarity about their personal values and convictions and are able to resist social pressure (Shamir and Eilam, 2005). Look at the following example:

Have a clear understanding of what your values are

'I think the first thing is to be aware when a decision is actually really starting to test your values. It's when – I think there's almost a gut instinct that maybe something you are being tempted to make a decision on is not really in keeping with what you've previously said about your values and what you stand for and what the company stands for. So it's almost – I don't know, I think again if you can listen

Do not be afraid to articulate your values

Use dialogue to gain situational clarity

Walk-the-talk

to the signals that you tend to produce as a human being, that this doesn't quite feel right, probably that's when you're starting to get into uncomfortable territory. I find that it's helpful to almost voice that and let people know that that's the dilemma that you're facing, to openly say this is a difficult decision because it's really challenging my values, the values of the business and I want to remain true to the values but I'm finding the decision quite difficult for these reasons. And I think almost by airing it, you can start to get other people to engage in the same dilemma and debate and almost become more supportive, to help find a solution that still allows you to make the decision that needs to be made but not lose your values. And I think sometimes it's about courage, to say that you're being true to your values and if those values are going to mean anything, if they're really going to be worth anything, then you will be judged on that, not by what you say but by what you do and to remind yourself that that's how people will judge you as a leader. Everyone can say fine words about their values but people judge whether you're true to those values or not by what you're then seen to do. So I think there's a need for consideration, thought, engagement of other people into the debate, potentially that dilemma that you're facing and then lots of communication afterwards to explain to people that this was the decision-making process that you went through, but to remain true to your values this is the decision that you've taken and to say to people in line with my values this is the decision that I've taken.'

Having a clear understanding of what your values are, knowing how your values influence your behaviour and a willingness to stick to your values are key components of becoming authentic. This also implies a willingness to take personal risks, articulating your values in hostile situations and environments.

Understanding and accepting who you are

Leader identity can be viewed as the knowledge a person has about him or herself and assists in organizing and give meaning to behaviour. Day and Sin

(2011) argue that identity integrates various elements of the self-concept and 'it helps to ground individuals in terms of who they are, what their major goals and aspirations are and what their personal strengths and challenges are'. A clear understanding of who am I?; that is, having self-concept clarity, may also lead to the experience of feelings of self-liking and self-acceptance (Kernis, 2003) as well as a positive perception of their ability to perform across a range of situations (Judge et al., 1998). Authentic leaders are not only clear on who they are but accept themselves with their strengths and weaknesses. Kernis (2003, p. 3) argues in this regard that these individuals 'are people who like, value and accept themselves, imperfections and all'. Look at the following examples:

Understand what is important to you

You do not always need to live up to expectations of others

Accept yourself with your strengths and weaknesses

'There are things that – actually there are things that I used to do that I have stopped doing; I used to apologize a lot for being regularly two or three minutes late which I wish I didn't do but I used to devote hours apologizing about it and I used to devote similar numbers of hours apologizing for being quite a chaotic person in relation to paper – hopeless! Hopeless with paper – my desk is covered in bits of paper and I cannot – I've never been very good at filing things because I think they all have a completely separate identity, I don't want to put them together because they don't really quite belong together. And I used to waste a lot of time feeling I was failing by not having a tidy desk and therefore demonstrating a tidy mind or whatever I thought I was doing and I would apologise for that and I've stopped it, and I stopped after the leadership programme. I think which was yes one thing that really dropped in for me which was yes, I can try harder to be a better completer/finisher, a better filing clerk, be on time and I do and I will continue to and it works sometimes but it's important that I'm me and I am better at starting things and I am being creative when I'm juggling 18 different bits of paper and I need to put structures in place that support that.'

Believe in yourself and your own abilities

'. . . so I've stopped worrying about that, I've got more confidence in myself that I know enough about what to do and how to get the best out of people and how to motivate people to think that I can make a

Make peace with your inner self

reasonable fist at most things. But it's only when you're really your own man can you really be yourself because the moment you're having to please other people and think am I going to get the promotion, am I now going to be able to move from this company to that company so I'm not going to piss anybody off along the way because I want them to recommend me, think I'm a nice person – no different than in your activity in a university, you don't want to go around being right but being confrontational by saying well that's not right and this and that . . . they'll say well he's a difficult bloke we don't want to – people used to think I was difficult – not difficult – people used to think I was very aggressive when I was younger – I was, so what? But you know, you are what you are! And I am what I am!'

Leaders who are able to make sense of their history and trigger events are also able to achieve high levels of self-awareness (i.e. understanding their values and motives) and these formed key building blocks in the formation of the leader identity. It is therefore the ability to learn and find meaning, not only from positive events but also from negative life events that shape us, inspire us and teach us to lead (Bennis and Thomas, 2002). Leaders who have a clear sense of their self may strive for open and truthful relationships with others (Spitzmuller and Ilies, 2010) and are willing to reveal personal information about themselves (Avolio and Gardner, 2005). This also means the leader accepts his/her strengths and weaknesses and is open and willing to share information. Regarding openness in interpersonal relationships, some leaders emphasized the following:

Be human – humans are allowed to make mistakes, feeling uncertain and inadequate

You do not need to have answers to all problems

'Be prepared to self-disclose, be prepared to talk to people about your strengths, but absolutely in equal measure be very prepared to talk to people about your limitations and where you need their help because the more that you do that, as a leader, the more they will identify with you as a human being and the more they'll be likely to help you when they realize you're in trouble because you're in an area you know nothing about or that you're weak at.'

Do not be afraid to ask for help

'I said because I have to ensure that I'm not frightened to ask for help and I'm not fearful of saying

"actually I don't know", or "could you support me in this, this and this?"'

The willingness of leaders to communicate personal learning and insights about themselves are very important, as these make followers aware of the leader's core values and beliefs. Many managers feel uncomfortable sharing personal emotions with others in the workplace. Traditionally it was frowned upon to express and demonstrate emotions in the workplace. An important component of organizational change is how employees experience change, that is, it is about feelings and emotions. The starting point in helping employees dealing with their emotions and feelings is the ability to understand and manage our own emotions. Making sense of your life story will help you to understand how your life events have shaped you as a leader and provide a better understanding of your behaviour in your interaction with others.

Making sense of your life story

Reflecting on the chapters of your life novel, answer the following questions:

What life themes/messages can you extract from the different chapters?

What are the five most important things you have learned about your life; how did you overcome the crucibles or transformative experiences in your life?

How did it shape you as the person who you are?

What are your values and how did your life experience help you to develop these values?

How did your life experiences shape you as a leader or putting it differently, how have your experiences inspired you, shaped you and taught you to lead?

What drives you?

To what extent was it possible for you to act according to your own values and be authentic in your interaction with others?

Do you need to do certain things differently? If so, what are they and how are you going to do it?

Strategies for becoming more authentic

Despite all the information available to improve leadership, for example self-help guides, books on self-improvement and so on, no quick fixes or recipes exist. Becoming more authentic is about a choice that you make – you need to choose to be you! The following narrative explains this 'personal choice' in more detail:

Making a choice to become authentic is the first step on the authentic journey

You have the power to make the choice

Are you willing to take personal risk?

How will you know if you act in an authentic manner?

'You know, you have to make a positive choice. No one else can do it except them, in other words, there's no rule book to follow, because everyone, by definition, is different, they are who they are. So it's about choice – you have to choose. I choose to be me and I'm fine with it. It's a bit like saying "I'm an alcoholic", and coming out with it at an AA meeting. You have to choose to be you. I'm OK with being me, me is fine, me is great, me is also not great in certain areas but I'm happy to talk about it. But it's a positive choice and I can encourage people to do that but ultimately it is their choice and if they choose not to, then, that's their choice, fine. But every single one of us has that choice and we have the power to choose to be ourselves. The great thing about being yourself of course is that you can't actually be dishonest then, it's marvellously secure, it's a bit like always telling the truth, it's a great place to be because you can never make a mistake, whereas if your leadership style is full of falsehoods and manipulations and misrepresentations, then I mean you're dead, because you just can't possibly remember by the time you get to my age what you said when to whom. I mean it's just hopeless. So it's just easier, just tell the truth, just be who you are, it's the easiest thing in the world then, you can't go wrong and people recognise that and people follow you more, people will be more loyal and they'll help you when you're down and they'll applaud you when you're up. So I think everybody – any CEO who's wondering how to be more authentic has got a real problem and whether they are a CEO or not, it should be the question because you just can't be a leader today without being authentic I don't think. It's a disaster. Certainly in our world – we see plenty of inauthentic leaders in other companies and that makes us pleased to be where we are because – I mean I couldn't bear to work for an inauthentic leader, it just wouldn't work for me at all and – it's vital.'

Becoming authentic is a journey you embark on and although there are no recipes, we can learn from authentic leaders in practice. It seems that not only do you have to make choices, that is, becoming more authentic, but you also need to understand and make sense of your life-story. It also involves a willingness to take personal risks and experimenting with behaviour in different contexts. The involvement of significant others, the creation of support structures and a willingness to invest resources in your own development are highlighted as helpful mechanisms in becoming more authentic. It also seems that (1) core values act as a compass that provides guidance in the development process and (2) you need to have confidence and a belief in yourself that you are able to change. Lastly, the importance of creating a work-life balance is emphasized and time for personal reflection is created. The following discussion explains these strategies in more detail:

Draw your life-line and make sense of your life-story

Becoming authentic is a journey

Be willing to experiment with behaviours

'Know themselves, look at – not examine – your history and what makes you the person that you are and you know, I'd never done the life chart before and when I drew it, it was like "Oh my God", you know, it wasn't this sort of soft undulating little curve it was this huge peaks and troughs, huge, like icicles, it was weird. And that was a revelation for me, it really was a revelation for me and – but try not to overanalyse it because I think if you do, you can become very introverted and also very risk averse. You don't want to get to a point where you're questioning all your decisions and all your actions and thinking "Oh my God," you know, "does that look authentic or doesn't it? Does it look like a transactional leader or a transformational leader?" If you get to that point – and believe me, I know some people like that! You've lost the plot if you get to that point, so I would just say know yourself and don't be too hard on yourself because you will make mistakes, you will, and I've made loads of them, loads of them, fortunately not many that have been catastrophic! I think if I had to play this over again, if I had to play this out again I'd be much easier on myself, I wouldn't continually strive for the perfection because the 10% gain that you get with a 90% time investment just isn't worth it.'

Have confidence in your own ability

'Have confidence in your ability, celebrate your successes, don't be too hard on yourself, don't drive for

	perfection, get support, put at least a coaching provi-
Create and make use of support structures	*sion in place for yourself, especially when you're first new in a Chief Exec job, always have an eye to the future and the long term, put yourself at the bottom of the inverted triangle; you're there to support the rest of the organization and the rest of the organization isn't there to support you. Be humble, be*
Use your values as a guiding compass	*guided by your values because usually they're right, usually people don't make it to a Chief Exec position unless they've got strong values and determination.*
Invest in your own development	*Invest – invest in your leadership skill and hone it as much as you possibly can. Try to get some work life balance – says she who doesn't have any work-*
Create work-life balance	*life balance at all! And create space to think, because your day can just get crowded out with stuff and you need space to think, because if you're not thinking, you can be damn sure the rest of the organization*
Create space for reflection	*isn't either! And they need you to think – if you're the Chief Exec they need you to be thinking things through.'*

Leading Change Authentically

From the previous discussion it should be clear that successful leadership is not about emulating somebody else but leading in a way that is aligned with you as a person. This means your leadership style needs to be consistent with your values and your personality and this should be evident in you behaviours. Making sense of 'who you are' also implies that you need to have a clear sense of purpose and in this regard George (2003, p. 2) highlights the following: '. . . it is essential that you first answer the question, leadership for what purpose? If you lack purpose and direction in leading, why should anyone follow you?' Complete the following exercise:

Leadership for what purpose?	What three or four words would describe you as a leader? What is your leadership purpose? What motivates you to lead? What are you passionate about?

Authentic leaders have a clear understanding of who they are, what their motivations and passions are, lead with purpose and demonstrate behaviours that are aligned with their values. They understand their strengths and weaknesses, are consistent in their interaction with others and lead with their heads as well as their hearts (George et al., 2007, p. 130). Integrating the different authentic leadership perspectives from authors such as Ilies et al. (2005); Avolio and Gardner (2005); Gardner et al. (2005) and George et al. (2007), we can make the following linkages between authentic leadership and leading organizational change (Table 1).

From Table 1 it should be clear that being authentic in leading change is beneficial as it influences followers in a positive way. Shamir and Eilam (2005) state in this regard that if a leader's behaviour is consistent and aligned with his/her values and beliefs, followers develop trust in the leader. This is possible because the leader provides behavioural cues that followers use to construct and interpret events and this guides their behaviour. Putting it differently, if the change leader establishes alignment between values and actions, he/she will say what they mean and mean what they say. Trustworthiness is therefore inferred by displaying characteristics such as fairness, dependability, integrity and honesty and this can affect work attitudes and behaviours. Authentic change leaders also

Table 1 Linkages between authentic leadership and change

Authentic leadership characteristics	Influence on the change process or change recipients
A high level of self-awareness may lead to an understanding of personal biases and a good understanding of they are perceived by others	The way we implement and lead change is influenced by our own mental models. If we understand how our mental models influence our thoughts and behaviours we can be 'aware' of how our mental models impact on the change process. This is also true for the way we interact with others. Understanding the impact we have on others will enable us to be sensitive to how people act and react in the change process.
Authentic leaders do not distort, exaggerate or ignore information and pay equal attention to positive and negative information The leader is open to feedback and allows for openness and honesty in conversations	Being open to feedback and information sends a signal to change recipients that they can be open and honest in sharing their change experiences, it is allowed to take risks and experiment with new behaviours. It is especially important not to distort information about the change process – be open and willing to share relevant information with change recipients. This does not only relate to the change process but also to feedback the leader may receive about his or her style of leadership. Authentic leaders use personal feedback as a mechanism to improve and develop themselves to become even better leaders.

(*Continued*)

Table 1 *(Continued)*

Authentic leadership characteristics	**Influence on the change process or change recipients**
The leader's motives, goals and values are transparent and evident to followers and is willing to disclose the 'true self' to followers Consistency exists between values and behaviours: for example, authentic leaders will say what they mean and mean what they say	Organizational change leads to uncertainty and followers need leaders who are consistent, trustworthy and leading by example. Being transparent creates trust between the leader and follower, fostering teamwork and cooperation. A key component of any change process is the creation of high levels of trust between change agents and change recipients. Articulating your values, goals and motives provides certainty – a much needed quality in any change process.
Authentic leaders are willing to share emotions and understand the role of emotions in other people	Change recipients experience different types of emotions during the change process. Before you are able to address their emotions, you need to understand and make sense of your own emotions. You need to reflect on questions such as 'why am I feeling this way'; what influenced my emotions'; how am I going to deal with it'. Putting it differently, you need to be able to recognize and understand your own emotions and their impact on others. It also means you need to be perceptive of the emotions of the change recipients. If you really understand how they feel, you will be able to assist them in managing their own emotions more effectively.
Authentic leaders have confidence, hope, self-efficacy and resilience and have an optimistic view of the future	In any change process, change recipients do not only need leaders they can trust, but also leaders who are able to show them the way forward. Being optimistic and hopeful about the change process creates energy and impetus for the change. Change is tough and if you are the change agent, you need to instil confidence in your followers that you are competent and the 'right' person to lead the change. You also need to demonstrate resilience – remember the proverb *when the going gets tough, the tough get going*, or putting it differently, when a situation becomes difficult, the strong will work harder to meet this challenge.
They are able to build long-term relationships with followers	Having personal integrity will enable you to build lasting relationships with your followers. Encouraging communication and dialogue, leading with purpose will enable you to forge relationships build on mutual understanding and values. They build strong relationships between individuals and teams and this leads to positive social exchanges.
A high emphasis is placed on the development of employees	Not only act the authentic leader as a role model for change recipients, but also places a high emphasis on developing authentic characteristics in followers. Furthermore, creating development opportunities for change recipients will support capacity and skills building that may be needed in the change process.

exhibit patterns of openness and clarity in their behaviour toward others by (1) sharing information needed to make decisions, (2) accept others' input and provide constructive feedback to their followers. As a result, followers develop higher levels of psychological capital. This means followers (1) have more confidence in their own abilities (self-efficacy) and invest effort to be successful to succeed in demanding tasks; (2) have positive expectations (optimism) about succeeding now and in the future; (3) persevere toward goal attainment and when needed, redirecting paths to goals in order to succeed (hope) and (4) when experiencing problems and set-backs, bounce back (resilience) to achieve success (Luthans, et al., 2007, p. 3). The starting point to becoming better at leading change is to develop and express authenticity. This means that you need to constantly reflect, make sense of your experiences and use your insights to increase your authenticity in leadership.

Chapter Summary

In this chapter we explored the processes used in authentic leadership development and emphasized the importance of being authentic in leading change. We highlight the importance of *synthesis* and *sense-making* (through the use of specific processes) as key mechanisms in understanding key life changing events. This sense-making ability leads to a heightened sense of self-awareness and self-insight, and provides not only a platform for value creation and motive development, but also for a construction of the self, that is, the forming of a change leader identity. This provides a platform for change leaders to be more open in interpersonal relationships, to be authentic, show compassion and demonstrate self-transcendent behaviours. These are key resources in leading and managing change. As indicated, individuals use different processes in making sense of history and trigger events. Self-awareness and self-concept clarity are functions of the ability of the leader to make sense of the past and present. Shamir and Eilam (2005) argue that leaders' life stories should be regarded as 'repositories of meaning' and should be analysed from a variety of perspectives. They argue that life stories should also be compared to others (e.g. family members, followers, and ordinary people) to determine if leaders' life stories are selectively constructed by the leaders. This means that you should develop mechanisms that assist you in distinguishing between authentic and inauthentic life stories. The life-story approach should focus on revisiting your life events and the development of self-knowledge and interpretation, that is, sense-making. Remember, becoming authentic is a highly individualized process and you can seek help in making sense of the past. Talking to somebody that you trust, or making use of mentoring and coaching serve as examples in this regard.

KEY INSIGHTS FROM PRACTICE

Understand your purpose.
Be true to yourself.
Live your values.
Accept yourself with your strengths and weaknesses.
Walk-the-talk – actions are based on values and convictions.
Authentic change leaders are originals – not copies.
Use open, honest, direct communication.
Seek feedback from and advice from colleagues and subordinates on your development journey.

References

Allport, G.W. (1955). *Becoming: Basic Considerations for a Psychology of Personality*. New Haven, CT: Yale University Press.

Armenakis, A.A. and Harris, S.G. (2002). Crafting a change message to create transformational readiness. *Journal of Organizational Change Management*, 15 (2), 169–183.

Avolio, B.J. and Gardner, W.L. (2005). Authentic leadership development: getting to the root of positive forms of leadership. *The Leadership Quarterly*, 16 (3), 315–338.

Avolio, B.J., Gardner, W.L., Walumbwa, F.O., and May, D. (2004). Unlocking the mask: a look at the process by which authentic leader's impact follower attitudes and behaviours. *The Leadership Quarterly*, 15 (6), 801–823.

Avolio, B.J., Walumbwa, F.O., and Weber, T.J. (2009). *Leadership: Current Theories, Research and Future Directions*. University of Nebraska: Management Faculty Publications.

Bennis, W. and Thomas, R. (2002). Crucible of leadership. *Harvard Business Review*, 80 (1), 5–11.

Block, P. (1997). Foreword. In Roger Harrison (ed.), *A Consultant's Journey: A Dance of Work and Spirit*. San Francisco: Jossey-Bass.

Cooper, C., Scandura, T.A., and Schriesheim, C.A. (2005). Looking forward but learning from our past: Potential challenges to developing authentic leadership theory and authentic leaders. *Leadership Quarterly*, 16, 474–493.

Day, D.V. and Sin, H. (2011). Longitudinal tests of an integrative model of leader development: Charting and understanding development trajectories. *The Leadership Quarterly*, 22, 545–560.

Gardner, W.L., Avolio, B.J., and Walumbwa, F.O. (2005a). Authentic leadership development: emergent themes and future directions. *Leadership and Management*, 3, pp. 387–406.

Gardner, W.L., Avolio, B.J., Luthans, F., May, D., and Walumbwa, F.O. (2005b). Can you see the real me? A self-based model of authentic leadership and follower development. *The Leadership Quarterly*, 16 (3), 343–372.

George, B. (2003). *Authentic Leadership: Rediscovering the Secrets to Creating Lasting Value*. San Francisco: Jossey-Bass.

George, B., Sims, P., McLean, A.N., and Mayer, D. (2007). Discovering your authentic leadership. *Harvard Business Review*, 85 (2), 129–138.
Goffee, R. and Jones, G. (2000). Why should anyone be led by you?, *Harvard Business Review*, September–October, 63–70.
Goffee, R. and Jones, G. (2007). Leading clever people. *Harvard Business Review*, 85 (3), 72–79.
Ilies, R., Morgeson, F., and Nahrgang, J. (2005). Authentic leadership and eudaemonic wellbeing: Understanding leader-follower outcomes. *The Leadership Quarterly*, 16 (3), 373–394.
Judge, T.A., Erez, A., and Bono, J.A. (1998). The power of being positive: the relation between positive self-concept and job performance. *Human Performance*, 11, 167–187.
Kegan, R. (1983). *The Evolving Self*. Cambridge, MA: Harvard University Press.
Kernis, M.H. (2003). Toward a Conceptualization of Optimal Self-Esteem. *Psychological Inquiry*, 14 (1), 1–26.
Kets de Vries, M. (1993). *Leaders, Fools and Imposters: Essays on the Psychology of Leadership*. Jossey-Bass: San Francisco, CA.
Klenke, K. (2007). Authentic Leadership: A self, leader and spiritual identity. *International Journal of Leadership Studies*, 3, 68–97.
Ladkin, D. and Taylor, S.S. (2010). Enacting the 'true self': Towards a theory of embodied authentic leadership. *The Leadership Quarterly*, 21, 64–74.
Luthans, F., Youssef, C.M., and Avolio, B.J. (2007). *Psychological Capital*. Oxford: Oxford University Press.
Machiavelli, N. (1992). *The Prince*. Everyman: London.
May, D.R., Hodges, T.D., Chan, A.Q.Y.L., and Avolio, B.J. (2003). Developing the moral component of authentic leadership. *Organizational Dynamics*, 32 (3), 247–260.
Murray, M. and Kujundzic, N., (2005). *Critical Reflection: A Textbook for Critical Thinking*. Québec, Canada: McGill-Queen's University Press.
Nicholson, N. (2013). *The 'I' of Leadership*. CA: Jossey-Bass.
Palmer, P.J. (1994). *Leading from Within: Out of the Shadows, into the Light*. In J.A. Conger (ed.), *Spirit at Work: Discovering the Spirituality in Leadership*. San Francisco, CA: Jossey-Bass.
Roberts, L.M., Dutton, J.E., Spreitzer, G.M., Heaphy, E.D., and Quinn, R.E. (2005). Composing the reflected best self-portrait: Building pathways for becoming extraordinary in work organizations. *Academy of Management Review*, 30 (4), 712–736.
Shamir, B. and Eilam, G. (2005). What's your story? A life-stories approach to authentic leadership development. *The Leadership Quarterly*, 16, 395–417.
Spitzmuller, M. and Ilies, R. (2010). Do they see my true self? Leader's relational authenticity and followers' assessments of transformational leadership. *European Journal of Work and Organizational Psychology*, 19, 304–332.
Swartz, S.H. (1994). Are there universal aspects in the structure and contents of human values? *Journal of Social Issues*, 50, 19–45.
Walumbwa, F.O., Avolio, B.J., Gardner, W.L., Wernsing, T.S., and Peterson, S.J. (2008). Authentic leadership: development and validation of a theory-based measure. *Journal of Management*, 34 (1), pp. 89–126.
Weick, K.E., Sutcliffe, K.M., and Obstfeld, D. (2005). Organising and the process of sensemaking. *Organization Science*, 16 (4), pp. 409–421.

CHAPTER 2

Change Readiness: Are You Ready for Leading Change?

Chapter at a Glance

This chapter builds on Chapter 1 where it was indicated that leading change in an authentic manner creates higher levels of change acceptance, collaboration and trust. It was highlighted that an understanding of *what* I am; *who* I am and *why* I am is the pivot point on which your change leadership depends . . . and without it, your orientation to your 'true north' is missing (George et al., 2008, p. 51). This chapter further explores individual attributes, behaviours and competencies that you, the change leader need to be aware of when leading and implementing change. These insights are captured in the CEO interviews and their insights. The first step, before implementing and leading change, is being introspective; for example, asking questions about (1) your own philosophy of change, (2) the attributes you have that may impact positively and negatively on your ability to lead change effectively, and (3) what can you do to become ready for change?

Beginning Cases: Preparation

Our orientation towards change, how we view change, is formed through sense-making of our past experiences with change and the influence of significant others in our lives. These experiences shape our perspectives and influence how we implement and lead change. Therefore, change starts with the change agent and a willingness to reinvent him or herself every day. This reinvention of the self is a conscious process; creating and experimenting with new learning experiences are key building blocks of any individual change process. This can be illustrated as follows:

Reinvention is a conscious choice

'My philosophy of change is straightforward. It starts with a strong belief that change is positive because I was educated that way and that developed my view on change. My parents brought me up with the idea that we are all human beings and must constantly reinvent ourselves. You need to reinvent yourself constantly just because the world changes whether you like it or not – that is a given. There are three ways to grasp this reality: You can accept it and get ahead of it, follow it by being just part of this flow or actually resist the change but then you lose a great opportunity. Let me give you an example of how I embraced the change. I went to business school in USA and one of my very first business classes was on leadership and change. The first five minutes we had the business professor told us to do an experiment: If you have to change three things about you in your life/daily habits/physical changes – what would you change? The assignment was "Start small with a focus on the short-term and change things more profoundly medium to long-term". What I did was to shave my head, put my watch on the right wrist and changed glasses for contacts.

Identify what you want to change and implement small and incremental changes

Be willing to take personal risks

'These were the three immediate changes I did and the learning was interesting because it was the first time I was bald and people were looking at me differently and I actually started to meet different people because different types of characters came to me and that gave me a different perspective on people. The lenses – I used to play basketball – with

Reflect on the new experiences and identify key personal learning and insights

glasses it was just a pain and it was frustrating. And now I have lenses and I was again able to play basketball. The watch was just a reminder of the different perspectives I was getting. So a couple of months later I continued with this philosophy of change and seeing how this impacts. I used to read every single morning the Wall Street Journal *in the same Starbucks. I then decided to l read a different newspaper – I read the* Financial Times. *Different newspapers have a different structure, different writers and different perspectives. If you read both – you get new perspectives. I also decided to change places to drink coffee and again I start meeting different people. I then decided to get eye surgery and it opened a new world for me as well, i.e. I was now able to participate in water sports. This was a very practical way for me as a student to understand how change can impact your life, can impact people's life. It brings more openness and more in-depth understanding about things. So you know, these are clear conclusions about change I learned: (1) you need to reinvent yourself every day and (2) you need to re-think things and reflect.'*

Have a strategy to record key learning and insights

'People do this in different ways. A lot of people when they go to sleep they think about one or two impactful findings of the day, about their learnings how they impacted on people. Other people actually write everyday in a diary three or four bullet points about things that impacted their way of doing things or perceiving things or some key learning – sometimes they read back even as far as three years ago and they remember – this helps change. For me the key learning and insights are: (1) Reinvent yourself everyday – otherwise you lose ground and (2) by doing so – you learn a lot more about yourself and get a much more in-depth understanding of what is possible. Now – why is all this important? I think nature is all about change and life is all about change. Life equals change and death equals you don't change any more. Question is do you want to be alive or dead?'

Chapter Introduction

The concept of readiness for change has received substantial attention in the literature (Prochaska et al., 1992) and it is generally accepted that organizational change readiness is an important building block for effective organizational change (Pellettiere, 2006; By, et al., 2008). Readiness for change can be regarded as a comprehensive attitude (Holt, et al., 2007) and is influenced simultaneously by the *content* (what is being changed), the *process* (how the change is being implemented), the *context* (circumstances under which the change is occurring) and individual attributes, that is, the characteristics of those being asked to change (p. 235). Readiness for change refers to the mindset of employees (Cunningham et al., 2002) and can either be defined as a psychological state; that is, attitudes, beliefs and intentions: or described in structural terms; organizational resources and capabilities. More specifically, Armenakis, et al. (1993, p. 683) regard readiness as an 'organisational member's beliefs, attitudes and intentions regarding the extent to which the changes were needed and the organisation's capacity to make those changes'. We know from research that variables such as self-efficacy (Eby et al., 2000; Armenakis et al., 2007); tolerance for ambiguity (Walker, et al., 2007); locus of control (Holt et al., 2007); and demographical characteristics (Weber and Weber, 2001; Spreitzer and Mishra, 2002) are *individual differences* that may impact on the willingness of recipients to support and implement organizational change. While the variables mentioned refer to things that may impact on the readiness levels of change recipients, they are also applicable to the change agent responsible for implementing the change. When being tasked as the person responsible for implementing the change, change agents often do not sufficiently reflect on (1) their own beliefs, attitudes and feelings about the proposed changes and (2) the skills needed to successfully implement and lead the change. For us, the starting point in leading change effectively, is the level of individual change readiness of the change leader.

Mental Models

A mental model or schema is a cognitive structure that represents organized knowledge about a given concept or type of stimulus and contains both the attributes of the concept and the relationship among the attributes (Fiske and Taylor, 1984, p. 140). Putting it differently, mental models help people to simplify, manage and make sense of their environment. Despite the usefulness of mental models, they can also have specific limitations. Barquero (1995 cited in Greca and Morereira, 2010, p. 3) puts it like this:

> . . . a mental model is a type of knowledge representation which is implicit, incomplete, imprecise, incoherent with normative knowledge in various domains, but it is a useful one, since it results in a powerful explicative and predictive tool for the interaction of subjects with the world, and a dependable source of knowledge, for it comes from the subjects own perspective and manipulative experiences with this world.

We have different mental models for different life domains which influence how we view and react to things. For example: we have mental models around what are the attributes of an effective employee or what constitutes effective leadership. The following examples reflect the 'output' of mental models that two leaders have about leadership success and philosophy about change:

Leadership success	*'I'd probably equate it to when I look at successful leaders, the qualities that I admire – I look for people who deliver consistently and deliver over the long term rather than short term because I think it can be quite easy sometimes to just look at somebody for something they've achieved over a short period of time, but what I really admire are those leaders who are successful over long periods of time. I admire leaders who have the courage to speak up on issues that you just know might've been easier for them not to have spoken up on, but who are articulate and who are thoughtful in what they're saying and who I think are saying things because they genuinely care.'*
Philosophy about change	*'Change is inevitable and it is critical to survive. You need to create a culture in the company that embraces change. The culture must be vibrant, you need an entrepreneurial approach to change – to manage and live with change you need a "can do" attitude. I believe you need to build in change as a normal phenomenon in the operating environment. You need to continuously ask, especially in your business cycle, or question what things should we do differently. But you also need to break change up in manageable chunks – it needs to be manageable but in a continuous way.'*

Therefore, mental models include what a person thinks is true (selective perception), not necessarily what is actually true. Irrespective of whether a mental model is true or untrue, it shapes and influences behaviour. However, we are not consciously aware of our mental models or the effects they have on our behaviour but they determine what we pay attention to and what we do. We also have specific mental models around change. Change mental models or schemata consist of three dimensions (Lau and Woodman, 1995) that is, *change salience* (cognitive affirmation of the need for change and the willingness to help make those changes), *change valence* (individual perception of the meaning and significance of the change) and *change inference* (conclusions about the reasons for the change and the probability of change success). Take a look at the following example:

A change mental model of an employee	*'They (management) announced their new 2018 vision for the organization using road shows. The CEO made a presentation and explained the purpose*
Change salience	*of our new vision is to position the organization for future external challenges. Attending the session was a waste of time – they are not interested in any*
Change valence	*comments or feedback – it was more a celebration of how clever they are. I really believe the top management team is delusional – good luck for them implementing their vision. The changes are substan-*
Change inference	*tive and people will definitely lose their jobs – it is not clear how their strategy is going to make the organization better. Things are going fairly well right now and maybe the change should start with them – a new management team may be a better strategy. They conveniently forget it is their current employees that have made them successful. This new vision is just more of the same – hopefully they will lose interest after some time.'*

The three dimensions provide a framework for understanding the reasons, significance and consequence of the change. The first step in creating successful organizational change is to investigate your own change schema. Putting it differently, you need to examine and understand your own mental models about change by finding answers to the following questions: (1) 'what is your perception of the meaning and significance of the proposed changes'; (2) 'do you believe there is a real need for change and (3) 'what do you believe are the organizational outcomes of the proposed changes?'. This is important because your predetermined ideas about the organizational change will influence your decision-making about implementation strategy, who to involve, networks to activate and so on. Discussing your answers with your peer group and manager will help to clarify your assumptions, mental models and expectations about the proposed changes. This sense-making process (i.e. interpretation of organizational change) helps you in communicating these interpretations to your subordinates who themselves have mental models of change. This sense-giving process will help you to frame the meaning and the impact of the change. This is sometimes described as the 'contextualization of the need for change'. Furthermore, you need to explore your emotions (e.g. fear, anxiety, inertia) and determine a plan of action that you can implement that will help you (on a personal level) to embrace the proposed changes effectively. Understanding *who am I?*, *what baggage do I bring to the change process?*, *what biases do I have?* and *what are my coping mechanisms?* will enable you to deal with change in a way that does not adversely affect others. Remember, the behaviour of individuals is primarily determined by past events and experiences, rather than what lies ahead. Don't make the change about yourself: it is about getting the people who are in the organization to understand the change that is needed. In this way you become the helper of the bridge builder, as opposed to it all being about you having the right answer. There never is just one answer to the problem. But the starting point in any change process is you, the change leader. This can be explained as follows:

The starting point of any change process is YOU

Use significant others to help you to make sense of the change

'The single biggest challenge about change is not recognizing that change is needed or having people not buy-into the fact that we have to change – because in theory it is easy – it is having people buying into the execution of the change. And there is only one way this happens – is that they need to change themselves. They have to buy in to the change themselves. The issue with people again is human nature. When you recognize things need to change – you always think your neighbour needs to change, the guy in front/behind you – everybody needs to change except for yourself – because you don't need to. The "don't touch me philosophy" kills change. The single biggest challenge about change is to have every single individual understand that change starts with himself. Not by his neighbour but with himself. It takes exchanges/communication and recognition by that specific individual that he himself needs to change.'

Change is a choice

'I think nature is all about change and life is all about change. I don't want be philosophical here – but life equals change; death equals you don't change any more. Question is do you want to be alive or dead?'

Therefore, it is important to reinvent yourself continuously and discover the possibilities that may be within you. Unfortunately, managers do not always believe that change starts with them; instead it is something that their subordinates or colleagues have to do. Everybody needs to change except them! Employees will notice when your behaviour and attitudes change in a visible manner – this will give you a lot more credibility when you ask employees to take ownership of the change themselves – provided you 'walk-the-talk'. They will buy-in to change more easily if you show them that you have changed as well. This is the key. You need to embrace, welcome and applaud change as being something good. Change may be frightening, because it is out of the ordinary, because it is different, because it is new, because it is worrying, because it is going to make you insecure: but successful change starts with you.

Identify your thinking traps

Revisit your values as you identified them in Chapter 1. What are your deeply held beliefs or assumptions about the following:

1. *People*: do you believe people are passive, need to be persuaded, rewarded, punished and controlled if they are to align their efforts with the needs of the organization? Or, do you believe that people are cooperative, able to take responsibility and set their own goals if leaders provide the conditions under which they can do this?
2. *Attitude towards change*: how do you view change? 'If it ain't broke don't fix it' Or do you find change is fun and good and want to change? Or, you may like the idea but want to think about it or, are you one of those in between – change things not working so long as it is practical? Understanding your attitude towards change and by completing personality profiling questionnaires similar to the Myers Briggs Type Indicator (MBTI), 16PF and so on will help you to determine the impact of your leadership style on change.
3. *Resistance to change*: how do you view people's reaction toward organizational change? Do you view it as feedback that you can use to improve the change process or do you view reactions as negative as people have a natural tendency to resist any change?

4. *About the organization*: What is the metaphor (i.e. a figure of speech containing an implied comparison, in which a word or phrase ordinarily and primarily used for one thing is applied to another, e.g., my organization operates like a well-oiled machine) you use for your organization? For example: do you view the organization as a machine, a mechanical metaphor? Your assumptions of the organization will then be as follows:
   - *Key aspects of metaphor:* Network of parts arranged in a specific sequence; standardization of output.
   - *Work process characteristics:* Well defined jobs and tasks; codified processes; vertical decision-making; formalization of roles and responsibilities.
   - *Human relations orientation:* Low individual initiative; managers plan and think, workers implement; adherence to rules and regulations highly valued; high monitoring of performance.

Your assumptions or metaphors of the organization will influence how you are going to implement and lead change. Reflect on your answers and ask yourself the following questions: (1) Are your assumptions still meaningful in the context of leading change? (2) Are they accurate and useful? (3) What assumptions do you need to revisit and make changes to?

The Dark Side of Leadership: Narcissism

Narcissism describes the characteristic of excessive self-love and the term is derived from the Greek myth of Narcissus. According to the legend, Echo was a young woman who fell in love with Narcissus, who was very handsome but also extremely vain. He rejected her expressions of love and she died of a broken heart. The god Apollo was angered by Narcissus' pride and condemned him to die without ever knowing human love. One day, Narcissus was feeling thirsty, saw a pool of clear water nearby, and knelt beside it in order to dip his hands in the water and drink. He saw his face reflected on the surface of the water and fell in love with the reflection. Unable to get a response from the image in the water, Narcissus eventually died beside the pool. Trapped in self-love, he could not distinguish reality from illusion, whether it was real or illusionary (Dunbar, 1985, p. 1). Unfortunately, narcissism is not confined to myths and stories. Most people have narcissistic tendencies but to work for a full-blooded narcissist who is responsible for leading change, may be difficult. Take a look at the following example:

Characteristics of a narcissist in action

Role of life experiences

Does not tolerate dissent

Demonstrate paranoid behaviour

Grandiose thinking

Status and prestige

Enforcing change

Dire consequences

'I worked for a true narcissist some time ago and it was a very difficult period in my life. He grew up in a country town, had an extremely strict father and didn't experience a lot of emotional support or recognition. Maybe it all started in his childhood? As a manager he was the most intolerant person I have ever met. His point of view was the only one that counted and any form of challenge or disagreement was classified as "negative". He was quite vindictive and believed people "were out to get him". The only way to survive was to agree with his point of view and to provide a lot of positive strokes. He truly believed in his own greatness and talked incessantly about his strategies, accomplishments. His understanding of participative management was quite interesting – he used it as an opportunity to manipulate or to force his viewpoint down your throat. Although the departmental budget was tight, there was always money to fund his needs. The refurbishing of his office is a good example – only the best and most expensive furniture was good enough. He even managed to put a few original paintings on the walls. He also had the ability to be quite charming when in interaction with his bosses – very much like a chameleon. As a change leader he was a disaster. He believed a good leader is forceful, knows exactly what is needed and people had to do what you say. Nobody was committed to any change but what was evident in his behaviour was that people are not important and their viewpoints are irrelevant. A lot of back stabbing and turf wars took place – there was no real feeling of belonging. He resigned after two years but his legacy was the creation of a toxic organization – internally focussed, low commitment and zero trust.'

Table 1 Narcissistic characteristics

Characteristics of narcissists (APA, 2000)	**1.** A grandiose sense of self-importance (e.g. exaggerates achievements and talents, expects to be considered superior without real evidence of achievement). **2.** Is preoccupied with fantasies of unlimited success, power, brilliance, beauty, or ideal love. **3.** Believes that he or she is 'special' and unique and can only be understood by, or should associate with, other special or high-status people (or institutions). **4.** Requires excessive admiration or adoration from others. **5.** Has a sense of entitlement, that is, unreasonable expectations of especially favourable treatment or automatic compliance with his or her expectations. **6.** Is interpersonally exploitative, that is, takes advantage of others to achieve his/her own ends. **7.** Lacks empathy: is unwilling to recognize or identify with the feelings and needs of others. **8.** Is often envious of others or believes that others are envious of him or her. **9.** Shows arrogant, self-important behaviours or attitudes. **10.** A history of intense but short-term relationships with others; inability to make or sustain genuinely intimate relationships.

This narrative illustrates narcissistic behaviour and the potential negative consequences for people and the organization. True narcissists or people with an excessive self-love exhibit the characteristics in Table 1.

Throughout history, narcissistic leaders were able to inspire people and shape history (Maccoby, 2003) and leaders such as Napoleon, Hitler and Jack Welch (Glad, 2002) serve as examples in this regard. Although narcissism may sometimes be useful, and we all demonstrate some narcissistic characteristics, there is also a downside to narcissistic leadership. Maccoby (2003, p. 203) states in this regard:

> . . . no matter what their strengths, productive narcissists are incredibly difficult to work for. They don't learn easily from others. They are oversensitive to any kind of criticism, which they take personally. They bully subordinates and dominate meetings. They don't want to hear about anyone else's feelings. They are distrustful and paranoid. They can become grandiose, especially when they start to succeed. Perhaps their most frustrating quality is they almost never listen to anyone.

True narcissists are fixated on power, prestige and status. It is important to distinguish between high levels of self-absorption or people with a high self-regard of themselves. Not everyone who exhibits *some* of the behaviour exhibited in Table 1 is narcissistic! However, in *excessive forms* it can be highly damaging to individuals, relationships and organizations (Kets de Vries, 2004). Lubit (2002) argues in this regard that managers with strong narcissistic tendencies (e.g. sense of entitlement, lack of empathy and exploitation of others) may destroy morale and motivation and force employees to divert their energy away from the task toward self-protection. Demonstrating the behaviours as discussed refers to 'bad' leadership, and can be regarded as abusive, tyrannical, inconsistent and petty (Judge and LePine, 2007). Obtaining feedback from various sources is a key mechanism to get a reality check on how people experience you as a leader. Take a look at the following example:

Obtain feedback

Ask challenging questions

Use not only work colleagues as sources of information but also friends, family

Be willing to hear the 'good and bad' news

Do regular reality checks

'And then I also have the non-Executive directors and the Chairman, who again, will give a view as part of my own performance review about how they think I'm doing but part of that will also be about my values and if you think they were instrumental in recruiting me, they also have, I think, a vested interest in making sure I'm getting feedback both good and not so good, if they think I'm either living the values in the way that I said that I would, or if they think I'm not living up to the values in the way that they were hoping for. I mean the other one that's very interesting about that is my children are very good at challenging me! Probably, you know, they do – as they've been getting older – they sort of understand the business more but equally they are quite challenging, probably because their friends will challenge them when they know what their father does. They can challenge quite hard so that's another, I think, way that you just get a reality check about your values. Then the other people who I think again are often forgotten – friends, as well as family, can sometimes be amazingly helpful at again, just making you sit back and think about your values and whether what you say you believe in and stand for, whether that's what they also see you do. I think there's something about, as a leader, having the antennae out so you're actually trying to pick up the signals and being conscious that that's what you're trying to do to get that feedback. I think sometimes, because there are a lot of pressures on me because I think it's almost – I can understand why some would

Avoid sycophants who tell you only what you want to hear

Don't shoot the messenger who tells you the truth

almost prefer not to get too much feedback – I tend to naturally want to hear what the feedback is and I think it goes right the way back because I want to do well and therefore I know the only way I know I'm going to do well is if I continue to seek out, listen and act on feedback about how I'm personally doing – albeit it can be at times challenging and uncomfortable. So I think it's something about attitude of mind and openness to receiving that sort of feedback but it's incredibly important. The danger with all of us as leaders, especially Chief Executive level, is that you only hear what you want to hear or people only tell you what they think you want to hear. So very quickly I think if you don't have the right approach to this you can lose touch with the reality and start to live in a bubble that isn't real.'

The 'dark side' refers to the part of ourselves that lies hidden in the shadows of our personality (Kets de Vries and Engellau, 2010) – it is usually a part of our personality that you don't know or don't want to know about. Your willingness or unwillingness to engage in self-disclosure, and listen to feedback, has a lot to do with your understanding of yourself and others' understanding of you. The following exercise may be helpful:

Understanding your 'dark side'

Answer the following questions:

What is known by you about yourself and is also known by others?

What do you know about yourself that others do not know about you? This may refer to private feelings, needs, and past experiences that you prefer to keep to yourself.

Ask somebody who you trust: What is unknown by you about yourself but which others know? This can be simple information, or can involve deep issues (example.g. feelings of inadequacy, incompetence, unworthiness, rejection) which are difficult for individuals to face directly, and yet can be seen by others.

What key insights did you identify?

What are the implications of your key insights for leading change?

So what does narcissistic leadership or bad leadership have to do with leading change? While the leadership of change is about having a vision, changing systems, structures and processes, it is more about leading people; that is, creating commitment, engagement and support for the change. Key to successfully leading change is the ability to form relationships, act on feedback, listen to people, not being overly sensitive to criticism and demonstrating empathy. Furthermore, you need to commit to telling the truth, reward those who disagree with you, admit when you are wrong and create support for being open and authentic. Kets de Vries and Engellau put it like this 'True leaders are merchants of hope, speaking to the collective imagination of their followers, co-opting them to join them in a great adventure. Great leaders inspire people to move beyond personal, egoistic motives' (2010, p. 11). This is only possible if you are willing to tolerate disagreement, deal constructively with criticism, consult with colleagues and share decision-making. What is also needed is a high level of emotional intelligence, that is, the ability to perceive accurately, appraise and express emotion; the ability to access and/or generate feelings when they facilitate thought; the ability to understand emotion and emotional knowledge and the ability to regulate emotions to promote emotional and intellectual growth (Mayer and Salovey, 1997, p. 10). Take a look at the following examples:

Express emotions in an authentic manner

'Frustration – they'll see frustration, I'm not a screamer, I don't shout! But they'll see me cross and impatient but I do have quite clear rules about if I start shouting at people that's inappropriate behaviour but if they see me frustrated with a situation or a piece of news then there's no point pretending I'm not frustrated, so they'll see that. They might see me rather low but I try to keep it to a minimum so it's the kind of balance thing but I don't censor myself in the course of a morning if for half an hour I'm fed up with a piece of news, they're going to see me being fed up about it and importantly, they see me absolutely delighted! We had two nominations for some awards last week and I stood on a chair in the office and told them about it – not because that's the best way to communicate it but because I needed to say it and I wanted them to see how delighted I was. You can't see that in an email! So yeah, I make a point of making sure people see that I'm proud and pleased for sure, when I am.'

Understand the impact of your emotions on others

'I think it's quite a difficult one this, our values are about being open and honest, it's quite difficult then not to show your emotions if you're going to be open and honest! I think what you also have to be very mindful of is I suppose just how people react to the position, to the office of being a Chief Executive and I think there is a real skill in knowing that if you are upset about something that's gone wrong, if you were to really show your emotions, that can have quite a dramatic impact on the whole organization and so you have to, I think, try and show the emotion, show that you are perhaps upset about something but do it in a measured way and I think that's a real art and very difficult because we are human beings and we feel emotion and it can be quite difficult to get that measure of emotion right but I do, I do – I think because of our values I do try and be open and honest with how I'm feeling but I'm also aware that people are looking to me as a leader and therefore will look at the emotions that I'm showing and it can have a very positive impact or it can equally have a devastating impact if you've not considered in what you're doing. And that's not me putting forward the notion that I think people, as Chief Executives, should be manipulative with their emotions, I don't think you should, but I think you do need to be aware of how your emotions land and they can land very heavily on people, especially those that perhaps don't know you personally very well and so might only see you very infrequently. So I think there is something almost about – it's not the best way to describe this – but being quite statesmanlike and just being very aware of the individual and how they are as individuals and how they are likely to react to the emotions that you're sharing. I think the emotions you have to be careful with are the negative emotions, I think it's OK – the positive emotions, I don't think people will criticise you for being too full of praise or too happy but I think people will criticise you if they think you've been too critical or too forceful in your views and I think that's one

Interpret your own emotions and decide when is it appropriate to display your emotions

Ask yourself what will be gained by showing your emotions

Your own resilience is critical if you are to display emotion in a useful way

Some emotions have to be managed privately

of the most difficult things for Chief Executives to master because again, I go back to the point, I think we are human beings and we're not robots and therefore emotions do come out from time to time. Even those who hide their emotions, bizarrely, by hiding their emotions they are giving out an emotional response which can be quite difficult to live with because it's somebody who almost appears very unfeeling and that is in itself an emotion. So, me personally as a leader, I'm a great believer that you should show your emotions but in a measured way and aware of the responsibility that you have. Probably asking yourself, what are you hoping is going to be gained for the good of the people or for the company by showing your emotions? I think when times are tough, like right now, it becomes much more difficult for leaders because I think some of the emotions that you might feel you wouldn't necessarily want to share openly with everyone. So, for example, fear and uncertainty may not be a good emotion to show when times are tough and people are looking to you as a leader for a way forward. And I think Chief Execs need a high degree of resilience to be able to absorb some of the emotions that they'll be feeling themselves about the challenges that the business faces; to then honestly present a belief that there is a way through. So some emotions for a Chief Exec are best done in private, some emotions I think is the reverse; are best done openly with your teams.'

High emotional intelligence leaders are better able to generate and maintain enthusiasm, confidence and optimism in employees (Goleman, 1998), enhance the leader's ability to deal with change (Huy, 1999) and manage stress (Cryer et al., 2003). The following exercise may help you identify behaviours that may impact on your ability to lead change effectively:

Understanding your A, B and Cs (Komaki, 1986)

Identify five problem behaviours (for example, 'negative reaction to feedback') that you would like to improve. To improve our ability to understand and influence our behaviour, we need a systematic approach. One approach to understanding our behaviour is known as the ABC analysis. The letters represent a behavioural equation which includes the following:

1. *Antecedents: What occurs before the behaviour? (And what may have triggered it or may be things that contribute to or cause the behaviour?)*
2. *Behaviour: What happens during the behaviour? (What does it look like?)*
3. *Consequences: What are the immediate and delayed reactions from everyone involved?*

The first step is to describe the behaviour that you would like to improve in clear, behavioural terms. Secondly, describe the antecedents that occur and the conditions that exist immediately before the behaviour happens. Thirdly, identify the consequences of the behaviour. Fourthly, analyse the antecedents, behaviour and consequences and identify the relationship between the components. Lastly, after gaining an understanding, develop new antecedents/consequences to learn new behaviours and evaluate the effectiveness thereof. The following serves as an example of the relationship between antecedents, behaviours and consequences:

Something to think about:

- What situations typically evoke emotions in you?

It is OK to have strong emotional reactions – it is what you do with those emotions (how you behave) that can be a problem.

Mental Toughness: Don't Give Up

There is growing research evidence that mental toughness can impact on performance in areas such as sport (Bull et al., 2005) and the military (Reivich et al., 2011). It is defined in many different ways: for example, ability to cope with or handle pressure (Goldberg, 1998), or to overcome failures (Gould et al., 1987). Clough, et al. (2002, p. 38) provide a more comprehensive definition and define mental toughness as those individuals who 'have a high sense of self belief and an unshakeable faith that they control their own destiny and these individuals can remain relatively unaffected by competition and adversity'. Jones et al. (2002, p. 209) refer to potential outcomes of mental toughness and argue that mental toughness will enable you to cope better than your opponents with the many environmental demands, and 'be more consistent and better than your opponents in remaining determined, focused, confident and in control under pressure'. Despite the different conceptualizations of the attributes that make up the ideal mentally tough performer, or put it differently, key dimensions of mental toughness (see perspectives of Jones et al., 2002, 2007 along with Clough, et al., 2002), it seems the following can be regarded as mental toughness attributes:

- High level of self-belief in own ability to achieve goals, that is, self-efficacy.
- Having a strong self-belief that they have unique qualities and abilities that make them better than their competition.
- Able to recover and not be affected by performance setbacks.
- Having a strong desire to succeed.
- Able to focus on the task despite environmental distractions.
- Accept anxiety as inevitable and is able to cope with it.
- Able to block out personal problems and focus on the task at hand.
- Ability to cope with pressure.

Mental toughness refers to the ability to handle setbacks and remain unfailing when the 'going gets tough', having self-belief, desire and motivation to perform, able to handle pressure and anxiety and the ability to perform consistently. This is described as follows by a number of CEOs:

Life challenge

Strong self-belief

'When I had my problems, I then had the collapse of the business and you just keep your head down and get on with it, that's the difference that makes champion fighters and guys who can go in and spar for three rounds but then end up getting knocked out, you know, you get into the ring if you're a real champion you'll have days when you will get a black eye, you'll have days you'll get a bloody nose, you'll get days that you'll get knocked down but you don't get knocked out, you then pick yourself up and get back into the fight. Now, that has to be in you.'

Strong desire to succeed

'The measure of a man is how you deal with your major problems in life and how you come through that because it has to affect you in different ways

Cope with pressure

Not be affected by setbacks

and if you come through it and you rise above it all and you don't get bitter and twisted, you don't allow it to corrupt you inside and you keep thinking positive, then – and you need the strength, you need that inner strength, you need that focus, commitment, dedication, then people do respect it. People respect it even if they don't like you, they say well you've got to respect the man because you know, look what he's achieved, and look what he's been through. It's like a soldier, it's like somebody in the SAS; he's fought all the battles, he's taken some bullets, he's been shot in the leg, he was shot in the arm – as long as he didn't get shot in the head and now he's recovered and how he's gone back in the front line and risen through the ranks, from being a private to being a general. But it takes time, young people have to understand it takes time, it takes commitment, it takes focus and it takes dedication and total commitment and if you're not prepared to do that, then you are not going to be very successful in whatever you do.'

In the fantasy idealized world of change management, the change process is linear, not too difficult to manage, people will support the change wholeheartedly and you will most probably be hailed as a change hero of your organization. However, change does not always run smoothly and according to plan. In reality, 7 out of 10 planned change efforts fail to achieve their intended objectives. In the real world of change management, people may desert you, your allies will make a run for it, resistance may come from the people you least expected and you may feel isolated and alone. This means that you need to believe in your own abilities, be able to recover from setbacks, have a strong desire to succeed, focus on the change task despite environmental distractions, be able to cope with pressure and manage your own uncertainties and anxieties. In short, you need to be mentally tough to manage and lead change effectively. Having the confidence that you have what it takes to manage change will also allow you to take risks. Taking risks means making a conscious decision to accept uncertain outcomes when change is introduced. Change is inherently uncertain and making a mistake is not the worst thing that may happen to you. It is only through our mistakes that we are able to identify problem areas and learn from it. Experiment with new behaviour and create a climate for your subordinates that is supportive of 'trying out new things'. This can be explained as follows:

Believe in what is possible

Create an environment where people are willing to experiment and take risks

'We have this little voice in our heads who tells us constantly we can't do certain things. If we help our employees to believe in the art of possibility, we may be able to shift mountains. It is such a simple philosophy that if you applied it at all stages of your life it's remarkable and may unleash the capacity of us as human beings. We tend to foster that in our organization. As managers we sometime allow people to be victims of structure and tradition. Do we encourage them enough to be more than that and take risks? We might create the greatest change of all if we encourage our employees to experiment and help them to believe in themselves.'

Do not get dejected when problems occur and be passionate in whatever you do. You cannot analyse everything to death. You have to make some leaps of faith, sometimes they are right, and sometimes they are wrong. This means that you need to have courage. Kouzes and Posner (2006, p. 137) state that

> . . . courage is a state of mind. It has to do with how we humans experience certain situations and how we deal with our fears. While there certainly is a physiological component when we encounter adversity, we can make choices [in] how we handle it. Acknowledging our fears, being appropriately confident that we can handle the situation, and taking initiative despite our fears can be an act of courage.

However, you need to believe in yourself, you have to be comfortable with making judgement calls and taking risks. Linking the previous with a sense of urgency and passion about what you are doing is what constitutes an effective change leader. Rather than getting bogged down comparing yourself to others, worrying about whether you are worthy to be making these risky decisions or whether someone else could be doing it better, instead realize that at this moment in time – right here right now – *you* are the gift and your message is the contribution (Zander and Zander, 2000).

Decrease catastrophic thinking

Catastrophic thinking is when a person imagines scenarios in his or her head that are way more intense or graphic than what can really be expected or putting it differently, when we devise irrational worst-case outcomes. Do you suffer from catastrophic thinking pattern syndrome, that is, always expecting the worst? The worst-case scenario almost never happen but increases anxiety and paralyses your ability to take action. Do the following:

- Identify one example of your own catastrophic thinking.
- Generate a best-case possibility.
- Identify the most likely outcome.
- Develop a plan for handling the outcome.

Concentrate your energy on what is possible. Focussing on the negative may reduce your own confidence. To think positive doesn't mean that you ignore unpleasant situations. It means, however, that you approach the unpleasantness in a more positive and productive way. You think the best is going to happen, not the worst. If the thoughts that run through your head are mostly negative or if you are depressed, your outlook on life is more likely to be negative. If your thoughts are mostly positive, you're likely an optimist – someone who practices positive thinking. Skiffington and Zeus (2000) propose the following strategy that may help you to analyse negative thoughts:

1. What is the situation?
2. What are your self-limiting beliefs about the situation?
3. What are the consequences of these thoughts?
4. Are these thoughts logical, do I have evidence and how helpful is it to have these thoughts?
5. Are the thoughts unfounded and illogical? Does someone stand to gain (monetarily or otherwise) from me thinking this way?
6. What are they doing for my life? How are these thoughts influencing my relationships, work and life?
7. What can I do about it?

Less Ego, More Humility

What does humility mean? Templeton (1997, p. 162–163) explains it as follows:

> . . . humility is knowing you are smart, but not all-knowing. It is accepting that you have personal power, but are not omnipotent . . . inherent in humility resides an open and receptive mind . . . it leaves us more open

> to learn from others and refrains from seeing issues and people only in black and white. The opposite of humility is arrogance – the belief that we are wiser or better than others. Arrogance promotes separation . . . It looms like a brick wall between us and those from whom we could learn.

True humility is, therefore, the ability to be grateful for your talents and successes but at the same time not being self-focussed or self-absorbed. Humility does not mean that you are overly modest or self-effacing or meek. In a change leadership context it means that you view your leadership as a position of trust and stewardship (Hunter, 2004) that is, taking care of the people entrusted to you, listening to their concerns and doing the right thing (Winston, 2002).

A difficult challenge for some leaders to overcome is to remain modest in light of the success that they have achieved. When managers get caught up in their egos, it makes them less effective. The real power of change leadership is making your subordinates powerful. The question to ask is not, *how good or powerful am I?* but rather, *what do I need to do to energize and engage my subordinates?*. This is also your role in the change process, helping others to discover, explore, making sense and meaning of the change. Assisting employees to discover possibilities in themselves is only possible if we are able to transcend ourselves. Victor Frankl (1985) in his book *Man's Search for Meaning*, puts it as follows:

> . . .being human always points, and is directed, to something, or someone, other than oneself – be it meaning to fulfil or another human being to encounter. The more one forgets himself – by giving himself to a cause to serve or another person to love – the more human he is and the more he actualizes himself.

Collins (2001) proposed that leadership by those who possess true humility and a professional strong will, bring significantly greater benefits to the organization relative to benefits realized from CEOs of the charismatic or celebrity variety. He found that people who demonstrate humility display respectfulness, willingness to admit imperfections and have a lack of self-focus or self-serving bias (Tangney, 2002; Peterson and Seligman, 2004). Putting it differently, humility is the capacity to recognize that leadership is about serving others instead of being served. Greenleaf (1977, p. 7) explains this further:

> The servant-leader is servant first . . . it begins with the natural feeling that one wants to serve, to serve first. This conscious choice brings one to aspire to lead . . . The best test, and difficulty to administer is this: do

> those served grow as persons? Do they, while being served, become healthier, wiser, freer, more autonomous, and more likely themselves to become servants?

On the one hand the leader needs to demonstrate personal humility but on the other, also needs to demonstrate resilience; the determination to follow through on an organizational vision, mission, or goal.

Humility involves honest self-appraisal, the ability to forget the self and to appreciate the value of all things (Tangney, 2002). Molyneaux (2003, p. 359) state in this regard that:

> . . . humility is a self-respect and self-regard that is secure, wise and large enough to take risk by sharing and blending discipline with compassion. Thereby it can embrace its own and others' needs – needs that include, but extend well beyond, simple economic needs and considerations.

Creating sustainable change is not being charismatic but demonstrating leadership that builds greatness, that is, the ability to demonstrate personal humility and exercising a strong professional will (Collins, 2001). Great change leaders have the ability to foster success in others and enhance the decision-making capabilities of others (Mintzberg, 2004, p. 38). This can be explained as follows:

The role of the leader as servant

'My own philosophy is that a leader needs to be a servant. The CEO can be regarded as a good tenant farmer. Cultivating the ground, etc. for the next person. It is very much a servant role – it is not about the person – it is about the organization. The leader can extract a lot of energy of the organization – serving the leader and not the organization – this is a waste of resources. I believe in the servant leader model and also selecting a senior team who think that the organization and not the individual is the most important. I have a very low tolerance for egos.'

Be careful of your own ego

'I admire leaders who have the courage to speak up on issues that you just know might've been easier for them not to have spoken up on, but who are articulate and who are thoughtful in what they're saying and who I think are saying things because

they genuinely care, so there's no sort of hidden agenda. It's a very personal one, I sort of have great admiration for those without an ego and that can be quite difficult, the more senior you are the more egos I think are potentially out there. Personally what I admire are those who don't seem to have an ego. I think we've all got it to some degree but those who don't seem to have an ego, who – almost the business and them as an individual are almost one and the same and what they stand for is their organization and it being successful and that's more important to them than personal success.'

Resuscitate Your Passion for Life and Work

Steve Jobs, in a speech to graduates at Stanford University said,

> . . . when I was 17, I read a quote that went something like: 'If you live each day as if it was your last, someday you'll most certainly be right'. It made an impression on me, and since then, for the past 33 years, I have looked in the mirror every morning and asked myself: 'If today were the last day of my life, would I want to do what I am about to do today?' And whenever the answer has been 'No' for too many days in a row, I know I need to change something. People with passion can change the world for the better. Passion is everything.

What do we mean by passion? Passion can be regarded as a strong inclination toward a self-defining activity that individuals like (or even love), that they value

Table 2 Types of passion source? (Adapted from Vallerand et al., 2003)

Obsessive Passion	Harmonious Passion
1. Never stop thinking about work and unable to disengage from work	**1.** Engage with work because it gives joy and is pleasurable
2. Is at higher risk of burnout	**2.** Work is in harmony with other activities in life and finding work-life balance
3. Persist with activities even when it is no longer logical to do so	**3.** Work does not conflict with other areas of their life – are in control of their passion
4. Experience conflict between their passion and other life activities	**4.** Increases psychological well-being and lead to the creation of positive emotions

(and thus find important) and in which they invest time and energy (Vallerand et al., 2003). This means the person is highly engaged in the activity, does it regularly, invests energy and likes what they are doing. Howard Schultz (CEO of Starbucks) describes this as follows:

> *'It took years before I found my passion, but getting out of Brooklyn and earning a college degree gave me the courage to keep on dreaming. After tackling seemingly insurmountable obstacles, other hurdles become less daunting. So many times I have been told that it can't be done. Again and again, I've had to use every ounce of perseverance to make it happen. When I wholeheartedly believe in something, I can be relentless in my enthusiasm, passion and drive to bring it to life.'*

Passion is an internal phenomenon. Finding a way to do what you love – even if that something is cutting grass or towing cars – is the secret to being great at what you do. It comes from the heart and for that reason, don't wait for anyone else to light the fire for you. Everyone has to find his or her own source for the fire. Two types of passion can be distinguished, that is, it can either be obsessive or harmonious (see Table 2).

Why should we care about having obsessive or harmonious passions in work or for that matter having a work-life balance when we lead change? The importance is highlighted by Marks and MacDermid (1996, p. 421) who are of the opinion that balanced individuals are primed to seize the moment when confronted with a role demand because no role is seen as less worthy of one's alertness than any other'. This can be explained as follows:

Create balance in your life

> *'I kind of think it's work-life balance, if you've got your balance right, your home life can really help make you realize that actually this work stuff is not really that serious. I mean don't get me wrong – I'm as ambitious and competitive as the next person, otherwise I wouldn't be where I am and I love being in the competition and I want to win and I want to grow and I've got high aspirations for the business – all of that, absolutely, vehemently, passionately – as I hope comes across – but, by the same token, you know I love my family and I know that family's hugely important to me and so this silly expression*

"I'm married to my work," for God's sake, just go get a life. That's just the land of hopelessness, it really is. So any CEO who's in that position, who thinks work is more important than anything else, they are wrong. Simply wrong.'

Balanced individuals approach every typical role and role partner with an attitude of attentiveness, care, time, and involvement and experience less role-overload, greater role ease and less depression. This provides the energy to implement and lead change effectively. Complete the following exercise:

Passion in practice

1. *Reflect on the past*: Look again at the results of your life-line exercise in Chapter 1. Look at the high and low points, what are the underlying themes? What kind of passions do you have?
2. *Analyse the present*: What has or has not changed at work, in your life? How do you see yourself? What kind of satisfaction do you get from your work? What needs to change?
3. *Envision the future*: What is your purpose, vision for yourself? What does the ideal future look like?

What do you need to do to reignite your passion for life and work?

Chapter Summary

The chapter highlights the importance of personal preparation for organizational change. Change agents do not consistently question their own beliefs, attitudes and feelings about the change. Nor do they determine how personal attributes such as mental models, change philosophy, personal characteristics and so on may influence how they implement and lead change. The core message of the chapter is that the change process starts with you, the change agent. You need to take a careful look at yourself and continuously ask questions around personal attributes you need to develop, what are your strengths and dysfunctional behaviours you exhibit, when leading change. Most importantly, ask yourself the question if you are ready for the organizational change you are responsible for. To become ready for change means you need to be (1) willing to cross boundaries, so take personal risks and venture beyond familiar territory, (2) behave according to your values, and (3) learn from and reflect on experiences. Use support structures such as peers, followers and even family members to give feedback around your personal impact, strengths and possible development areas.

KEY INSIGHTS FROM PRACTICE

A need to reinvent yourself everyday.
Examine and understand your own mental models about change.
Be tough – be willing to make difficult decisions.
Be empathetic and understand the impact of your actions on others.
Show optimism and look for the potential in any challenge.
The real power of change leadership is making your subordinates powerful.
Resuscitate your passion for life and work.
Trust yourself and others.

References

APA (American Psychiatric Association) (2000). *Diagnostic and Statistical Manual of Mental Disorders* (DSM-1-IV-TR, 4th edn, Text revision) Washington, DC: American Psychiatric Association.

Armenakis, A.A, Harris, S.G., and Mossholder, K.W. (1993). Creating readiness for organisational change. *Human Relations*, 46 (6), 681–703.

Armenakis, A.A., Bernerth, J.B., Pitts, J.P., and Walker, H.J. (2007). Organisational change recipients' beliefs scale: Development of an assessment instrument. *Journal of Applied Behavioural Science*, 43, 495–505.

Bull, S.J., Shambrook, C.J., James, W., and Brooks, J.E. (2005). Towards an understanding of mental toughness in elite English cricketers. *Journal of Applied Sport Psychology*, 17, 209–227.

By, R.T., Diefenbach, T., and Klarner, P. (2008). Getting organizational change right in public services: The case of European higher education. *Journal of Change Management*, 8 (1), 21–35.

Clough, P., Earle, K., and Sewell, D. (2002). Mental toughness: The concept and its measurement. In I.M. Cockerill (ed.), *Solutions in Sport Psychology* (pp. 32–45). Thomson, London.

Collins, J. (2001). Level 5 leadership: The triumph of humility and fierce resolve. *Harvard Business Review*, Jan, 66–76.

Cryer, B., McCraty, R., and Childre, D. (2003). Pull the plug on stress. *Harvard Business Review*, 81 (7), 102–107.

Cunningham, C.E., Woodward, C.A., Shannon, H.S., MacIntosh, J., Lendrum, B., Rosenbloom, D., and Brown, J. (2002). Readiness for organizational change: A longitudinal study of workplace, psychological and behavioural correlates. *Journal of Occupational and Organisational Psychology*, 75 (4), 377–392.

Dunbar, R. (1985). *Narcissistic Dilemmas and Studies of Organizations*. Paper presented at the Conference on alternative perspectives on organizations, Baruch College, New York.

Eby, L.T., Adams, D.M., Russel, J.E.A., and Gaby, S.H. (2000). Perceptions of organizational readiness for change: factors related to employees' reactions to the implementation of team-based selling. *Human Relations*, 53 (3), 419–442.

Fiske, S.T. and Taylor, S.E. (1984). *Social Cognition*. Reading MA: Addison-Wesley.

Frankl, V.E. (1985). *Man's Search for Meaning*. New York: Washington Square Press.

George, B., McLean, A., and Craig, N. (2008). *Finding Your True North: A Personal Guide.* San Francisco: Jossey-Bass.

Glad, B. (2002). Why tyrants go too far: Malignant narcissism and absolute power. *Political Psychology*, 23, 1–37.

Goldberg, A. (1998). *Sports Slump Busting: 10 Steps to Mental Toughness and Peak Performance*, Champaign, IL: Human Kinetics.

Goleman, D. (1998). *Working with Emotional Intelligence.* London: Bloomsbury Publishing.

Gould, D., Hodge, K., Peterson, K., and Petlichkoff, L. (1987). Psychological foundations of coaching: Similarities and differences among intercollegiate wrestling coaches. *The Sport Psychologist*, 1, 293–308.

Greca, I.M. and Morereira, M.A. (2010). Mental models, conceptual models and modelling. *International Journal of Science Education*, 22 (1), 1–11.

Greenleaf, R.K. (1977). *Servant Leadership: A Journey into the Nature of Legitimate Power and Greatness.* New York: Paulist Press.

Holt, D.T., Achilles, A., Armenikis, Feild, H.S., and Harris, S.G. (2007). Readiness for organizational change: The systematic development of a scale. *Journal of Applied Behavioural Science*, 43, 232–255.

Hunter, J.C. (2004). *The World's Most Powerful Leadership Principle.* New York: Crown Business.

Huy, Q. (1999). Emotional capability, emotional intelligence, and radical change. *Academy of Management Review*, 24, 325–345.

Jones, G., Hanton, S., and Connaughton, D. (2002). What is this thing called mental toughness? An investigation of elite performers. *Journal of Applied Sport Psychology*, 14, 205–218

Jones, R.A., Jimmieson, N.L., and Griffiths, A. (2005). The impact of organizational culture and the reshaping capabilities on change implementation success: The mediating role of readiness for change. *Journal of Management Studies*, 42 (2), 361–386.

Judge, T.A. and LePine, J.A. (2007). The bright and dark sides of personality: Implications for personnel selection in individual and team contexts. In J. Langan-Fox, C. Cooper and R. Klimoski (eds), *Research Companion to the Dysfunctional Workplace: Management Challenges and Symptoms* (pp. 332–355). Edward Elgar Publishing, Cheltenham.

Kets de Vries, M. (2004). Organizations on the couch: A clinical perspective on organizational dynamics. *European Management Journal*, 22 (2), 183–200.

Kets de Vries, M. and Engellau, E. (2010). *Clinical Approach to the Dynamics of Leadership and Executive Transformation.* Harvard Business Press Chapters.

Komaki, J.L. (1986). Toward effective supervision: An operant analysis and comparison of managers at work. *Journal of Applied Psychology*, 71, 270–279.

Kouzes, J.M. and Posner, B.Z. (2006). *A Leader's Legacy.* San Francisco: Jossey-Bass.

Lau, C.M. and Woodman, R.W. (1995). Understanding organizational change: A schematic perspective. *Academy of Management Journal*, 38 (2), 537–554.

Lubit, R. (2002). The long-term organisational impact of destructively narcissistic managers. *Academy of Management Executive*, 16 (1), 127–138.

Maccoby, M. (2003). *The Productive Narcissist: The Promise and Peril of Visionary Leadership.* New York: Broadway Books.

Marks, S.R. and Macdermid, S.M. (1996). Multiple roles and the self: A theory of role balance. *Journal of Marriage and the Family*, 63, 417–432.

Mayer, J.D. and Salovey, P. (1997). What is emotional intelligence? In P. Salovey and D. Sluyter (eds), *Emotional Development and Emotional Intelligence: Implications for Educators* (pp. 3–31). New York: Basic Books.

Mintzberg, H. (2004). *Managers, Not MBAs.* San Francisco: Berrett-Koehler.

Molyneaux, D. (2003). Blessed are the meek, for they shall inherit the earth: An aspiration applicable to business. *Journal of Business Ethics*, 48, 347–363.

Pellettiere, V. (2006), Organization self-assessment to determine the readiness and risk for a planned change, *Organizational Development Journal*, 24, 38–44.

Peterson, C. and Seligman, M.E.P. (2004). *Character Strengths and Virtues: A Handbook and Classification*. New York: Oxford University Press.

Prochaska, J.O., DiClemente, C.C., and Norcross, J.C. (1992). In search of how people change: Applications to addictive behaviors. *American Psychologist*, 47 (9), 1102–1114.

Reivich, K.J., Seligman, M.E.P., and McBride, S. (2011). Master resilience training in the U.S. Army. *American Psychologist*, 66 (1), 25–34.

Skiffington, S. and Zeus, P. (2000). *The Complete Guide to Coaching at Work*. McGraw-Hill: Australia.

Spreitzer, G.M. and Mishra, A.K. (2002). To stay or go: Voluntary turnover following and organisational downsizing. *Journal of Organizational Behaviour*, 23, 707–729.

Tangney, J.P. (2002). Perfectionism and the self-conscious emotions: Shame, guilt, embarrassment, and pride. In P.L. Hewitt and G.L. Flett (eds), *Perfectionism* (pp. 199–215). American Psychological Association: Washington, DC.

Templeton, J.M. (1997). *Worldwide Laws of Life*. Philadelphia: Templeton Foundation Press.

Vallerand, R.J., Mageau, G.A., Ratelle, C., Léonard, M., Blanchard, C., Koestner, R. et al. (2003). Les passions de 1'Âme: On obsessive and harmonious passion. *Journal of Personality and Social Psychology*, 85 (4), 756–767.

Walker, H.J., Armenakis, A.A., and Bernerth, J.B. (2007). Factors influencing organizational change efforts: An integrative investigation of change content, context, process and individual differences *Journal of Organizational Change Management*, 20 (6), 756–767.

Weber, P.S. and Weber, J.E. (2001). Changes in employee perceptions during organisational change. *Leadership and Organisational Development Journal*, 22, 291–300.

Winston, B.E. (2002). *Be a Leader for God's Sake*. Virginia Beach, VA: Regent University School of Leadership Studies.

Zander, R.S. and Zander, B. (2000). *The Art of Possibility: Transforming Professional and Personal Life*. New York: Penguin.

CHAPTER 3

Leading Change: Winning Hearts and Minds

Chapter at a Glance

This chapter focusses on specific actions that you, the change leader need to be aware of when leading and implementing change. Managers must lead, not merely aspire to manage change. Mobilizing employees through effective communication is at the heart of leading change. Leaders need to set direction, create alignment and maintain commitment towards the change but they do not control the change. Their role is to enable others and to create the conditions that will facilitate organizational change.

Beginning Cases: Preparation

What does it mean to lead change in such a way that we are able to capture the hearts and minds of our employees? What do we need to understand in order to be able to create conditions that will make the implementation of organizational changes more successful? Answers to these questions are evident in the CEO and executive reflections that follow. We explore these and other issues in the rest of the chapter.

Change is continuous

'Well, I suppose currently as a leader you are talking all the time about changing and preparing the organization for moving on. Change is very much a constant now in business. For many years we had periods where there was very little or relatively little change but over the last 10–15 years there probably have been very significant changes. Where we are at this point in time, I'd say it is even increasing and the rate of change is more continuous than it has been. So the challenge for us as a leader and for me in my role is to help the organization to move its change capability onto a different level and try to develop the culture within the organization so that it doesn't think of change as a block but as a continuous sort of evolution. We tried quite a number of stepped phases of change over the last 15–20 years and now our need is more to be moving all of the time ahead of the change but we haven't fully transitioned in terms of our capability to do that.'

Rate of change is accelerating

Is your organization built for change?

'So there comes a point where, I suppose, you have to look at who you're competing with, what the easiest way to respond faster to customers is going to be and realize what has worked very successfully for many years probably was now starting to become a bit of a threat to the company. And, also you start to build in inefficiency, for example the way we choose to refit our shops and to open up new shops – if you had eight directors, all at a local level deciding what equipment they would put in, who they would purchase that equipment from, the layout of the shop – before you know it you're building in complexity which also builds in cost which means you're not getting the benefit of and the reason to think about the key question: why did the organization need to change? If you were to look at who the competitors are now, compared to five to ten years ago, there's been quite a transformation in the competitors. We were actually going to be disadvantaged, we were competing suddenly with brands

Complex systems and processes impact on change agility

What is happening in your external environment?

who were much bigger, probably financially much stronger and therefore if we were going to maintain a value reputation and also continue to grow and to grow well, we had to look at how do we actually run as a business much better and more efficiently than we've done previously.'

Employee involvement and participation is the key to change success

'I think it's very hard for people when they can see that they're working harder than ever that, sales are still harder to come by. When people are spending less, again our people have to do more, just to stand still and then what you're saying on top of that is if you look further out, we're not predicting a return to sort of the sales growth that we've experienced in the last decade. How are you going to spend more but also then grow profitably? How do you do more but for less? And our people you know, when you say that they sort of look at you as if you've slightly lost the plot you want us to work harder but we're going to do everything for less, you want us to do more for less? It's not until you say yeah but there are ways to do it and actually you've probably got the answers – that's when a lightbulb moment happens when you say you must sit here day after day thinking management just don't know what's going on. Why are we doing this way because there must be a better way of doing it, you're closer to it at the sharp end, you're actually physically making product or you're actually selling and you see the way that we are running – you will hear great ideas every day. And when you ask them that, do you think we're doing everything perfectly or do we ask you to do things that you think are slightly mad and they say, well actually, now you come to mention it there are certain things that I wonder why you ask us to do it this way. There's something about capturing the power of our people, our customers – they do tend to see things that they question and they wonder why do we do things in the way that we do it and actually if we did it in a different way, we probably would have a benefit.'

Involve employees

Identify best practice, contextualize it for your business and implement.

'The other thing is if you are not too proud, you can actually learn from others and if you go around the world you will see other businesses that are doing things where they are doing them better and they are doing them in different ways and if we can bring that learning back to the UK. So, how do you make it better for customers? Simpler for your people and then ultimately cheaper for the organization? And if you start out by saying, "look, that's what you have to achieve" and you get that right, everybody wins but too often what happens is people have a reaction which is "I've got to do more for less" and that equates to "I've got to strip cost out which means I'm just going to have to do more for less" and what happens is you get real tension within the business because it starts to creak and people feel the pressure because you are in effect only asking them to do that. You're saying I want you to do more but there's going to be either less funding, less people, less investment and that won't grow sustainable business. So I much prefer a sort of how do we get the whole mindset around better simpler cheaper. If you start out with that, whatever we're doing has got to pass those three tests you won't go far wrong. By the way it's not easy to do. Because you do have to tick those three boxes, but when you do it, you'll actually have your people saying this is great because actually it's simpler; our business is much simpler to run today and therefore although times are tough, it's a more enjoyable workplace because you've made life simpler and easier for me. Your customers are saying – well this is great because whatever you've done, it's better for me as a customer and we should be sitting there saying and as a result of all of that it's cheaper and therefore we're actually going to have hopefully pleased shareholders and you've ticked all the boxes.'

Successful change requires thinking out of the box

Chapter Introduction

There is growing consensus that the leader plays an important role in shaping employees behaviours and attitudes towards change implementation (Kotter,

1996; Higgs and Rowland, 2005). Behaviours such as setting direction, employee involvement in the change process, communicating the change rationale and providing support are linked to increased employee support for the change (Kotter, 1995; Burke, 2002). Adding to this, House and Adita (1997) view change leadership as the ability of the leader to operationalize the change and to manage it from a tactical point of view. That is, creating change readiness, enabling the change strategy and implementation (Kanter, et al., 1992). Despite the purported role and importance of the leader in change success, 'no consensus exists on the specific leadership competencies critical to change success' (Wren and Dulewicz, 2005, p. 296) Exceptions to this are studies by Higgs and Rowland (2000; 2001) who group leader behaviour into three categories: framing change, shaping behaviour and creating capacity for the change, which includes developing leadership competencies associated with successful change implementation. The leadership competencies identified are associated with areas such as communicating the context for change, implementing and sustaining the change, facilitating and developing change capability. This refers to the structural components of leading change often termed the *hard side of change*. Normally, managers are more familiar with and have experience with the 'hard side' of leading change. Less attention, however, is given to the 'soft side' of leading change, the people component. Both the hard and soft sides of leading change are equally important. Leaders also need to focus on engaging employees in the change process, supporting them through a process likened to that of mourning: letting go of the past, building hope and learning (Michelman, 2007). Irrespective of the type of change, initiating and implementing change is a function of managerial behaviour (planning, budgeting, organizing and staffing, controlling and problem solving) and leadership behaviours (establishing direction, aligning people and motivating and inspiring your employees). This is explained in the following quotes:

Take personal ownership for the change

Change communication is a key success factor

'In terms of buy-in to the change – people will notice when management change – this will give you a lot more credibility when you ask them/suggest taking ownership themselves. They will buy-in more easily into change if you show them that you have changed as well. This is key and then it is really communication, communication. I will be uncomfortable with change if there is no change – because I know what the consequences/medium or long-term may be. I really think it is about change or die. In terms of my managers and change: middle management is key – if you don't get buy-in from them – there is no way you get the organization to change. You need to get

Understand the role of middle managers in implementing change

Successful change integrates the 'hard' as well as the 'soft' side of leading change i.e. head + heart = change acceptance

Participating in any change process is a choice

Understand what you want to achieve

your middle-management on-board. They are the ones that are going to drive the change. They are the pillars of execution of the change – if you do not get buy-in from them – forget about the rest of the organization. The second point is again – because of the human challenge – they need to have manager qualities – to make it happen within their teams. They need to have human management skills – to drive the change. So number 1 is buy in and number 2 is execution competence through human management. It is human – it is not technical. Technical, who cares – we can get consultants to show the tools. The buy-in and the belief in that it is human, only human is crucial. For example, 10 years ago you had to move employees from handwriting things to computer. It was not about teaching the guy to do it on the computer (you can send him on a course to increase his technical proficiency) but if you do not get the buy-in and that desire to change he will go back to the handwriting – because he does not want to change – so it is the human factor.'

'To create enthusiasm for change – well first of all it is the combination of two things. First question is do you want to be on the boat or not – if you are on the boat you have to change. Second is not to threaten people per se because that is not my way of doing it- an organization that does not change will die – there are different ways to die by-the-way – get bought out – IBM 30 years ago is a good example of not be able to change – they said "we are the best – we do not need to change" when you are the best that is when you really have to ask yourself the questions. Because when you are the best everybody else wants to beat you up. It is easier to be on the challengers list. So I really think – once the analysis is done – you will have people that say let's go for it – that are really enthusiastic about it. Leadership is not being no. 1 in an industry – leadership is about leading an industry – bringing innovation in the industry, keeping on top of things and this generates momentum, this generates enthusiasm

> *and therefore the boat goes ahead. And if you do not do this – yes you die. Question is what legacy do you want to leave?'*

Given the complexity of change it is not possible for one person to lead change – leadership exists at all levels in the organization – your task is to identify, develop and utilize the leadership skills of the whole organization. Kouzes and Posner (2002, p. 77) articulate it as follows:

> . . .it is not enough for leaders to simply deliver a rousing speech or talk about lofty ideas or promising futures. Compelling words may be essential to lifting people's spirits, but leaders know constituents are more deeply moved by deeds . . . leaders take every opportunity to show others by their own example that they are deeply committed to the values and aspirations . . . in the process of setting an example, leaders lead their constituents form what *I believe* to what *we believe*. In the end it wasn't about me, it was about what all of us did by working together. Leadership is a relationship.

Framing the Change

Sense-making

In Chapter 1 the importance of making sense of life events was highlighted and emphasized as a key building block in the authentic change leader development journey. However, the leader does not only need to make sense of the self but also need to understand why the change is needed, that is, making sense of the change. The leader needs to understand and interpret the environmental triggers of change (Senior and Fleming, 2006) and 'define a revised conception of the organisation' (Gioia and Chittipeddi, 1991, p. 434). The relationship between leaders as sense-makers and the effectiveness of strategic change in the organizations has been well established (Gioia and Thomas, 1996). An important role of the leader is assisting employees in the sense-making process and helping employees finding answers to: what is the change about?, *how is it going to impact on me as an individual?* and *what is my role in the change process?'* From an individual perspective, the leader needs to gain insight into the reasons why the organizational change is needed and important, to consider the end result of the change, as well as the nature of the change. Weick et al. (2005) argue in this regard that sense-making starts with noticing and bracketing; that is, 'inventing new meaning' and this process is guided by available mental models (as discussed in Chapter 2), the cognitive meaning structures of the leader. These simplified representations of reality provide a conceptual framework for 'describing, explaining and predicting future system states' (Rouse and Morris, 1986, p. 359). Johnson (2008) argues in this regard that mental models serve as a basis for perception, analysis and understanding, and direct individual behaviour. This means that the leader needs to understand 'any intended change in a way that fits into some revised interpretive system of meaning' (Gioia and Chittipeddi, 1991, p. 434).

For example, teams and boards develop a shared mental model of their world through debate and discussion. Alignment between members of an executive team or board cannot be assumed and on occasion the 'development of the shared mental model' is assisted through skilful facilitation by an organizational development specialist. Secondly, sense-making is also about labelling and categorizing (Weick et al., 2005) of events in order 'to stabilize the streaming of experience' (p. 411). Sense-making does not take place in isolation but can be regarded as a function of various social factors (Weick et al., 2005). This means that the leader needs to share and express feelings and emotions about the change event, identifying potential and foreseeable problems as well as identifying solutions to overcome possible barriers. This may also include the use of helping relationships; that is, being open and trusting about problems with someone who cares (Levesque, et al., 1999). Weick et al. (2005) argue that sense-making is also about action and answering the question *what do I do next?*. This refers to Prochaska and Velicer's (1997) concept of self-liberation where the individual chooses to and commits to a specific course of action. To make sense of an event is also about connecting the abstract with the concrete (Weick et al. 2005). This implies the leader needs to do an environmental evaluation which is based on an affective and or cognitive assessment of how one's thoughts, feelings or behaviours may affect/impact upon changing the environment (Prochaska, 1984). This also relates to what Gardner et al. (2005) refer to as 'emotional self-awareness', an important component of effective change leadership. Finally, change sense-making is 'about continued redrafting of an emerging story so that it becomes more comprehensive, incorporates more of the observed data, and is more resilient in the face of criticism' (Weick et al., 2005, p. 415). This means the individual needs to engage in continuous self-evaluation, assessing feelings and emotions about the change (Levesque, et al., 1999). Reflexivity, so called reflection in action (Schön, 1983), can be regarded as an important component of the sense-making process and includes behaviours such as questioning, planning, exploratory learning, analysis, diverse exploration, and reviewing past events with self-awareness (West, 2002).

The CEO needs to understand and interpret the external and internal environment of the organization and 'define a revised conception of the organisation'

(Gioia and Chittipeddi, 1991, p. 434). We asked participants to tell us about the main drivers for change in their organizations and it seems that external drivers such as the economic recession, technological innovation and demands from stakeholders are key challenges facing their organizations. Take a look at the following example:

Identify external challenges

'The single biggest challenge I think is the economy and how our organization is both a retailer and a manufacturer so we have both the challenges that the retail sector are facing and also the challenges that the manufacturing sector face. So how, with low sales growth, rising costs, do you find ways of actually competing, innovating, but also growing profitably in a very challenging marketplace?'

'Well I think in our particular industry of technology, there is a monstrous disruptive change taking place which is, in shorthand, the transition from the world of the PC and the client server installation to the world of the cloud and we're not through the transition yet, but it's clearly one of those systemic structural changes in the environment which is going to change the landscape forever and consequently, for an organization like ours, which has built its success on the old world, it faces monstrous challenges in addressing its shape for the new world.'

The leader needs to gain insight into the reasons why the organizational change is needed and is important, and needs to consider both the results of the change as well as the nature of the change. Sense-making starts with *inventing new meaning* and this process is guided by available mental models, the meaning structures of the leader. These simplified representations of reality provide a conceptual framework for 'describing, explaining and predicting future system states' (Rouse and Morris, 1986, p. 359). Some CEOs explain the result of their sense making as follows:

Making sense of the external environment

'Well as ever, before we start worrying about the organizational shape, the right thing to do – at least in our view – is to make sure that our strategy is right. So having assessed where the market is likely to go, and having understood what our vision should be and having recognized what assets we have at our

What actions do you need to take to position your organization?

disposal, which are timeless and will help us combat whatever the future challenges might be, then we need to work out what our strategy is to get to the vision. And once we've identified that strategy, then that will dictate what form of organizational reshape we should consider.'

Have a clear understanding of the end goal

Understand the 'here and now' but take a long-term perspective

'And then I suppose the last piece in that is having an eye to what it is we look like at the end of it, so what I keep trying to focus on is what we're going to be like in year five. We will look very different to what we are now, we're going to work very differently, the terms and conditions of some staff are going to be very different, we're going to have to be a lot more flexible, we're going to have to prioritize much better, all that kind of stuff. So really focussing on the long game, even though the here and now – managing the here and now is difficult because, if you like, there's nobody else doing that "what do we need to be like in five years' time?" because they're all focused on the here and now and managing through what is a very difficult environment.'

In the previous chapter the role of interpretative schemas or change mental models in understanding change was highlighted. Change mental models not only inform the participant's philosophy about change, so how change is viewed, but also how change is implemented and managed. Lau and Woodman (1995) argue in this regard a change schema 'may not be the only cognitive variable that affects attitudinal and behavioural responses towards change but can be regarded as an important guide for actions' (p. 537). This may affect the manner in which the leader creates organizational readiness for the change, how the need for change is communicated, how employees are mobilized to support the change and how the initiative is evaluated (Battilana, et al., 2010).

Setting direction

Following from the leader's *sense-making process*, an abstract change vision is formulated, and it is this vision that is disseminated to change recipients through symbols and symbolic action (Gioia and Chittipeddi, 1991), that is, *the sense-giving process*. This is important because during organizational change there is uncertainty, ambiguity in roles and information overload (Cummings and Huse, 1989). Change recipients respond to what is happening in the environment and make assumptions about the change process. The purpose of the leader's sense giving process is to create readiness for change and is comparable with Lewin's (1951) conception of unfreezing (Kotter, 1995; Luecke, 2003). This refers to disturbing the status quo by 'either strengthening or weakening the forces for change' (Cummings and Worley, 2005, p. 22) or putting it differently, changing employee beliefs and attitudes about an imminent change. It incorporates two important components: motivation to implement the change, so an action component; and the perceived behavioural capability of the recipients, such as levels of self-efficacy in implementing the change effectively. This can be explained as follows:

Formulating a vision is a team effort
A vision creates shared understanding

Understand the role of values as drivers of the vision

'We went back to basics, we developed a vision, a mission and a values type of statement, where taking my top executive team we went through a series of away workshops over a period of about six months to develop our views of what the organization was, where we wanted to be and what its role would be and to create a series of values to try and distil the organization's operation into a series of values. So we did that and we did it successfully. We had acceptance and approval from the board, we then had to embark on the more important mission of launching it and getting it going and part of that was establishing a brand for the organization.'

The purpose of the change vision is to inspire, provide direction, motivate others and maintain commitment (Kotter, 1996; Van Velsor and McCauley, 2004; Landau, et al., 2006; Cole, et al., 2006). The change vision has to be achievable, be clear and understandable (Christenson and Walker, 2004) and aligned to the culture and values of the organization (Landau et al., 2006). The change vision needs to be shared as this creates a framework of common understanding (Christenson and Walker, 2004) and assists in shaping the values and standards of the organization (Lafley, 2009). The importance of creating a change vision is highlighted and emphasized by key change – leadership prescriptions found in the literature. Table 1 provides an overview of key change leadership approaches where the formulation of a change vision is seen as a key component of the change process.

A clearly articulated change vision therefore assists in mobilizing employees and creating emotional alignment (Hooper and Potter, 2000) towards the envisaged change process. The importance of effective communication in the change process has been well researched (Paterson and Cary, 2002; Bordia et al., 2004;

Table 1 Change leadership approaches

Lewin 1951) Change process	**Kanter, et al. (1992) Ten Commandments for executing change**	**Cummings and Worley (2005)**	**Ulrich (1998) Seven step model for managing change**	**Luecke (2003) Seven Steps**	**Kotter (2012) Eight- stage process for successful organizational transformation**
Unfreeze	Analyse the organization and its need for change	Motivate change	Lead change	Mobilize energy and commitment through joint identification of business problems and their solutions	Establish a sense of urgency
Movement	**Create a vision and a common direction**	**Creating a vision**	Create a shared need	**Develop a shared vision of how to organize and manage for competitiveness**	Create the guiding coalition
Refreeze	Separate from the past	Develop political support	**Shape a vision**	Identify the leadership	**Develop a change vision**
	Create a sense of urgency	Manage the transition	Mobilize commitment	Focus on results, not on activities	Communicate the vision for buy-in
	Support a strong leader role	Sustain momentum	Change systems and structures	Start change at the periphery, then let it spread to other units without pushing it from the top	Empower broad-based action
	Line up political sponsorship		Monitor progress	Institutionalize success through formal policies, systems, and structures	Generate short-term wins
	Craft an implementation plan		Make changes last	Monitor and adjust strategies in response to problems in the change process	Never let up
	Develop enabling structures				Incorporate change into the culture
	Communicate, involve people and be honest				
	Reinforce and institutionalize change				

Oreg, 2006). Armenakis and Harris (2002) further highlight the importance of change communication. Change strategies often fail because information is not effectively communicated or the quality of the information falls short of expectations and requirements (Bordia, et al., 2004). Quality of communication is regarded as a key mechanism in creating change readiness (Kotter and Cohen 2002, Elving, 2005) and can influence how employees perceive the change and may facilitate their readiness for the change initiative (Bordia et al., 2004). Communicate by a factor of 10 is the recommendation of Kotter (2012), that is, repeat the message at least 10 times. Employees need to understand why the change is necessary, be able to predict what is going to happen next and what is expected of them. The contextualization of change is absolutely critical. Failure to address change recipients' predictive and explanatory needs (Berger, 1987) may lead to feelings of uncertainty and emotional reactions to the change (Oreg, 2003).

The purpose of the vision is therefore to inspire, provide direction, motivate others and maintain commitment (Van Velsor and McCauley, 2004; Landau, et al., 2006) towards the envisaged change. Kotter (2007) argues in this regard that 'without a sensible vision, a transformation effort can easily dissolve into a list of confusing and incompatible projects that can take the organisation in the wrong direction' (p. 7). Regarding the importance of direction setting, the majority of leaders emphasized the importance of having (1) a clear understanding of the reasons for change, or putting it differently, have a clear understanding what will things look like when the change is completed (2) involvement of key role-players in determining the direction of the change, (3) disseminating the vision to the different stakeholders and (4) showing visible support. These points were emphasized by our CEO respondents:

Define the end state

Have a clear roadmap of how to reach the end state by formulating specific objectives

'And then I suppose the last piece in that is having an eye to what it is we look like at the end of it, so what I keep trying to focus on is what we're going to be like in year five; we will look very different to what we are now, we're going to work very differently, the terms and conditions of some staff are going to be very different, we're going to have to be a lot more flexible, we're going to have to prioritise much better, all that kind of stuff. So really focussing on the long game, even though the here and now – managing the here and now is difficult because, if you like, there's nobody else doing that "what do we need to be like in five years' time?" because they're all focussed on the here and now and managing through what is a

very difficult environment. So I keep asking myself – am I clear about what year five looks like? And then tracking back through my own head, "right well what I have to do today and tomorrow is this, this and this," because it all helps me to get to year five.'

Revisit your vision regularly

Test your vision for clarity and acceptance

'Well I think there's no one simple way of doing this and I think it's a continuous journey, to be honest, I don't think it's a one-off event. I think it's really a way of being, it becomes what you stand for and every time you have an opportunity to talk to people, reinforcing and confirming what the vision is and reminding people why it's still the right vision. I suppose my style was actually to sit and work with the existing team and to go out and spend a lot of time when I first arrived listening to people within the organization about what their views were . . .'

The importance of creating a change vision is highlighted and emphasized by key change – leadership prescriptions (e.g. Kanter, et al., 1992; Kotter, 2012) found in the literature. From the narratives, it seems the leaders we interviewed specified the general direction of the change and tried to mobilize commitment to the change through listening, involvement, and through exhibiting relationship-directed behaviour. It is important to remember that the change vision needs to be specific and should be able to describe closely what things will look like after the change. This can be explained as follows:

Understand the purpose of a *vision* i.e. to guide employees

Translate the vision into an inspiring message

'I think goals are different, goals are pretty easy to set, I would be advocating anyway that a confused vision with goals and all sorts of set things is easy enough to write down goals and targets and to say, this is how we're going to achieve it, and this is what's going to happen, and you can train people into that and you can coach them and guide them and do all sorts of things. Indeed you can nearly force people to go towards achieving targets and all that sort of stuff, but I suppose the vision thing is deeper than that, and it's wider than that and it's more complex than just setting targets. The vision thing is being able to picture something that you haven't firmed up yet. And that's where the difficulty is in trying to communicate that particular

vision, so you have to explain, you have to demonstrate through explanation and through training and through education and through all the different ways of trying to get that picture across. Then you're talking about people at different levels, some people are very quick to be able to pick it up. Others will always struggle, they just cannot . . . they need to see it on the table every time. Let me see before I can visualize it. So, you have to have patience and you have to have endurance and a whole lot of absolute belief in it, you have this belief that . . . and so I felt over the years that part of it was listening to people, trying to explain it, listening to their difficulties, sometimes just holding your counsel, shutting up and just listening, getting frustrated to hell. Because you have repeated it time and time again but unless again you come back and sit down and say look; that's where the person is at, I think the reality is important in leadership. Where are they at? Because you can assume that people are here there and everywhere, you have to find out, where exactly are they first? And it's only then you can start moving them along.'

Implementing a vision needs passion, resilience and optimism

To summarize, a vision provides a clear picture of the future, it addresses not only the minds of employees but also their hearts and employees should be able to assess it as achievable and specific. Key to any vision is to get buy-in not only from your top management team but also from your employees. This means that the vision should be translated into language that employees are able to understand. The vision is not an abstract statement – it should be easy to understand and inspire employees to take action. This is also what Cohen and Tichy (1997, p. 63) called 'the teachable point of view' or putting it differently, what it takes to lead employees. The leader needs to be motivated and able to motivate employees irrespective of difficult times they may experience. Furthermore, they need to be able to (1) articulate and shape values that are supportive of the organizational change and (2) be willing to make tough decisions. The change vision should be shared and communicated authentically and consistently for example during staff-meetings, one-on-one conversations, on the organization's intranet and so on. However, the vision provides a clear picture of where we are going, but does not tell the employees how we are going to achieve our vision. We need to articulate and communicate specific steps or goals to explain to employees the actions needed to reach the end state. Breaking the goals into bite-size chunks not only helps employees to understand what is going to happen (i.e. reduces uncertainty) but may also act as an empowering mechanism as they provide input on how to implement the vision. Understanding the road ahead enables employees to (1) understand their role in the implementation process and (2) prepare themselves for what lies ahead.

Strategic reflection

One of the most important things for those contemplating change is to step back and ask if they have the right overall strategy before they begin to implement. Hard data on market share, trends, cost and revenue projections are often neglected in change and are key factors to consider. Patterson, et al., (2005) emphasize the importance of continuously reviewing and reflecting upon objectives, strategies and work processes in order to adapt to changes in the wider environment. Reflexivity, reflection in action (Schön, 1983), can be regarded as an important component of the sense-making process and include behaviours such as questioning, planning, analysis and reviewing past events with self-awareness. CEOs also expressed the importance of (1) creating time for reflection and (2) reflecting on past experiences, and put it this way:

Be merciless when managing time – create opportunities for reflection

Asking the 'right questions' will help in raising the bar and stretching your employees

'I have half my diary always free so that I can think and that demands of course that I am ruthless with meeting management. So there are certain techniques and tools that I have that ensure that I prize the time that I have fantastically. I mean there's nothing I hate more than having – what some people are very proud about – having a back to back day, I mean I think a back to back day is a disaster because you have no time to think, you have no time to add value. Shareholders are getting no return if I'm not thinking. But if I'm thinking, I can be thinking about asking the right questions which are going to push the boundaries and stretch people more and raise the bar and take us across this massive transformational chasm of structural change that we have to get through.'

Use the vision as guiding principle

Reflect continuously

'How do we stay ahead of change? The pre-requisite to stay ahead of changes is to constantly reflect on in-depth issues and always have your vision on top of your head. You know – this in-depth analysis has to be constant. If you get bogged down into details and you never see the big picture – you never will be able

to take a step back and re-think about things. Every single industry faces its own challenges – but you will always identify future trends today by having this in-depth analysis. I will take an example – there are two ways to deal with it: There is today and deal with the crises short-term/cut costs. To stay ahead you need to ask yourself what is going to come out of this crisis – and these are the questions we need to ask ourselves. The fundamental questions I would ask myself continuously "what next/what after?" How do you want to come out of this crisis much stronger – clear headway and be ahead of the others? Then you start analysing your industry, your consumer behaviour after the crisis. What impact is this crisis having on your consumers that will change their behaviour when things will be back to life when it is nice. Will they still buy the same way? Will they still perceive the value of the brands they buy the same way? I think not, by the way.'

Do not become complacent – always ask what is the next challenge?

Reflection should provide insights around pressing business problems

At its most basic level the narratives refer to the questioning of taken for granted assumptions, frames and mental models and is aligned with Raelin's (2001, p. 11) idea of reflective practice as 'the practice of periodically stepping back to ponder the meaning of what has recently transpired'. This retrospective evaluation of the past assists CEOs to make choices about what they will and will not do, that is, doing a post mortem on past decisions and this will influence their orientation of choices and approaches towards the change process. This allows them to identify possible improvements and to implement changes if necessary. Of course some CEOs have an incapacity and unwillingness to discuss mistakes and failures which creates a major stumbling block in the top management team – the 'the elephant in the room' syndrome. This arises when team members do not have a sense of psychological safety in the team and as a result catastrophic errors can occur as the forces of conformity in the team are marshalled to block out dissenting voices. Well-known examples of this include the *Challenger* shuttle disaster and the Bristol infirmary cases.

Shaping Behaviour

Leadership in action

There is sufficient evidence that leadership characteristics and behaviours influence change implementation effectiveness (Higgs and Rowland, 2001; 2005;

Berson and Avolio, 2004; Bommer, Rich and Rubin, 2005). The relationship between transformational and charismatic leadership characteristics and change implementation success is well-known. Transformational leadership behaviours demonstrated in the change process were related to lower employee cynicism, improved perception of procedural justice and higher levels of change readiness (Berson and Avolio, 2004; Waldman, Javidan, and Varella, 2004; Bommer, et al., 2005). Trying to understand the leadership behaviours that are demonstrated in practice, we asked the CEOs questions around their change leader role. Aspects such as authenticity, openness in interactions, demonstrating behaviour that is aligned with their own values, demonstrating compassion and self-transcendent behaviours are highlighted as examples of typical behaviour patterns. Some leaders emphasized the following:

Authenticity is a key attribute in leading and managing change

Ensure congruence between values and behaviours

'It's the authenticity of an individual and whether people really believe that what they see versus what they hear a leader saying they believe in and what they're going to do and how closely those two correlate. I think it's very easy to say things but people will see you doing things, hear you saying things that they then will look at your body language, will look at what actions you then take, will look at your history and question whether, in their minds, it all adds up to genuineness and whether you really are a leader that does exactly what you say you're going to do and the minute you cross that line and don't, I think people then question how authentic you are.'

Do not underestimate your employee's ability to recognize inauthentic behaviour

'If you don't believe in that and if others just feel that you are saying something for the sake of saying it; saying the right things because it's politically correct. If you're not true to yourself and you're trying to be something you're not, it's amazing I think how people see through it. Even if you think you sound real. So I think, be yourself. Sure, you have to shape the message to suit the particular audience but that doesn't mean to say you change who you are. I can't stand it when I see people hiding behind the mask, I can't stand it and I see straight through it, as do their people of course, you know, followers are not idiots, followers – what do they look for in a leader? They want someone who is

authentic. Authentic and an authentic role model that they can follow.'

Model the change *'So I think for me it is about probably what comes from the heart, what you genuinely stand for and particularly when things are tough, whether you're true to everything you talk about and say is important to you. So I think it's very much around the emotions that you share, that you show, the vision that you have, the values that you have and then what people actually see you doing and then they will make judgements based on that.'*

Employees may exhibit high levels of change commitment when leaders exhibit authentic behaviours, that is, openness, expressing themselves and leading in ways that are consistent with their inner thoughts and feelings, acting with integrity and being aware of the impact of actions. This may lead to higher levels of support and commitment for the articulated change vision. The majority of leaders emphasized the fact that it is important to act according to their own values and to act as a role model. This is supportive of the viewpoints of Gardner et al. (2005, p. 350) who argue that the leader needs to be true to his or her core values and should be resistant to social or situational pressures and not compromise his or her values. A CEO explains:

Promise only what you can deliver *'It also means only promising what you can deliver, and not falling into the trap of over-promising – people hate that, they hate it. It means – for me, it means being utterly true to your own sense of purpose and belief and value.'*

It seems that aspects such as openness in interactions, demonstrating behaviour that is aligned with their own values, demonstrating self-disclosure, are highlighted as examples of typical leader behaviour patterns. This behaviour pattern may lead to greater employee identification with the leader (George, 2003) and should engender greater commitment towards the envisaged change vision. Leaders have to enact the required behaviours in deeds as well as in words and need to demonstrate their commitment and involvement (Kanter et al., 1992). Being authentic in interactions with employees, and thereby enhancing personal credibility, causes employees to trust, identify and admire the leader (Yukl, 2006), and to develop a compelling vision, is only part of the story. Whereas authentic leadership can be regarded as a root construct to any form of positive leadership and is 'the highest end of leadership' (Avolio, 2005, p. 194), it is also

Table 2 Transformational behaviours (adapted from Popper and Mayseless, 2007)

1. Focusses on individual needs of employees, gives personal attention and acts as role-model for imitation and identification. Also builds feelings of self-worth, competence and enables employees to make use of their individual potential. In practical terms it means the leader identifies individual strengths, treats employees with respect and is willing and available to give advice to employees.
2. Sets challenges for employees and helps employees to believe these challenges are achievable. Sets clear goals and standards but is non-judgemental.
3. Provides intellectual stimulation by promoting critical thinking and problem solving encourages innovation through challenging existing paradigms. Also provides opportunities for experiences and reinforce success. They get employees to think about issues, encourage non-traditional thinking and help employees to look at problems from different angles.
4. Motivates and inspires employees by showing enthusiasm, optimism, pointing out positive results, stimulating team work, talking about the purpose of the change and having a clear vision of the future.

important to demonstrate other transformational leadership behaviours in the leadership of change. The behaviours required to be truly transformational are indicated in Table 2.

From Table 2 it is clear that employees should have a clear understanding of the end state of the change (i.e. change vision), be empowered through involvement in the change initiative (this improves understanding and ownership) and the leader should be sensitive to employee needs. Understanding employee needs in the change process is important as personal consequences of the change will influence and shape the employees reaction towards the change (Caldwell, et al., 2004). In the end, what we want from our followers is commitment towards the change. It is also important to remember that any change in behaviour starts with you – ask yourself the following question 'If I want to lead change in an authentic way, how should I act and what are the observable behaviours my employees will look out for?' A good starting point is to get out of your office and talk to your employees. Despite the fact that we all know and acknowledge the fact that we need 'to be visible' we normally have a number of excuses why this is a good theory but difficult to put into practice. Reasons such as 'I am too busy'; too many meetings to attend and so forth may be legitimate reasons for not being visible but this is not supporting your cause! Getting out there and speaking to your employees provides information that may be useful for the change process but also to for your employees to get to know you. This builds trust and trust is crucial for any change process.

We worked with many organizational leaders and it is astonishing how few of them take the time to really know their employees. The conversations are superficial, formal; framed around the agenda of the manager and is dysfunctional. It is good practice to reflect after each conversation with employees and ask yourself the following questions (1) what did I learn from the conversation; (2) what was my impact; (3) if I have the opportunity to the conversation again, what will I do differently and (4) what have I learned about this individual as a person? Such knowledge is invaluable in unlocking the goodwill that is central to motivation, discretionary behaviour and support for change. Look at the following example:

Be accessible to your employees

Make time to discuss what is important to employees

Be open and honest

'I'm also trying – although not necessarily succeeding – to be a lot more visible and a lot more accessible; I operate with the open door policy and all that kind of stuff and walk the floor, but I'm taking a bit more time to do the corridor conversations, when people – you know when they walk past you that they actually want to stop and just chew the fat for a bit, and I'm just being a little bit more sensitive to when people do want to stop and have a chat and they'll usually start off with a conversation about the weather and that's actually been very helpful over the last few weeks, even though it's been a nightmare. So you start off a conversation about the weather and then they'll start to talk about what's really concerning them or trying to get – trying to pick my brains about what's happening nationally or whatever and it just gives them the opportunity to sort of offload things and get things off their chests.'

Herold, et al. (2008, p. 347) explains this as follows 'commitment goes beyond just positive attitudes toward the change to include the intention to support it as well as a willingness to work on behalf of its successful implementation'. It seems then that effective change leadership consists of the demonstration of two types of behaviour: task-orientated and person-related (Bass, 1990). Task-orientated skills are related to establishing organizational routines to attain goals and objectives, organizational design and control and problem solving. This can also be regarded as the 'hard-side' of change leadership where the leader for example needs to create the change vision, allocate resources and evaluate the effectiveness of the change. In contrast, person-related skills refer to the 'soft-side' of change management. This refers to behaviours that, for example, stimulate collaboration among employees, create a supportive organizational climate and ensure that employees are treated fairly and equitably. It also signals to employees that you understand the importance of showing direction, aligning employees and being able to motivate employees to accept the change. It is the use of these skills that builds commitment towards the change. Managers are usually able and competent in planning and structuring the change but less so when it comes to the people component of the change: implementing the change and building commitment towards the change.

Communication and creating a need for change

When examining the prescriptions for leading change (for example, approaches advocated by Kotter, 1995; Ulrich, 1998; Luecke, 2003), the importance of disconfirmation (Schein, 2004) or putting it differently, establishing a sense of urgency (Kotter, 1996) is highlighted. This means that employees must be mobilized to accept, commit and adopt the proposed changes. Different mechanisms can be used to mobilize acceptance. Kotter (1995) suggests in this regard that leaders need to (1) create a burning platform and (2) create a guiding coalition to support the change. Various factors may also influence the willingness of employees to accept the change. In fact, leading consultants such as Niall Saul at Symbio Business Solutions would argue that you need both external and internal forces for change where the latter are represented by middle managers who have a strong appetite for change. Factors such as the perceived need for the change (Barrett et al., 2005; By, 2008) and previous history of the organization in implementing change successfully (Hailey and Balogun, 2002), serve as examples in this regard. However, key to any change process is creating a real sense of urgency, that is, everyone in the organization needs to understand the reason for change. Creating a real sense of urgency is not only about numbers and the business case – it is also about touching the hearts of employees. This means the business case needs to be translated in a language that every employee can understand and 'feel' the necessity to change (Carroll and Flood, 2010). Structure the message in such a way employees can understand the impact on them personally. A way to do this can be explained as follows:

Use stories and analogies to bring the message to life

'Personally, I try to do it through communication, through the art of story-telling. I often think that Chief Executives really should be Chief Story-telling Officers! CSOs. Because it's through stories that you bring difficult subjects to life. If you just use dry case study type strategic business school language stuff, you're going to leave everyone cold. But if you put things in a personal perspective or you give a point you're trying to make an understanding, a rooting in a story or a parable or an analogy of some kind, you get people to see it, you get people to live it and breathe it. So that's how I do it but I think every

Ask well-formulated questions to help employees to think and reflect on an issue

Inspire employees and help them to feel good about themselves

Empower employees and hold them accountable

leader has got different ways. I mean I think you play to your own strengths, you've got to be authentic to who you are as an individual and you use the skills and the assets that you have to achieve the goal of inspiration. Another thing, another technique that I use is to constantly remind myself not to tell, but to ask questions. So again, great leaders ask questions all the time, they don't give any answers, they just ask questions because if you ask questions, by definition you put the responsibility for the answer in the person of whom you're asking the question. Whereas if you give the answer you've taken the responsibility away, which is why managers, who do telling all the time – tell, tell, tell, come on, come on, come on, control, control, control – managers end up working unbelievably long hours because they do all the work, because they take responsibility away from their people. Whereas leaders, who ask questions, and therefore empower their people, tend to go home at 6 pm and no one can understand how the hell they've managed to go home and yet they're successful. But the reason they can do that is because they understand the power of inspiration; make people feel great, make people understand what they can do to take ownership and accountability for themselves to make a success of whatever it is that they're being asked to do.'

Structure and communicate the message so that it is relevant for the target audience

'I think one of the things we have been emphasizing particularly in the last year since we launched our recent strategy, our 20/20 strategy. We identified at the outset a very clear need to communicate the strategy and to be clear about what we intended as an organization to achieve. The message has to be clear and pitched to a relevant audience and then it is about communication. It's probably the key aspect of delivering the changes by communication. Outlining where you are going and how you are actually going to do that.'

The role and impact of communication on the change process, that is, creating a need for change, has been well established (Amiot, et al., 2006; Holt et al.,

2007). Change communication should be enthusiastic, frequent (Lewis, et al., 2006) and needs to communicate realistic expectations (Lovallo and Kahneman, 2003). It needs to communicate the future direction with honest answers to the what, why and the how of the change. Change recipients need to have a clear understanding of (1) what is going to change and (2) how will they contribute towards the change, that is, what are the change expectations? There is consensus in the literature that to effect change readiness, employees need to understand the need or reasons for organizational change (Barrett et al., 2005; Jones et al., 2005; By, 2008). Authors such as Kanter et al. (1992); Kotter, (1995) and Ulrich (1998) agree that the leader needs to create a context for the change and establish a sense of urgency. Putting it differently, if people do not understand the reason or need for change, they will resist (Lewin, 1951).

Test your communication effectiveness

1. Do you understand the viewpoints of employees regarding the change?
2. Have they heard the change message?
3. Do they believe it?
4. Do they know what the change means?
5. Have they interpreted the change for themselves?
6. Have they internalized the change message?

Inaccurate communication or predictions may lead to feelings of resentment and violations of trust (Tomlinson, et al., 2004) and therefore it is important that communication is honest and should address the positive aspects as well as the possible negative consequences of the change. Bordia et al. (2004) argue in this regard that accurate and balanced communication may assist in creating positive attitudes and this may lead to change acceptance (Wanberg and Banas, 2000) and increased trust in management (Paterson and Cary, 2002). Armenakis et al. (1999) and Armenakis and Harris (2002) argue that the content of any change message should consist of five key areas. Firstly, it is important to clarify why the change is needed by explaining the gap between the current state of the organization and the desired state. Efficacy is the second component and expresses confidence in the organization's ability to successfully implement the proposed changes. The third component refers to appropriateness and refers to the content of the change, that is, the type of change that is applicable. Fourthly, demonstrating management commitment and support for the change and explaining individual level outcomes of the change.

While the content of the message is key to help create readiness amongst employees, the way in which the message is conveyed, is also important. Aiken and Keller (2007) argue it is through storytelling that the CEO unlocks significantly more energy from change recipients to pursue the change. Language is a powerful tool leaders use to create change readiness: acceptance and accomplishment

(Conger, 1991). Robichaud, et al. (2004, p. 630) argue in this regard that it is 'through language that leaders establish the identity of objects, events, and actors that constitute their social environment'. Language is a powerful tool leaders use to create change readiness, acceptance and accomplishment, and to create shared understanding, leaders need to use words that are expressive and inspirational (Conger, 1991). As already indicated, in order to destabilize the *status quo*, that is, unfreezing of employees (Lewin, 1951), leaders need to describe and communicate the need for change: share their vision of the need for change. Armenakis and Harris (2002) highlight the importance of change communication as change strategies often fail because information is not effectively communicated. It also influences how employees perceive the change (i.e. their mental models) and may facilitate their readiness for the change initiative (Bordia et al., 2004). The CEOs describe how they communicate change as follows:

You cannot communicate enough

Be visible and communicate face-to-face

'I say the way you do that as a leader is through communication, it's something that leaders never ever spend enough time and effort on, which is communicating cogently and sensibly – not through webcasts and emails and stuff, but actually getting out there, talking, meeting, being visible and using anecdotes and story-telling to show people that change is not a bad thing, change is a good thing, in fact it's a necessary thing, in order to get to the future that we all wish to have.'

Share own personal experiences

Communication should create hope and optimism

'The way that I do this quite a lot is painting pictures, talking about different organizations and different sectors that I've worked in, talking about how things can be different, talking about opportunities, if you like, trying to illustrate what a changed organization can look like and feel like and what it can deliver and how it can be better performing, how it would look different for the public, how we could create better value for money.'

Change is a journey

Reflect on your own style of leadership and the impact it may have on followers

'The key to it is to empower the people around the strategy of the company. I did it in a way that I wasn't seen as one who talked down on people saying this is the way it will be but as one who said I would like to embark on a journey and I would like you to join me. I suppose my philosophy and the process I follow to bring about change is a process of involvement and facilitating it.'

This reflects the importance of communication. Leaders use and interpret symbols, rituals and other cultural artefacts as power tools that provides richer insights into the what, the why and the how of the change. The impact of the change as well as personal consequences of the change influence how employees frame the change (Armenakis and Harris, 2002) and therefore it is important for leaders to give relevant change information, elaborate on personal benefits (Gilley, 2005) and answer employee questions in order to increase change acceptance (Green, 2004). This also means that employees understand what their role in achieving the change objectives is. Some CEOs articulated the importance as follows:

Do your employees understand the real reason for change?

Does the reason for change grasp their hearts and minds?

'You need to create a platform internally to make people sit up and recognize that there's a time and a need to change. And that's very difficult. If you're in a successful organization, in an industry that's always grown, sometimes that can be tough. Because people can't understand why we need to change if we are so successful. The old phrase is "if it ain't broke, don't fix it." So you need to really put a context in place for people that explains why, if you roll the clock forward – a year, 18 months – whatever the time period is, that life won't be like that anymore.'

Personalize the change for your employees – what does the change mean for them?

'Because the next thing people will ask you is "I get the reason but what does it mean for me? What are we going to do? How are we going to get there?" And the more you can think that through, then the more you can stand up and say with conviction what you are going to do, the more people will start to believe and then start to come around to the idea of change.'

Give recognition of things that is working well. Recognize their contribution of past successes

'I think one of the things that often gets missed is – don't forget to praise the things that have been working well that don't need to change, because it almost says there is a foundation here that you're building on, what's been working well, what you want to keep, what you like. So don't forget to tell people not just about the change that's required and the things that aren't working well, but also

things that are working well that are going to stay the same, because I think knowing that there are some solid foundations to build on can be very helpful to actually allow you to do significant change.'

Tell the employees what is going to stay the same

The leader has to address two fundamental needs of employees, that is, their *predictive needs* (concerned with the ability to predict what is going to happen next) and *exploratory needs*, that is, explain why things are as they are (Berger, 1987). From the data it seems the leader places emphasis on reasons why the change is needed, and explaining the nature of the change. To reduce feelings of confusion, uncertainty and change anxiety, it is also important for the leader to draw on the past: linking the new to the old (i.e. what worked well, what is going to stay the same) as this will contextualize the change and assist in making sense of the change. Communication is therefore a powerful lever that can be used in creating readiness for change. The leader needs to communicate the change message repeatedly to ensure that momentum and enthusiasm for the change is created and maintained. Equally important is the ability to listen to feedback from your employees and to act purposefully on the feedback received. This also includes not only formulating an appropriate response, but also taking into account your body language, tone of voice and emotion conveyed when responding to employees (Carroll and Flood, 2010).

How do you respond to feedback from followers?

Gable, et al. (2006, p. 905) argue that responses can be divided into four types:

1. Active constructive (e.g. enthusiastic support)
2. Passive constructive (e.g. quiet, understated support)
3. Active destructive (e.g. demeaning the event)
4. Passive destructive (e.g. ignoring the event)

For example, as Head of a Department, one of your managers tells you that employees are not supportive of your proposed changes, that is, reduction in overtime payment in the organization. How do you respond? See Table 3 for possible responses.

While it is important to listen to feedback from your employees, you need to be conscious of 'how' you give feedback and the impact this may have on your employees (Carroll and Flood, 2010). This can be explained as follows:

Table 3 Examples of possible responses

	Constructive	**Destructive**
Active	*Active constructive* (e.g. enthusiastic support) *'This is an opportunity to really understand how the employees feel about the changes and we should explore ways where we can reduce costs but also help employees to find work-life balance.'* (responding positively, maintain eye contact and displaying positive emotions)	*Active destructive* (e.g. demeaning the event) *'This is exactly what I am paying you for – it is your job to sort it out, if you are not able to get them on-board I will find somebody who is able to do it.'* (negative and displaying negative non-verbal cues)
Passive	*Passive constructive* (e.g. quiet, understated support) *'Give them time, they will understand the reasons why we need to cut overtime.'* (lacking enthusiasm and downplaying, little to no active emotional expression)	*Passive destructive* (e.g. ignoring the event) *'Not supportive you say – I have to go, I am late for my next meeting.'* (lacking interest, displaying little to no eye contact, turning away and leaving the speaker)

Do the following: Reflect on two previous conversations that you can use to analyse your responses.

Event/feedback	Your response	Type of response (active/passive; constructive/destructive	Reaction to your response	If you can do it all over again, how would have you responded

The story . . .

'One of my previous bosses was an astounding leader . . . sitting at my desk, the phone rang, I picked up the phone and he said "Hello, its John here," – this was like talking to God! – so I said "Hello John," and he said "would you mind awfully writing an article for me for a newspaper on Topic A - 400 words, unfortunately I need it on my desk tomorrow morning, I'm terribly sorry, but would that be possible?" "Absolutely no problem John," I'm a Master of the Universe, I can do anything! So I was 23 at the time, 24, perhaps a bit older? I spent all night writing it, it was brilliant, it was a masterpiece; 400 words you have never read anything in your life that was like this, absolutely perfect – handed it in, knackered, the

following morning, I think I went home to bed then and of course it wasn't for the paper that day it was for the paper the following day so that intervening night, I went to my nearest tube station, all the papers appear on the racks at midnight and I went to grab the newspaper and feverishly made my way through it and found the article, there it was! I noticed two things, the first thing was it said it was by John and me – I couldn't believe it, I mean I remember going around the tube station saying "My God! I've arrived! I'm here, this is me! I've done it! I've cracked it! I'm in the newspaper!" and then of course I calmed down a bit and I started to read the article and I then realized the second thing, which was that not one word of this article bore any resemblance whatsoever to anything that I'd written, there was an occasional "and" and a "the" and a "but" but the rest was unrecognizable. So I went home to bed a bit perturbed actually because I couldn't understand it at all. I went in the next day, the phone rang, John said "I wonder if you wouldn't mind popping up to my office, just to talk about a couple of things to do with the article?" I thought oh my God, here we go, I'm for the high-jump. And you've got to remember I was – I don't know how many levels below John, but N where N is a very large number and I went into his office and he bade me over and he sat me down and he then took me through, for 20 minutes, him and me, the art of writing and he showed me what I had done which was now covered in red ink, it was just a sea of red, and what he had written and how he had moved from where I had gone to where he had gone. Now, I have to say, I don't remember much of what he said, looking back, I don't remember much of what he did, but this is the point: As an inspirational leader I remember how he made me feel, and I can remember it like it was yesterday, and it was 30 years ago. I can remember he made me feel like a billion dollars, he made me feel like I could do anything, simply because he took the time out, time out to give me time, to give me his time, and I never forgot it, I never forgot that, it was a turning point for me.

Lessons learned . . .

Invest personal time in employees

Negative feedback should not diminish the self-esteem of your employees

Are you able to inspire employees when you give feedback?

'Roll forward 25 years, so it was about three or four years ago and I did a – so it's a long time forward – and I did one of these director magazine profiles that you know, and it was on the organization but of course inevitably the journalists love to write about "the leader", and so it was your favourite car and your favourite film and your favourite food and your favourite restaurant and your best ever leader, and I wrote "John". Thought no more about it, two months later it got published, on the day it got published, on the day, my PA said to me "I've got this bloke called John on the phone, would you like to speak to him?" "STOP THE COMPANY, STOP EVERYTHING, PUT HIM THROUGH!!!" "Hello John," I was like a little boy again, it was pathetic, and he said "I just wanted to call you because I am so humbled that you have chosen me as the best leader you ever worked for," and he did it all over again, he made me feel a billion dollars all over again! And that time was only 90 seconds. So the story's important though because in it, is not only something that shaped me and my thinking, but it's the power of inspiration. Inspiration is not a long term programme, inspiration can be in the moment, typically it's one to one, typically it's personal and typically it's because you give time and because you're present and it's a great gift, it's a great gift and those who understand it and nurture it and value it can change people's lives, as John did mine.'

Creating Capacity for Change

Get the right people on-board

Leaders need to mobilize employees to accept and institutionalize the proposed changes (Kotter, 1996; Oreg, 2003). This can be achieved through different means for example: creating a coalition to support the change (Kotter, 1996; Higgs and Rowland, 2000), through participation (Amiot et al., 2006; Holt et al., 2007) and implementing appropriate structures, systems and processes. Change participation, that is, the active involvement in the planning and implementation of organizational change, has been linked to higher support for the change (Holt et al., 2007), the experience of positive emotions (Bartunek, et al., 2006) and less employee stress (Amiot, et al., 2006). Involving organizational members in the planned change process may reduce barriers to change by creating psychological ownership of the change. The key lesson is to allow organization members to participate in planning the change and involve as many employees as possible in making decisions. This creates understanding, motivation and ownership of the change. Higgs and Rowland (2009, p. 48) argued that it is not only about shaping behaviour or framing change but it is also about creating capacity or putting it differently, creating capabilities and allocation of resources, for the imminent change. Conversely, Hubbard, et al. (2007) argue that effective leaders also have the ability to remove employees who do not have the right attitude or values to fit with the organizational culture and to hold all employees accountable for results. This implies that leaders need to evaluate the degree to which organizational members are performing the routines, practices or behaviours targeted in the change process (Luecke, 2003; Yukl, 2006) and reflect on the impact of the change of organizational effectiveness (Patterson, et al., 2005). Do we start the change journey by announcing *where we are going* (change vision) or 'with who do we start the change journey?'. Traditional change models normally start with creating the change vision, building a burning platform and communicating the vision. Answers to these two questions will fundamentally influence the way in which you are going to implement and manage the change. Making sure that you have the 'right' people in the organization, the people who add high value, who have energy, passion and who are committed to the organization, is a first step in this process. Collins (2001) summarizes this issue by stating 'great vision with mediocre people still produces mediocre results'. Some leaders put it like this:

Get the right team on-board

'So the first thing about "get the right team on the bus" – wow. If there's anything that's so true it's that; forget strategy and vision and mission and anything else, if you haven't got the right team on your bus, you ain't going to go anywhere. By contrast, if you've got the right team on the bus, with the right attitude, you can do anything, anything at all and that has been taught to me time and time again. If you're going to recruit somebody into your team, recruit first for attitude – don't even look at their CV, don't even look at it, there's just no point. Talk to them as people, understand them as individuals first, hire for "fit" – worry about the skills and the competencies and all that stuff later, as a filtering device but get people for "fit" first. So team on the bus – absolutely the most vital thing of all.'

Recruit for attitude and organizational 'fit'

Capability can be developed through interventions

Employees with the wrong attitude kill change

Empower employees by allocating sufficient resources for the change

'When it comes to change, I always talk to the leadership teams about three things that could be the biggest blocks to change: capability, being one of the big fundamental ones but I always tell people that we can do almost anything with capability, we can train, we can up skill, we can learn, we can bring new people in, so I'm a great believer that capability shouldn't be the block to change but that you might need to invest, you might need to make sure you have got the capability. I then talk about having the right attitude and what I say there is, you either have the right attitude and want to make the changes or you don't and if you don't there is a danger that if this is the right change for the organization then you are going to become out of line with the organizational needs and that could be very unhelpful or very dangerous. So how do you make sure that people actually go into change with the right attitude? By the way that's not to say that everybody has to agree with everything that you're doing because you do want people that will challenge but if somebody's going in absolutely adamant that it's the wrong thing then having had the debates, and if you're still sure that the change that you're making is right, if people still have the wrong attitude, especially leaders, there may come a point where you have to say this obviously isn't the company for you anymore because you don't agree with the changes that we're making but we've heard your view but we're absolutely sure this is still the right change. Because otherwise people could become blockers to change or worse, they could de-rail the change and harm the whole organization. And then the third one for me is whether we allow people to make the change and that can be about giving them the right resources, the right equipment, the right tools, the right funding or time, you know, are we allowing people to make the changes that we set out to?'

In practical terms, it means that you need to assess (1) capability of employees and (2) attitude of employees, that is, their mindset about the change. You can do almost anything with capability, you can train, up-skill, or hire new people but you might need to invest in your employees to create the capability to add real value. However, if people do not have the right attitude, commitment or passion for the organization, there may come a point where you have to say this obviously is not the company for you anymore. Finally, the leaders' role in the change process is therefore to act as a change enabler (Weick et al., 2005) as 'leaders cannot control the future because in complex systems such as organisations, unpredictable internal dynamics will determine future conditions' (Marion and Uhl-Bien, 2001, p. 391). Although leaders need to set direction, create alignment and maintain commitment towards the change (Van Velsor and McCauley, 2004), they do not control the change. Their purpose and role is to enable others and to create the conditions that will facilitate organizational change. Kanter et al. (1992) and Kotter (1996) argue in this regard that the role of leaders is to empower others to act, provide tangible support, use recognition and rewards to gain support as well as putting in place appropriate systems and structures. This can be explained as follows:

Understand what objectives need to achieved

Align employees to objectives

The top management team need to demonstrate their commitment

Ensure processes, systems and procedures support the change

'There are three legs to the process: Targets, engagement of people and systems and processes. The first layer of it is around targets. Looking at for example the amount of energy that we're using as a company; how we manage diversity etc. and then putting hard targets in place: by 2012 we're going to reduce the amount by 15%, so we formulate objectives so that we can physically do things to deliver our targets. Making sure that the leadership buys into it because then the organization becomes committed automatically because you have to do it and report on that. The second leg is around the people and getting them committed. As well as calling on the people at the bottom and involving them, I also got my fellow directors to sign up to a number of commitments that they would make, leadership actions that they would take through their own behaviour – because you should talk-the-talk and walk-the-walk. The third leg is around processes and procedures and systems. Revising, reviewing the way we work and make decisions around procurement, the things we take into consideration when we're buying equipment is important when you want to create capacity for change.'

Chapter Summary

The chapter highlights the importance of leadership practices and aims to answer the question 'what kind of leadership is best for leading change effectively?'. The importance of actual behaviours such as *framing the change* (sense-making, setting direction and strategic reflection); *shaping behaviour* (authenticity and communication) and *creating capacity* (employee involvement and engagement), are highlighted. However, for leadership to be effective, it has to be spread throughout the organization. This also refers to the ability to develop leadership in others on an ongoing basis and to enhance the decision-making capabilities of your subordinates. Effective change leaders are able to inspire employees by making them feel significant, communicate through vivid models and examples and motivate their people through joint identification with collective goals, rather than through rewards and punishments. To lead change effectively, you must encourage dissent and disagreement and use feedback to improve the change process.

KEY INSIGHTS FROM PRACTICE

Engage employees through a common purpose.
Help your employees to believe that they make a difference in the organization's success.
Learn from your employees.
Build capacity for the change.
Manage meaning and manage trust.
Develop a leadership style that builds trust through authenticity.
Lead to make a difference.
Manage the structural ('hard side')as well as the people component ('soft side') of change.
Change is different in every organization – the bigger the organization and the more complex the change – the longer it is going to take.

References

Aiken, C.B. and Keller, S.P. (2007). The CEO's role in leading transformation. *McKinsey Quarterly*, Feb, 1–4.
Amiot, C., Terry, D., Jimmieson, N., and Callan, V. (2006). A longitudinal investigation of coping processes during a merger: Implications for job satisfaction and organisational identification. *Journal of Management*, 32, 552–574.
Armenakis, A.A. and Bedeian, A.G. (1999). Organisational change: a review of theory and research in the 1990s. *Journal of Management*, 25, 293–315.

Armenakis, A.A. and Harris, S.G. (2002). Crafting a change message to create transformational readiness. *Journal of Organizational Change Management*, 15 (2), 169–183.
Avolio, B.J. (2005). *Leadership Development in Balance: Made/Born*. Mahwah, NJ: Lawrence Erlbaum Associates.
Barrett, J.H., Haslam, R.A., Lee, K.G., and Ellis, M.J. (2005). Assessing attitudes adn beliefs using the stage of change paradigm – case study of health and safety appraisal within a manufacturing company. *International Journal of Industrial Ergonomics*, 35 (10), 871–887.
Bartunek, J.M., Rousseau, D.M., Rudolph, J.W., and DePalma, J.A. (2006). On the receiving end: Sensemaking, emotion and assessments of an organisational change initiated by others. *Journal of Applied Behavioural Science*, 42, 182–206.
Bass, B.M. (1990). From transactional to transformational leadership: Learning to share the vision. *Organizational Dynamics*, (Winter), 19–31.
Battilana, J., Gilmartin, M., Sengul, M., Pache, A.C., and Alexander, J. (2010). Leadership competencies for implementing planned organisational change. *Leadership Quarterly*, 21, 422–438.
Berger, C.R. (1987). Communicating under uncertainty. In M. Radloff and G. Miller (eds), *Interpersonal Processes: New Directions in Communication Research* (pp. 39–62). London: Sage.
Berson, Y. and Avolio, B. (2004). Transformational leadership and the dissemination of organisational goals: a case study of a telecommunications firm. *Leadership Quarterly*, 15, pp. 625–646.
Bommer, W.H., Rich, G.A., and Rubin, R.S. (2005). Changing attitudes about change: Longitudinal effects of transformational leader behaviour on employee cynicism about organisational change. *Journal of Organizational Behavior*, 26, 733–753.
Bordia, P., Hunt, E., Paulsen, N., Tourish, D.J., and DiFonzo, N. (2004). Uncertainty during organizational change: Types, consequences, and management strategies. *Journal of Business and Psychology*, 18 (4), 507–532.
Burke, W. (2002). *Organisational Change: Theory and Practice*. Thousand Oaks, CA: Sage.
By, R.T., Diefenbach, T., and Klarner, P. (2008). Getting organizational change right in public services: The case of European higher education. *Journal of Change Management*, 8 (1), 21–35.
Caldwell, S.D., Herold, D.M., and Fedor, D.B. (2004). Toward an understanding of the relationships among organizational change, individual differences and changes in person-environment fit: A cross-level study. *Journal of Applied Psychology*, 89, 868–882.
Carroll, S.J. and Flood, P.C. (2010) *Change Lessons from the CEO: Lessons from the Arts*, Chichester: John Wiley & Sons, Ltd.
Christenson, D. and Walker, D. (2004). Understanding the role of vision in project success. *Project Management Journal*, 35 (3), 39–52.
Cohen, E. and Tichy, N. (1997) How leaders develop leaders. *Training and Development*, 51 (5), 58–73.
Cole, M.S., Harris, S.G., and Bernerth, J.B. (2006). Exploring the implications of vision, appropriateness, and execution of organizational change. *Leadership and Organization Development Journal*, 27 (5), 352–367.
Collins, J. (2001). Level 5 leadership: The triumph of humility and fierce resolve. *Harvard Business Review*, Jan, 66–76.
Conger, J. (1991). Inspiring others: The language of leadership. *Academy of Management Executive*, 5 (1), 31–45.
Cummings, T.G. and Huse, E.F. (1989). *Organization Development and Change*. West Pub. Co. (St. Paul).

Cummings, T.G. and Worley, C.G. (2005). *Organizational Development and Change.* Mason, OH: South-Western.

Elving, W.J.L. (2005). The role of communication in organisational change. *Corporate Communications.* 10 (2), 129–138.

Gable, S.L., Gonzaga, G.C., and Strachman, A. (2006). Will you be there for me when things go right? Supportive responses to positive event disclosures. *Journal of Personality and Social Psychology*, 91 (5), 904–917.

Gardner, W.L., Avolio, B.J., and Walumbwa, F.O. (2005). Authentic leadership development: emergent themes and future directions. *Leadership and Management*, 3, pp. 387–406.

George, B. (2003). *Authentic Leadership: Rediscovering the Secrets to Creating Lasting Value.* San Francisco: Jossey-Bass.

Gilley, A. (2005). *The Manager as Change Leader.* Westport, CT: Praeger.

Gioia, D.A. and Chittipeddi, K. (1991). Sensemaking and sensegiving in strategic change initiation. *Strategic Management Journal*, 12, 433–448.

Gioia, D.A. and Thomas, J.B. (1996). Identity, image and issue interpretation: Sense making during strategic change in Academia. *Administrative Science Quarterly*, 41, 370–403.

Green, S.E. (2004). A rhetorical theory of diffusion. *Academy of Management Review*, 29, 653–669.

Hailey, V.H. and Balogun, J. (2002). Devising context sensitive approaches to change: The example of GlaxoWellcome. *Long Range Planning*, 35 (2), 153–178.

Herold, D.M., Fedor, D.B., Caldwell, S., and Liu, Y. (2008). The effects of transformational and change leadership on employees' commitment to a change: A multilevel study. *Journal of Applied Psychology*, 93 (2), 346–357.

Higgs, M. and Rowland, D. (2009). Change leadership: case study of a global energy company. *Strategic Change*, 18, 45–58.

Higgs, M. and Rowland, D. (2005). All changes great and small: Exploring approaches to change and its leadership. *Journal of Change Management*, 5 (2), 121–151.

Higgs, M.J. and Rowland, D. (2000), Building change leadership capability: The quest for change competence. *Journal of Change Management*, 1 (2), 116–131.

Higgs, M.J. and Rowland, D. (2001), Developing change leadership capability. The impact of a development intervention. *Henley Working Paper Series*, HWP 2001/004.

Holt, D.T., Achilles, A., Armenikis, Feild, H.S., and Harris, S.G. (2007). Readiness for organizational change: The systematic development of a scale. *Journal of Applied Behavioural Science*, 43, 232–255.

Hooper, R.A. and Potter, J.R. (2000) *Intelligent Leadership: Creating a Passion for Change*, Random House: London.

House, R.J. and Aditya, R.N. (1997). The social scientific study of leadership: Quo vadis? *Journal of Management*, 23, pp. 409–473.

Hubbard, G. Samuel, D., Cocks, G. and Heap, S. (2007) *The First XI Winning Organizations in Australia.* Indianapolis: John Wiley & Sons, Inc.

Johnson, H.H. (2008). Mental models and transformative learning: The key to leadership development? *Human Resource Development Quarterly*, 19 (1), 85–89.

Jones, R.A., Jimmieson, N.L., and Griffiths, A. (2005). The impact of organizational culture and the reshaping capabilities on change implementation success: The mediating role of readiness for change. *Journal of Management Studies*, 42 (2), 361–386.

Kanter, R.M., Stein, B.A., and Jick, T. (1992). *The Challenge of Organizational Change.* New York: Free Press.

Kotter, J.P. (1995). Leading change: Why transformation efforts fail. *Harvard Business Review*, 73 (2), 59–67.

Kotter, J.P. (1996). *Leading Change.* Boston: Harvard Business Press.

Kotter, J.P. (2007). What leaders really do. In R. Vecchio (ed.). *Leadership; Understanding the Dynamics of Power and Influence in Organisations* (2nd edn). Notre Dame: University of Notre Dame Press.

Kotter, J.P. (2012). Accelerate. *Harvard Business Review*, 90 (11), 43–58.

Kotter, J.P. and Cohen. D.S. (2002). *The Heart of Change: Real-Life Stories of How People Change their Organizations.* Cambridge, MA: Harvard Business School Press.

Kouzes, J.M. and Posner, B.Z. (2002). *The Leadership Challenge* (3rd edn). San Francisco: Jossey-Bass.

Lafley, A.G. (2009). What only the CEO can do. *Harvard Business Review*, 73 (2), 1–9.

Landau, D., Drori, I., and Porras, J. (2006). Vision change in a governmental R&D organization. *Journal of Applied Behavioral Science*, 42 (2), 145–171.

Lau, C.M. and Woodman, R.W. (1995). Understanding organizational change: A schematic perspective. *Academy of Management Journal*, 38 (2), 537–554.

Levesque, D.A., Prochaska, J.M., and Prochaska, J.O. (1999). Stages of change and integrated service delivery. *Consulting Psychology Journal*, 4, 226–241.

Lewin, K. (1951). *Field Theory in Social Science: Selected Theoretical Papers.* New York: Harper.

Lewis, L.K., Schmisseur, A.M., Stephans, K.K., and Weir, K.E. (2006). Advice on communicating during organisational change. *Journal of Business Communications*, 43, 113–137.

Lovallo, D. and Kahneman, D. (2003). Delusions of success: How optimism undermines executive decisions. *Harvard Business Review*, 81 (7), 56–63.

Luecke, R. (2003). *Managing Change and Transition.* Boston: Harvard Business School Press.

Marion, R. and Uhl-Bien, M. (2001). Leadership in complex organisations. *Leadership Quarterly*, 12 (4), 389–418.

Michelman, P. (2007). Overcoming resistance to change. *Harvard Management Update*, 12 (7), 3–4.

Oreg, S. (2003). Resistance to change: Developing an individual differences measure. *Journal of Applied Psychology*, 88 (4), 680–693.

Oreg, S. (2006). Personality, context and resistance to organizational change. *European Journal of Work and Organisational Psychology*, 15, 73–101.

Paterson, M. and Cary, J. (2002). Organizational justice, change anxiety and acceptance of downsizing: Preliminary tests of an AET-based model. *Motivation and Emotion*, 26, 83–103.

Patterson, M.G., West, M.A., Shackleton, V.J., Dawson, J.F., Lawthom, R., Maitlis, S., Robinson, D.L., and Wallace, A.M. (2005). Validating the organizational climate measure: links to managerial practices, productivity and innovation. *Journal of Organizational Behavior*, 26 (4), 379–408.

Popper, M. and Mayseless, O. (2007). The building blocks of leader development: A psychological conceptual framework. *Leadership and Organization Development Journal*, 7, 664–684.

Prochaska, J.O. (1984), *Systems of Psychotherapy: A Transtheoretical Analysis*, Homewood, IL: The Dorsey Press.

Prochaska, J.O. and Velicer, W.F. (1997). Misinterpretations and misapplications of the transtheoretical model. (Invited paper). *American Journal of Health Promotion*, 12, 11–12.

Raelin, J. (2001). Public reflection as the basis of learning. *Management Learning*, 32, 11–30.

Robichaud, D., Giroux, H., and Taylor, J.R. (2004). The meta conversation: The recursive property of language as a key to organizing. *Academy of Management Review*, 29 (4), 617–634.

Rouse, W.B. and Morris, N. (1986). On looking into the blackbox: Prospects and limits in the search for mental models. *Psychological Bulletin*, 100, 349–363.
Schein, E. (2004). *Organizational Culture and Leadership* (3rd edn). San Francisco: Jossey-Bass.
Schön, D.A. (1983). *The Reflective Practitioner: How Professionals Think in Action*. New York: Basic Books.
Senior, B. and Fleming, J. (2006). *Organisational Change*. Oxford: Pearson Education Limited.
Tomlinson, E.C., Dineen, B.R., and Lewicki, R.J. (2004). The road to reconciliation: Antecedents of victim willingness to reconcile a broken promise. *Journal of Management*, 30, 165–187.
Ulrich, D. (1998). A new mandate for human resources. *Harvard Business Review*, 76 (1), 124–134.
Van Velsor, E. and McCauley, C.D. (2004). Our view of leadership development. In C.D. McCauley and E. Van Velsor (eds). *The Center for Creative Leadership Handbook of Leadership Development* (pp. 1–22). San Francisco, CA: Jossey-Bass.
Waldman, D.A., Javidan, M., and Varella, P. (2004). Charismatic leadership at the strategic level: A new application of upper echelons theory. *Leadership Quarterly*, 15 (93), 355–380.
Wanberg, C.R. and Banas, J.T. (2000), Predictors and outcomes of openness to change in a reorganizing workplace, *Journal of Applied Psychology*, 85 (1), 132–142.
Weick, K.E., Sutcliffe, K.M., and Obstfeld, D. (2005). Organising and the process of sensemaking. *Organization Science*, 16 (4), pp. 409–421.
West, M.A. (2002). Sparkling fountains or stagnant ponds: An integrative model of creativity and innovation implementation in work groups. *Applied Psychology*, 51 (3), 355–387.
Wren, J. and Dulewicz, V. (2005). Leader competencies, activities and successful change in the Royal Air force. *Journal of Change Management*, 5, 295–309.
Yukl, G. (2006). *Leadership in Organizations* (6th edn). Upper Saddle River, NJ: Pearson-Prentice Hall.

CHAPTER 4

Getting Employees Ready for Change

Chapter at a Glance

Organizations are constantly confronted with changes in their external environments which necessitate the need to make changes to their strategy, structure, culture and organizational processes. Change is inevitable and employees react differently towards change. This chapter builds on Chapter 3 'Leading change: winning hearts and minds', and explores additional change variables that may impact on how employees react to change. Many people are afraid of the unknown or do not understand the real need for change and may react negatively towards organizational change. Conversely, change may also be viewed in a positive light, especially where employees can see how the change is going to improve their organizational life. This chapter focusses on how elements of change, that is, the content (what we change), the process (how we implement the change, the context (where we implement the change) as well as individual variables may influence employees reactions towards the change. Understanding the role and impact of these variables will enable you to lead and implement change more effectively. This is achieved by creating change readiness and potentially reducing resistance to change.

Beginning Cases: Preparation

Accepting change begins with an understanding of your own attitudes towards change and the reasons for organizational change. Change acceptance on a cognitive level is fairly easy; getting employees and indeed managers to accept it on an emotional level is far more difficult. It is therefore important to anticipate potential reactions towards the change and formulating strategies that may reduce the level of resistance. The following quotations provide a further perspective:

Embracing change is influenced by your personal mindset

An awareness and understanding of the external environment facilitates change

If the urgency for change is low, it may be more difficult to convince employees of the need for change

'When is it easier to change and how is change easily implemented? During the good times it is difficult to change – why – times are good so why change? You have this saying – Why change a winning team or why change a winning combination? It is winning so why change it? Because if you don't the day they stop winning they are in big trouble – and then to get back to where you were initially can take a long, long time. But it is still difficult – when your perception, your superficial perception, that things are OK – your natural tendency is – and that is purely human – to ask 'why make that extra effort?' But you need to move beyond superficial analysis – this enables you to see what the future is going to be like if you don't change. If you stay at a very superficial level – you won't notice change. You know the experience of the frog and the boiling pan – when the water is cold and you keep him in – once the water is boiling he will die because he won't have noticed the change, because it (change) is certain but slow. But if you put the frog into some boiling water – he will jump back out. And we are the same – if you do not move beyond a superficial analysis, and you say, well everything is going OK – why change/why make this effort/you won't change and one day you will die. So that is why I say it is never easy to change.

'So that is why I said it is never easy to change – so how to make it still happen despite the perception people may have about the changes that are needed.

If it is not easy to change when everything is OK I do think it is easier to agree with the fact that we do need to change if things go bad. But, in both cases, to implement it is a challenge. To have people recognize that change is necessary is easy when things don't go well that when things do go well – they do not have to do any in-depth analysis to see that things do not go well – and they will say – of course we need to change. But in both cases whether people perceive a change being necessary or they don't perceive it because they don't have the in-depth analysis of the rationale – in both cases there is big difference between people who are saying "we need to change" and people succeeding in change – for me there is a world apart. It is easy for somebody to say "yes/yes we need to change" – and two months later "we need to do this/we need to do that". So how to make it happen? For me this is the biggest challenge. The single biggest challenge about change is not recognizing that change is needed or having people not buy-into the fact that we have to change – because in theory it is easy – it is having people buying into the execution of the change. And there is only one way this happens – is that they need to change themselves. Is to buy-in that they themselves have to change.'

It is easy to understand the need for change on a cognitive level; it is much more difficult to accept it on an emotional level.

Organizational change is always mediated through individual level change

'Change is mandatory – it is all about execution. We all know we have to change – we need to invest money in change – it all about how efficiently you can get this done. Change is about execution rather than change itself. Nobody argues anymore that there is a need for change. There are also people who do not want to change – we call this the "slow no". So you go to a meeting – everyone – yes it can be done, let's do it. Then the slow no starts – a week later – it can't be done.'

Change success is all about execution

Anticipate potential resisters and formulate resistor management strategies

'We had invested a lot over the last 6–7 months on the analysis of the situation – we are very clear about the vision, mission, having very clear objectives, a clear strategy with clear qualities, a

re-organization adapted to today's environment and now it is all about change. So we have been through all the elements and we will see next year – it is going to be very tangible. I am pretty optimistic – the way the group reacts. There are two ways for a group to react – you don't really get any reaction – that will be a concern for me because that means yeah yeah/ blah blah things will not really change. The other option is you get clear attention from the team and you know what – some people may get upset, and they think about it and then they buy-in to it, it is very dynamic and this is what is happening. I get very positive vibes of what I have seen over the last couple of days – we will see but I think for the first time ever we have a dramatic change in the way that we do our business.

Experiencing strong reactions from your employees does not mean they are resisting change – it shows they still care

'I guess – we don't think of it in those terms – I mean I think- we think that – we are constantly changing, we have to – change has to be almost a norm for us because we're in a technological world and we're right in the middle of the technological industry where things shift very quickly. So we don't think of "Oh my God, how are we going to organize ourselves for change?" We have to be organized for change all the time, we have to be able to take it on-board, we have to have a leadership culture which embraces the new, which embraces challenging the status quo which is constantly saying "Hang on, are we going in the right direction, let's just reassess, let's revalidate, let's reflect, let's bear in mind what's going on outside ourselves and let's bring that knowledge back in and inform our behaviour as leaders."

Is your organization built for change?

Chapter Introduction

Organizations today operate in a state of 'permanent white water' where changes, for example, in information, technology and markets happen at an incredible pace (Marshak, 2002) and organizations have to keep pace with, adapt to and, where possible, anticipate the change. Despite the importance of adapting to internal and external changes, organizations have a poor track record of change implementation. Why is organizational and individual change so hard? Many reasons for this are purported in the literature and one potential reason is a failure to recognize and plan for possible employee reactions towards the change intervention. Normally, people are reluctant to change their habits – what worked in the past is good enough and if there is no compelling reason to change, employees will carry on what they have always done. There is agreement in the literature and practice that understanding employee reactions towards and making people ready for any organizational change is often the most important part of any change process. In Chapter 3 'Leading change: winning hearts and minds', the leader's role in creating change readiness was explored. It indicated that through the development and implementation of effective change implementation strategies, leaders in an organization may increase the possibility of successful change. In this chapter the employee reactions towards change will be further explored. An important question, therefore, to answer is, *what do we need to do to get employees ready for change and that they are willing to accept and implement organizational change?*

Understanding Readiness for Change

Understanding employee's attitudes towards change and factors that may impact on the formation of positive or negative reactions towards change may increase the likelihood for successfully implementing change in an organization. Porras and Robertson (1992, p. 724) argue in this regard that change in individual employee's behaviour is at the core of organizational change. Putting it differently, organizations only change through their members and successful change will only happen if individuals change their on-the-job behaviours. Therefore, organizational change is always mediated through individual level change (Schein, 2004). Most employees will think about changing their behaviours if there is a clear need and compelling reason for the change. It is also important to remember that while change involves learning something new, for example, learning new behaviours or attitudes, change is also about unlearning old behaviours or attitudes. The unlearning of old behaviours or attitudes may be very difficult for employees, as these behaviours are most probably well-integrated into the personality of the employee and changing may be experienced as traumatic. An individual's attitude towards a change intervention will influence their behavioural support for the change. Change efforts will fail if change agents underestimate the important role individuals play in the change process. As one CEO pointed out:

Compassion can take you a long way when you implement and lead change

'I suppose what we expect them to understand is that change is a personal issue for people. That quite often people, in terms of resistance to change, in reality people resist the pain to go through with it they don't resist the change; so it's the pain, the discomfort and the loss that people resist. We need to have managers who understand the people that go through the change and the skills that they need and what the credibility and personal influence would be used for.

The first step in influencing employee's attitudes towards the change is to create readiness for the change. The concept of readiness for change has received substantial attention in the literature and has been defined (see Table 1) in many different ways. Despite the many ways in which the concept is defined, it is generally accepted in the literature that organizational change readiness is an important building block for effective organizational change. Its importance is highlighted by Armenakis, et al. (1993, p. 681) who argues that organizational readiness for change can be regarded 'as the cognitive precursor to the behaviours of either resistance to or support for, a change effort'. This means that if people are not ready for change, they will resist the change initiative. Readiness for change then refers to the mindset of employees and can either be defined as a psychological state, so attitudes, beliefs and intentions or described in structural terms: such as organizational resources and capabilities. Most change models highlight the importance of creating an awareness of the need for change and supporting employee's perceived ability to change effectively.

Table 1 Conceptualizations of change readiness

Authors	Definition
Holt et al. (2007)	Organizational members' beliefs, attitudes and intentions regarding the extent to which changes are needed and the organization's capacity to successfully make those changes
Eby et al. (2000)	An individual's perception of the extent to which the organization is perceived to be ready to take on large scale change
Jones et al. (2005)	The extent to which employees hold positive views about the need for organizational change as well as the extent to which employees believe that such changes are likely to have positive implications for themselves and the wider organization

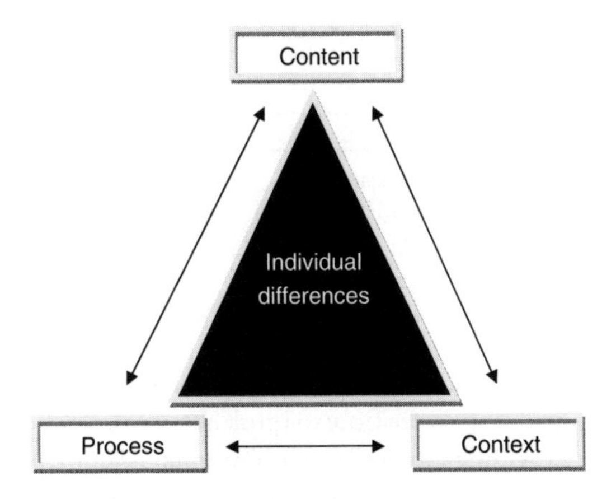

Figure 1 Variables influencing reactions towards change

Holt et al. (2007) provide a more comprehensive definition and define readiness for change:

> . . . as employees' beliefs that they are capable of implementing a proposed change (change self-efficacy); that the proposed change is appropriate for the organization (appropriateness); that the leaders are committed to the proposed change (management support) and that the proposed change is beneficial to organizational members (personal value).

Readiness for change can be regarded as a comprehensive attitude and is

> . . . influenced by the *content* (what is being changed), the *process* (how the change is being implemented), the *context* (circumstances under which the change is occurring) and individual attributes i.e. the characteristics of those being asked to change.

The four variables depicted in Figure 1 influence how employees feel about the change (affect), what they think (cognition) and what they intend to do (behaviour) in response to the change (Oreg et al., 2011). Viewing resistance as a multifaceted concept (i.e. emotional, behavioural and mental resistance) provides a more comprehensive view of resistance (Piderit, 2000) and interventions addressing resistance should also address the appropriate level of resistance (see Table 2).

However, it is important to remember that successful change is about feeling (emotional), not just thinking (mental). Combining the two, head and heart, is the key to change success. It seems, however, that managers still believe

Table 2 Examples of resistance

Affective resistance	Behavioural	Cognitive
Refers to moods and emotions such as anger, fear, anxiety etc.	Refers to intentions to act in response to the change and may involve behaviours such as complaining and procrastination.	This refers to employees thoughts about the change and comes about as a mental evaluation of the change e.g. what are the benefits of the change?

successful change is achieved by giving facts (i.e. stating the business case) and expect that if they give employees time to think about the implications that they will then change. Providing employees with rational arguments is only part of the story. We need to give people time to reflect; enable them to understand what the future is going to look like and to explore their feelings about the change. We need to build a bridge to the future that people can envision and walk across. Therefore creating change readiness is always about integrating two elements: head and heart. The following quotations provide a further perspective:

Creating change readiness does not happen overnight

'How do you create change readiness? Well my first comment on that would be it doesn't happen overnight and if I look back over probably the last two years, I've been creating change readiness and that's not because I had any more gift than anybody else did to see into the future to see what was coming, I think it's because I came into the organization with a view to changing it anyway, trying to achieve culture change and behaviour change and organization change. So, if you like, the organization's got used to me changing things but over the last two years I've been much more focussed on the areas of the organization that need some radical step change.

Use different communication symbols to facilitate understanding of the change

Creating the change readiness for me is – and the way that I do this quite a lot is painting pictures, talking about different organizations and different sectors that I've worked in, talking about how things can be different, talking about opportunities, if you like, trying to illustrate what a changed organization can look like and feel like and what it can deliver and how it can be better performing, how it would look different for the public, how we could create better value for money without I suppose trying to – and I actually said this, I had a full staff briefing on Monday when we were talking about the whole

Service Transformation Programme (this is what it's been called internally for the last 12 months) and what I said – and we've issued "at risk" notices to people who are at risk of redundancy – 64 people – and what I'm saying to them is we've got to be leaner, we've got to be more efficient, we've got to reduce the bureaucracy, we can't gold-plate everything from here on in because we just can't afford it, but that's not to say that what you have been doing as individuals is wasteful or inefficient or not very good. This is not a criticism of you as people, it's saying what we have in the organization, our processes and systems which are wasteful and which are bureaucratic and which we can't afford to do anymore and that's what we have to address. So if you like it's creating that space for change and painting a different picture, whilst at the same time saying oh and by the way, you're very good at what you do, you're very professional, you're very committed, you're very hardworking, but some of you aren't going to be here anymore and trying to get that balance on the change readiness is difficult.'

Be open and honest in your communication with employees

'I think my personal view is that change management is most fundamentally about how people are managed and if people are managed well on a day to day basis and in a positive HR sense – then I think readiness for change is always higher.'

Creating change readiness should be a continuous activity

To summarize, individual level readiness for change is influenced by an individual's beliefs that change is needed, that he or she has the capacity to successfully undertake change, and that change will have positive outcomes for his or her job/role. In the next section, variables impacting on reactions of employees toward change will be explored.

Variables Influencing Reactions Towards Change

Individual differences

Personal characteristics are sometimes ignored when change is implemented as managers perceive this as a given that cannot be influenced or managed.

Although these personal characteristics may be difficult to change, specific strategies, for example coaching, and the manner in which the change message is structured and communicated can be employed to increase individual level awareness and support. A number of research findings demonstrated the role and impact of individual characteristics in the change management process (Holt et al., 2007; Herold et al., 2007; Amiot et al., 2006). Differences in characteristics, for example, *levels of self-esteem, coping styles used to deal with change* and *locus of control* influence how employees react to and experience change. Differences in personality can predict employee's attitudes towards change and their willingness to accept and implement change. As managers we cannot change the personality of our employees but we need to be sensitive to and understand the impact of individual difference when we communicate and implement change in our organizations. Employees, for example, who have low levels of self-efficacy, or low tolerance for ambiguity, may experience high levels of uncertainty (i.e. inability to predict something accurately), anxiety, fear and an unwillingness to accept the change. Demographic variables such as age, tenure and level of education may also influence how individuals view and react towards the change. The differences between individuals highlight the importance of demonstrating managerial behaviours such as employee support, empathy and coaching of employees. A CEO explains this as follows:

Demonstrate transformational behaviours
Involve employees
Build their levels of self-efficacy
Provide recognition

'Talking, explaining, involving, and then energizing, I suppose if you've instilled the confidence that the change is logical, involve them and you provide sufficient support, then they'll make the step. It also means that you demonstrate an understating of where they are in the process. Then play back the fact that (a) they did that and (b) look how good they've been, you know, and doesn't it feel great now, that that thing that you didn't necessarily think you could do, you could do.'

Context

The context refers to the internal environment of the organization or as explained by Johns (2006, p. 386) it refers 'to the situational opportunities and constraints that affect the occurrence and meaning of organisational behaviour'. Many change efforts fail because organizations implement or impose change in an environment that is not ready to change. Aspects such as a lack of management support (Rafferty and Griffin, 2006), low organizational commitment (Lee and Peccei, 2007) and job characteristics (Hornung and Rousseau, 2007) serve as examples in this regard. Change management is not just about changing systems, structures or processes but it is all about managing the people factor. The leadership of an organization plays an important part in creating the context for change. The way they view and frame organizational change, mechanisms used to create an organizational context that is susceptible to change, plays an important role in how employees view and react towards organizational change. This can be explained as follows:

Frame change in a positive manner	*'I think in large part we do it by embracing and welcoming and applauding change as being something good. Lots and lots of organizations run away from change because it's frightening, because it's out of the ordinary, because it's different, because it's new, because it's worrying, because it's going to make me insecure. We have always tried to communicate that change is good, that if we are changing and prepared to be flexible and agile, then that*
Create an organization that is built for change	*is a good thing. We have, as an organization, five guiding principles which are very important to us which are indicative of the kind of behaviour and culture we wish our people to demonstrate and they*
Organizational values is a powerful mechanism to create an organization that is built for change	*are simplicity, agility, innovation, trust and integrity. So the last two are kind of pretty predictable but the first three are very important. With innovations we mean – actually almost from a change perspective so innovation of process, innovation of thinking, innovation of challenging the* status quo, *innovation in product definitely, innovation in service, innovation in the way we provide customers*
Reward value aligned behaviour	*with an experience. So the way we think of innovation and reward it and recognize it through award programmes and prizes and so on, is all around change, change is for good. And then agility – again is all about change, how agile are we as an organization to react to changing market circumstances? So I think people internally don't expect things to stay the same and that must be advantageous to us, that if something does change it's not seen as a threat,*
Any change should be linked to strategy	*it's seen as "OK, that's changed". Change for change's sake is not a good thing, so we're always careful to make sure that change is understood in the context of strategy. All our change is based on our strategy and therefore has more immediate understanding*

and resonance with our people because there's a context which makes sense.'

A very important contextual consideration is the level of trust that exists between employees and management. Oreg (2006) for example found that trust in management was the only variable that notably influenced the affective, cognitive and behavioural components of resistance to change. Rousseau et al. (1998, p. 395) define trust as 'a psychological state comprising the intention to accept vulnerability based upon positive expectations of the intentions or behaviour of another'. A trusting relationship is therefore characterized by feelings of confidence and support, and a certainty that that both parties will follow through on promises. Trust can, therefore, be seen as the basis for effective interpersonal relationships and De Ridder (2004, p. 21) argues that trust is an important generator of social capital and of supportive attitudes. Management practices such as participative decision-making, organizational support and meeting expectations are likely to influence employees' levels of trust. Behaving authentically, that is, acting according with values, preferences and needs, as well as valuing openness and truthfulness in relationships, can be regarded as the foundation of building trust. Authentic leaders understand the importance of being transparent in their interaction, demonstrating consistent behaviour and taking into account the needs of their employees. Gardner et al. (2005, p. 357) state that relational transparency involves presenting one's genuine, as opposed to a fake, self through selective self-disclosure to create bonds based on intimacy and trust with close others, and encouraging them to do the same. There is also empirical support for the role of trust in change communication (Rousseau and Tijoriwala, 1999). Employees who trust management may be more willing to trust change communication as well as acceptance of the reasons for change. Lack of trust in management has been associated with employee anger, frustration and increased cynicism. The creation of high levels of trust is not only important between management and employees, but also between team members and the level of support they receive from each other. Unfortunately, depending on the type of change, change alters the content of the psychological contract, that is, employee's and employer's beliefs or perceptions regarding the terms of the employment relationship (Robinson and Rousseau, 1994). If employees perceive the change as violating or breaching the psychological contract, the level of trust between employer and employee is negatively influenced and may emerge as a serious change barrier. Zhao et al. (2007, p. 669) write 'when the other party fails to fulfil its promises, the focal person's immediate response is mistrust, which will further produce negative attitudes and behaviours'.

Psychological contract breach

Understanding the implicit expectations employees have of the organization and how change interventions are going to impact on these expectations, can increase change success. How are proposed changes in your organization going to impact on the following elements?

- *Employee job satisfaction?*
- *Commitment of employees?*
- *Employee engagement?*
- *Relationships?*
- *Levels of trust?*
- *Accepting and supporting change?*

What actions can you take to minimize the impact of the change?

The change history of the organization also influences employee reactions towards change. Isabella (1990) found that change recipients compare the new change event to previous organizational changes they have experienced and draw certain conclusions about the change event. Negative experiences with historical organizational change will have an impact on future expectations of the change. For example, an experience of poorly managed change in the past may lead to expectations that the new change will also be poorly managed. Negative previous experiences with change may also lead to cynicism about organizational change (Bernerth et al., 2007) and normally involves loss of faith in leaders, a pessimistic viewpoint about change efforts being successful and the placement of blame for the failure of change on the facilitators of change, usually management (Rubin et al., 2009). The dangers of high levels of cynicism towards organizational change may lead to high levels of resistance (Stanley et al., 2005) and may activate a self-fulfilling prophecy. In a change context a self-fulfilling prophecy can be explained as follows: An employee has a belief that the change is going to be unsuccessful. As a result of this expectation the employee exhibits behaviour that is not supportive of the change and as a result of this behaviour, the change is unsuccessful: the prophecy is fulfilled. The ever-present danger of cynicism towards organizational change is explained by Bommer et al. (2005) who state that when cynicism about organizational change leads to unsuccessful change implementation, the failure reinforces the cynical beliefs and consequently, later change efforts are less likely to succeed. Cynicism about change can spill over into other areas of work life, for example, a decrease in employee motivation, organizational commitment and engagement. The key to avoiding cynicism in employees is to first make sure that your own managerial actions are consistent and based on integrity – you must walk-the-talk.

What does the change history of your organization tell your employees of the probability of future change success?

Reflecting on past organizational changes in your organization, write your organization's change story. What deductions can you make in terms of the following:

- Change successes
- Change failures
- Employee experiences with change
- Level of management commitment towards the change

Given your understanding of the past change history, what actions do you need to take to influence employees' perceptions of the organization's ability to implement change successfully?

A further contextual variable that may impact on the employee's reactions towards change is organizational culture. The concept of culture can be broadly defined as a

> . . . pattern of basic assumptions and beliefs, developed by a given social group throughout its history of internal integration and external adaptation, that has worked reasonably well in the past to be considered by the group as valid and important enough to be passed on to new members as the correct way of interpreting the organization's reality (Schein, 2004).

Organizational culture comprises different components; for example, social norms which define appropriate and inappropriate behaviours, values that guide decision-making and create a general atmosphere in the organization. It shapes, for example, the speed and efficiency with which things get done and the organization's capacity for and receptiveness to change. The culture of the organization creates an atmosphere, or what Ghoshal and Bartlett (1994) refer to as the 'smell of the place' and this influence employees' readiness and openness for change.

Understanding your culture: identify cultural variables that may impact on change implementation success

Explore the following elements of your organizational culture and determine to what extent these elements are supportive/not supportive of your change initiative:

1. Power structures in the organization
2. Rules and regulations
3. Informal networks
4. The way the organization is structured for example reporting relationships, roles and responsibilities

5. Control mechanisms used in the organization
6. Which behaviours get rewarded, what do you need to do to get punished?
7. Rewards systems used in the organization
8. Organizational routines, that is, how do people behave and react towards each other?
9. What do you need to do to get promoted in the organization?
10. Change leadership ability
11. Senior management support for change in the past?
12. What constitutes status, power and prestige in the organization?
13. What are the underlying assumptions people have about the organization? What are their assumptions around people, leadership, work, change, risk-taking and success?

Finding answers to the above questions will create a 'cultural story' of the organization. What do you need to do to overcome some of the identified barriers that may impact on change success?

Putting it differently, the culture of the organization provides employees with cues in terms of which behaviours are regarded as important and should be conformed to. Employees, for example, who perceive their organizational culture characterized by high levels of control, enforcement of compliance and lacking employee support, are more likely to hold negative views towards organizational change. In contrast, employees who perceive their organizations as open, flexible and participative, are more likely to possess positive attitudes towards the change. The role of organizational culture and climate in facilitating or inhibiting change can be regarded as key factor in creating organizational change readiness. One way of thinking about the power of culture is to imagine planing a plank of wood. If you work the plane 'with the grain' you will have nice shavings of wood coming out of the plane. If you work 'against the grain', however, then your plane will quickly lodge and stick to the plank. Experienced managers work with the culture as much as possible. As a strategic change enabler management should have a clear understanding of how elements of culture fit together, so artifacts and creations, values and beliefs and basic assumptions, are supportive of the proposed change.

Change process

The change process refers to methods used to implement organizational change and in Chapter 3 the importance and role of formal communication practices were highlighted. Formal change communication practices are controlled by the leadership of the organization and transmit information about the change process and how the change is to be implemented. With formal communication practices the change message is designed and standardized by the organization. In contrast, the role of informal communication or ad hoc conversation is often overlooked in the change process.

Use the water cooler moments wisely . . .

Informal communication, for example rumours, can make or break a change effort. The informal communication channel can be used as a powerful tool to influence employee perceptions. Think about the following actions that you can take:

- Visit the coffee machine regularly and engage in conversations with employees. Provide relevant change information that you would like to be distributed.
- Engage with the smokers in the smokers' corner and provide relevant change information that you would like to be circulated;
- Engage with employees in lifts, on the stairs or in the coffee shop and share information
- Engage actively with powerful individuals who have 'connections' in the organization irrespective of their level in the organization.

Using the informal communication channel to distribute information should be a planned process – have a clear understanding of the information you would like to send through the grapevine at different phases of the change process.

What other informal communication opportunities are available in your organization that you can use to distribute change relevant information?

Routine work conversations between employees and managers and the rumours that accompany change efforts (Bordia et al., 2004) also influence how people understand and react to change. Weick (1995) states in this regard that employees are not passive recipients of the change but play an active role in creating and reacting to the change. Co-workers and leaders provide cues, for example, talking informally about the change event, exploring issues, offering personal opinions and these conversations convey messages about the change event. Peach et al. (2005) have found that social support significantly influenced how the change is viewed and change recipient's intention to support the change.

Identify your informal communication and change champions?

The real change agents in organizational change are those employees who are influential with colleagues and who are positive towards the change. People pay different roles in groups and it may be beneficial to identify the following individuals to help you to spread the change messages can be seen in the following diagrams:

1. People who link different groups together fulfil a broker role.

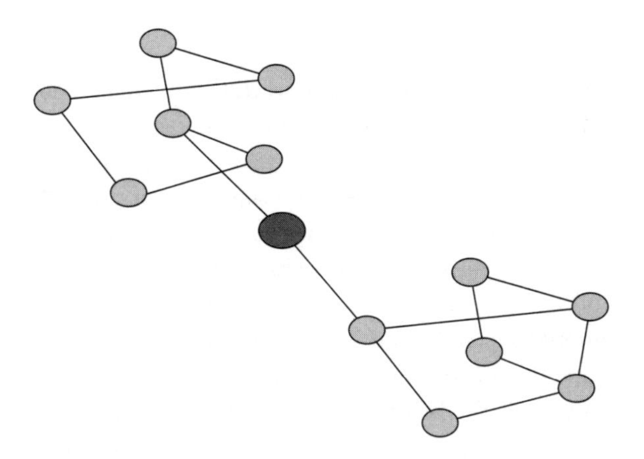

2. People with many links within a group are central people.

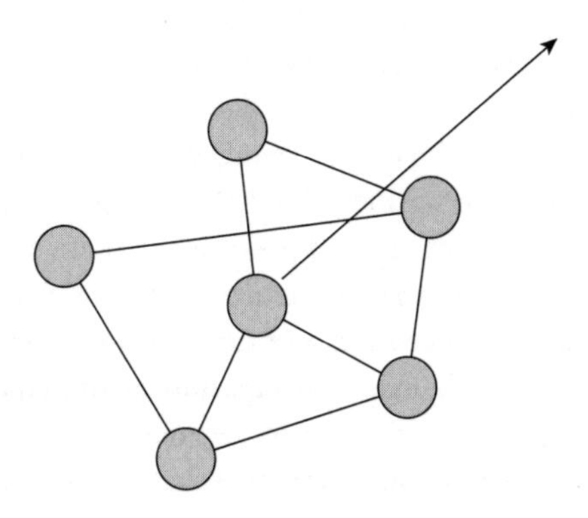

3. Where every member of the group has links to every other member, this represents cliques.

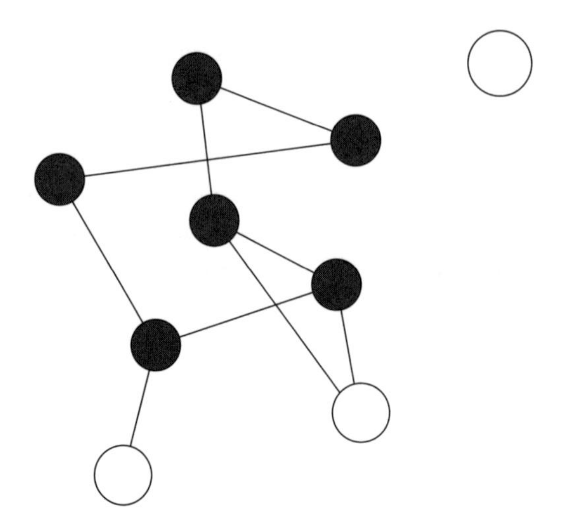

By engaging relevant and powerful individuals and involving them in change decision making can be a first step in engaging their hearts and minds. Organizational change 'involves individual and group sense-making processes taking place in a social context that is a product of constant and ongoing human interaction in organisational settings' (George and Jones, 2001, p. 421). Discussion with team members is how change recipients make sense of imminent changes and compare and evaluate the intensity and appropriateness of their own felt emotions (Carroll and Flood, 2010). In this regard it is also important to understand the role of emotional contagion, that is, the process in which an individual influences the behaviours and emotions of others (Barsade, 2002). In practical terms it means that if an individual is cynical about the change, he/she may re-evaluate their view if team members are more positively inclined towards the change. The opposite is also true. If team members are more negative about the imminent change, the individual (although initially positive about the change) may change his/her position and may also resist the change. The social environment is therefore used to create and interpret change events. In uncertain situations, employees try to make sense of the events, actively seek information and make assumptions about the change. Social cues from others have a determining influence on final positions that are taken. There is also broad consensus in the literature that participation in the change process and the experience of distributive, procedural and interactional justice impact on how change recipients react to change. Participation in the change project and decision-making processes creates a sense of urgency, contribution and overall support for the change. Participation may also decrease employees' change related stress and withdrawal behaviours. In implementing and managing change it is important to understand change recipients perceptions of the fairness of the outcomes (e.g. new responsibilities, remuneration) of the change process; fairness of procedures used to determine who gets what and fairness of the interpersonal treatment received in decision-making processes.

Change content

The nature or type of change may also influence change recipients reactions to it. Organizations today operate in a state of 'permanent white water' where changes, for example, in information, technology and markets happen at an incredible pace (Marshak, 2002) and organizations have to keep pace with and adapt to the changes. Changes in the environment may refer to events or activities external or internal to the organization that forces the organization to bring about changes in order to adapt to a rapidly changing environment. These events, or putting it differently, triggers for change can be divided into two broad categories: internal and external triggers for change. *Internal* triggers refer to those factors or conditions internal to the organization that necessitate change. Financial constraints such as changes in organizational strategy, a decline in profitability, low employee morale, mergers and acquisitions serve as examples in this regard and can cause organizational change. Putting it differently, internal triggers for change can be regarded as organizational changes in response to influences in the organization's environment. As these triggers are linked to changes in organizations, they are also directly under managerial control.

External triggers refer to variables originating from outside the organization, for example, change in customer requirements, increased or new competition, new technology and economic factors. The external triggers for change normally influence the organization to change its internal strategies, processes and practices. Changes in operational processes to increase operational efficiencies or quality improvement strategies serve as examples in this regard.

The external and internal triggers create a need for organizational change and it is the responsibility of management to interpret these changes and devise appropriate change strategies. Why is it important to understand the triggers for change? On the one hand they can be regarded as the forces which drive change and on the other, they inform us how fast we need to implement it. The forces for change may be strong or relatively weak and will determine if we are in a position to implement proactive change (if the forces are relatively weak) or if the forces are so strong that we need to act in a reactive manner. A well-known method to represent these forces is through the use of a force-field analysis. Lewin (1951) argues that for organizational change to happen, it may be more useful to reduce the forces maintaining the *status quo* than it is to increase the forces driving change. Change can generally be categorized in many different ways and Nadler and Tushman (1989) argue that change can be considered on two dimensions:

Scope of change — A change can either be small (incremental) and addresses only a small part of the organization or 'big' which addresses the whole organization – the latter is usually referred to as strategic change. It is important to note the key differences between the two types of change. Incremental changes do not change for example the organizational strategy, culture, power relations, etc. The purpose of incremental changes is normally to help the organization to become more effective. In contrast, strategic changes have a major impact on an organization, e.g. when the strategic direction of the organization is changed and these changes are also called transformational change.

Positioning or timing of the change — We can either anticipate change – i.e. not in response to events but in anticipation of external events that may occur or respond to an external event – i.e. reactive change.

Combining the two dimensions (scope of change and timing of change) – we can identify four classes of change (Nadler and Tushman, 1989):

- *Fine-tuning and adaptation*: Fine tuning refers to small operational changes (that alter certain aspects, looking for an improvement but keeping the general framework) in the organization, normally in anticipation of changes in the external environment and is also known as pro-active change. In contrast, adaptation refers also to small operational changes in the organization but usually to a response to changes in the external environment, that is reactive change.
- *Re-orientation and recreation*: These changes refer to strategic, transformational and revolutionary changes and can be regarded as radical transformations, where the organization totally changes its essential framework. Re-orientation refers to radical changes in anticipation of changes in the external environment and recreation refers to changes in response to changes in the external environment.

The type of change, incremental of transformational, will influence how people react and respond to change. A CEO offers the following viewpoint:

Irrespective of the type of change:

Attack organizational inertia with a vengeance

Help employees to move out of their comfort zone

Frame the change in a positive manner

Be authentic

Be clear on how employees react to change

'One of the ways we're trying to do it is to approach this mantra of "We've always done it that way" and we almost use that now as a ridicule so that if we are sat in a meeting and somebody proposes something it's more – and then you can almost hear the various people say "Ah, but we've always done it that way" – so you kind of, this self-deprecating piece of it. So yeah, we do try to introduce change as much as we can. There was the problem a couple of years ago, having hit the buffers basically, where we knew we couldn't change anything because we frankly couldn't afford it. We changed some of the big ones such as the perceptions and values and things like that but actually changing systems, procedures, processes and all that we just couldn't afford to do it. Interestingly now, having got to that point in it and had the real horrors and now just about to peep the head up again, we are trying to introduce change as a positive. So one of the things for instance, we sat down and talked to the managers at the end of last month and talked to them about a new IT system and very much using that change as the positive because what we're saying to them was we're about to invest somewhere about two to three million pounds in an IT system and that sounds like a lot of money but from your point of view, (a) it's going to be a lot of work but (b) actually just think of the positive message because the positive message is we think we've actually got through the worst and we're now starting to invest in the future – your future. So it's trying to use it from that point of view. But you've just got to be honest, that most of us hate change, we just say that we don't!'

Creating Change Readiness: Leadership Behaviours

In the previous section variables impacting on reactions of employees towards change were explored and some managerial behaviours that may minimize the impact of these variables highlighted. It should be clear from our previous

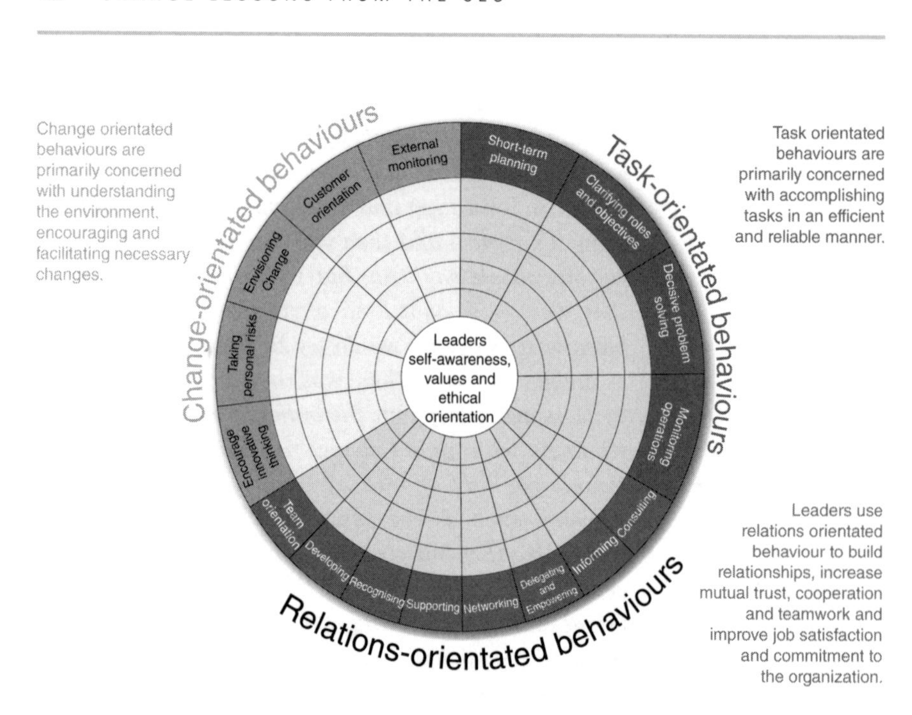

Figure 2 Leadership behaviours

discussions that the starting point of leading and managing change is having high levels of leader self-awareness, understating your own values and behaving in an ethical manner. This can be regarded as your own personal operating system and will influence your ability to use leader behaviours effectively. Figure 2 illustrates the central position of authenticity in leading and managing change. Yukl, et al. (2002), in an attempt to identify relevant leadership behaviours, argue that effective leaders need to demonstrate three types of behaviours: task, relational (relations) and change orientated behaviours. Building on the work of Yukl et al. (2002) and authentic leadership perspectives (e.g. Avolio et al., 2004), these behaviours can be graphically illustrated as Figure 2 shows.

In order to minimize the potential influences of the content, context and process of change, the leadership style of the leader should be flexible and adaptable. Yukl and Mahsud (2010) state in this regard that this 'involves changing behaviour in appropriate ways as the situation changes' (p. 81). Effective change leaders need to be able to use a variety of behaviours that are appropriate for the situation. Putting it differently, the situation determines the patterns of effective leader behaviours, that is, the amount of task, relational and change orientated behaviours demonstrated. Understanding the variables that may influence employees' reactions toward change necessitates the ability to diagnose a situation accurately and demonstrating appropriate leader behaviours. Examples of appropriate behaviour patterns are as follows:

1. Be authentic: understand your values, be self-aware and operate in an ethical manner.
2. Provide direction: have a clear understanding of where you want to go, inspire employees and communicate effectively. Have mechanisms in place that provides feedback on progress, role clarification and accountability but above all, inspire employees to support the change.
3. Empower your employees: understand that leadership should be shared, it is a relationship between yourself and followers, it is about collaboration and building trust. You need to be willing to share your power, provide visible support and allow your employees to get on with it.
4. It is not only about the head but also about the heart. Have compassion for your employees, provide recognition and rewards and celebrate achievements.
5. Be willing to take personal risks: allow your employees to experiment with new behaviours, create a climate where people are willing to contribute, challenge and taking individual risks.

Employee reactions to change may be a function of your ability to use appropriate behaviours when you lead and implement change. This can be explained as follows:

Change should not be an add-on, it should be integrated in organizational life

Create and develop employee capacity to change

Be visible and communicate

Know 'why' the change is needed and where are you going

'I would certainly say make change a normal part of corporate life; encourage, train and educate your people to understand that change is a good thing, that they need not be frightened of it, that change brings with it opportunity and progress and if you stay still too long these days, or you have a workforce that feels you ought to stay doing the same thing because that must be better mustn't it? You're going to get disintermediated, disenfranchized or just beaten in the market, you have to – and I say the way you do that as a leader is through communication, it's something that leaders never ever spend enough time and effort on, which is communicating cogently and sensibly – not through webcasts and emails and stuff, but actually getting out there, talking, meeting, being visible and using anecdotes and story-telling to show people that change is not a bad thing, change is a good thing, in fact it's a necessary thing, in order to get to the future that we all wish to have. I think, again, change for change's sake is a very dangerous thing so first off,

Demonstrate behaviours such as communication, coaching, counselling and listening

Walk-the-talk

as a leader, you have to set the vision, its got to be clear. Then you've got to set the objectives very clearly for the organization and for every part of the organization, then you've got to set the framework of behaviours within which you expect people to behave. But beyond that, as a leader, your job is to communicate, to counsel, to support, to coach, to listen, to observe, to enthuse, to inspire – that's the job of a leader and if you've got the vision, the objectives and the framework of behaviours, then actually, change is fine, because you've always got to shift your way towards that elusive vision that you have. The more comfortable you get talking in those terms the more comfortable your people will be. And I think the other thing is behaviour breeds behaviour, if you as the leader behave in a way that's perfectly comfortable with change; "Change is just a great thing! I love change, it's fantastic!" then that behaviour will be breeding behaviour in your own people and their people and you know, it cascades down the organization.'

Rethinking Resistance to Change

Resistance to change is frequently used as a reason why transformation efforts fail and managers have many terms to describe resistance for example not buying into the change, people are negative, they are dragging their feet and so on. They classify resistance using a range of behaviours they don't like and this may range from employees asking an innocent question (to clarify), to a roll of the eyes or to blatant sabotage. Davidson (1994, p. 94) states that the term resistance has come 'to include anything and everything that workers do which managers do not want them to do, and that workers do not do that managers wish them to do . . .'. The concept remains loosely defined, allowing some managers to see it almost everywhere and others almost nowhere (Weitz, 2001). The concept has been defined in many different ways, for example: resistance can be regarded as opposition, reaction or force that inhibits change (Piderit, 2000), a restraining force (Lewin, 1951) or as a positive force that can be used to challenge and refine change strategies (Mabin et al., 2001). It is also possible that 'resistance to change is an interpretation assigned by change agents to the behaviours and communications of change recipients, or that these interpretations are either self-serving or self-fulfilling' (Ford et al., 2008, p. 362). By labelling change recipient behaviour as resistant, the change agent negates to a certain extent his/her responsibility in creating resistant behaviour. Breaking promises or violation of the psychological contract; poor communication about the change or misrepresenting the possible advantages of the change serves as examples of change agent behaviours that may be the cause of change recipient resistance.

Resistance to change can either be conceptualized as a negative force or an important source of information. However, the belief that people may resist change may impact on our understanding and the way we deal with real organization problems. For example, if you view employee resistance as negative, you will most probably manage resistance in a forceful manner, using coercion or the use of verbal threats. Your perception and interpretation of employee behaviour will definitely influence how you are going to manage it. Treating resistant behaviour as irrational and not as a form of feedback or a resource may reduce the chances to improve the change process. The change agent should investigate his or her own motives and reflect on why specific employee behaviour *should* be classified as resistant *before* employee behaviour is classified as resistant. This is important because the employees might have a point! There may be sound business reasons for resistant behaviour and exploring the behaviour may actually provide insights about the change process and actions that may be taken to improve the change intervention. This can be explained as follows:

Understand the reasons for resistance:
Change is not needed
Employees do not understand it

'I think resistance to change is in 99% of the cases either fear of the unknown or fear of what it might mean for me. Resistance to change that is coming from the other place is about either I don't understand why change is necessary or I don't agree with it, and I'm not going to support it, to the degree that that is the thing that is holding back the change. That is in most cases is the lesser point. Even though if sometimes that is the way it might be articulated

Need to save face

that might be a face saving way of articulating something that is much more personal. It is a deep rooted fear that I actually don't understand some of the stuff this guy is talking about, whatever he talks about, strategy, competition, unique selling point all those buzz words. There will be people who won't

Help people to embrace and not fear change

make it and you have to get rid of them, move them, whatever. The real focus will still be on the 95% whose resistance or their capability of cutting back change is actually about personal fear, so you got to find a way of taking the fear out. That's what I'm saying by open communication, whether it has to be me with the board and then the board with managers and then all the way down to people whose individual performance conversations, performance contract, performance reviews and all of that stuff that says the future is not a certain place but it's going to be different and we will figure it out together, we want to try some stuff. In some cases the thing you have to change may be self-evident, it may be very clear and you know what you want to put in and it is a much more certain place. For example, if some of poor service, be it finance or HR or whatever, it is we are going to be outsourced or centralized, that model is probably well understood to the degree that it will affect individuals and individuals' jobs, it is fairly discrete. And in that case again it is about communicating and engaging, what we are doing, why we are doing it. Communicating as much as you could as soon as you could and I think in those situations dealing with the individuals who are affected by it and being seen to deal with the individuals that are affected by it and are responsible in an ethical way which I genuinely would think is a very good job. You know if someone is going to be displaced the support they would be given, the package they would be given and all that stuff for the individual themselves but also for how it is seen within the organization. Provided you have got the confidence that you have the right people sitting beside you and sort of taking the job together. I do think managing change is all about managing people. You have to make a determination at some point particularly in this change situation and new management situation that you have got people with you that are capable of moving and making the change intellectually. I guess the surprise for me was coming in here and it is very easy to say this but it is actually palpable when you see an organization that it is just not in their way of thinking.'

Creating alignment and support is all about communication

Be authentic, open and honest

Have the 'right' team on-board

Managing change is all about people

Resistance should be viewed as a natural part of the change process – change asks employees to move from the known to the unknown and people differ in terms of their ability to adapt to change. People do not necessarily resist the change itself, but resist the consequences of the change. Jick and Peiperl (2003) argue that we need to rethink the term resistance – it should be viewed 'as natural as self-protection; as a positive step towards change; an energy to work with; as information critical to the change process and that resistance is not necessarily a roadblock to the change process'. There are numerous consequences that may influence how employees are going to react to the change: for example; a fear of the unknown, fear that they do not possess the skills and knowledge necessary for the change, possible threats to power and influence, inconvenience, and so on. People may also resist change if they think they will lose something of value or if they do not understand the real implications of the change and perceive that the change will cost them more that they will gain from the change. Once resistance is articulated it becomes a force that you can work with. Unarticulated resistance is by far the worst kind as it undermines the change effort. A CEO put it as follows:

Invest time to prepare your employees for change

Create alignment on all organizational levels

Make change part of normal organizational life

'Sometimes you underestimate the peoples' ability to take the change and to understand the need for the change. At times we've just concentrated on agreeing something formally with the staff representatives, not investing the time with staff to actually bring them to the place we actually want them to be. The other message is the degree of preparation is very important. What normally happens in our organization in the past is that you have your standard organization and then you try to introduce a change project or change strategy in parallel with it. You need the intensity brought by people who are allocated to the change. You also need that the change is not seen as their change but that it's part of the business, it can't be delivered without the whole hearted conviction of the manager and ultimately the staff and the business. It needs to focus to get over the resistance and to build the energy for the change and to anticipate the different road blocks and issues of concern that will surface.'

To really understand resistance, we need to view resistance as a multidimensional attitude towards change (Oreg, 2003; 2006) comprising of an affective (how one feels about the change, e.g. angry, anxious), cognitive (what one thinks about the change, e.g. is it really necessary, will it be beneficial) and behavioural (actions or intentions to act in response to the change, e.g. complaining component). The components are not independent of each other but are distinct to one another and each highlights a different aspect of the resistance and gives us a better understanding of the relationships between sources of resistance, resistance to change and consequences of resistance. For example, Oreg (2006) found that changes in job security were associated with affective resistance, changes in power and prestige were associated with cognitive resistance and threats to intrinsic rewards were associated with cognitive and affective resistance. However, trust in management was the only variable that was associated with all three levels of resistance. Lack of trust significantly influenced the level of anger, frustration and anxiety experienced by employees and influenced employee's perceptions of the need and value of the change (Oreg, 2006). This can be explained as follows:

Build trust by being open, communicative, and provide honest feedback

'I would start by saying I don't think people generally particularly like change, so I think one of the first things you have to do is help people to realize there really is an absolute need for change, because if they don't really believe there is a need for change then you're going to find it hard. I think you have to be really honest with people. The big enabler is communication and engagement and regular reviews.'

Understand different types of resistance

'The resistance was very visible, a lot of resistance to change in organizations that are going through this is quite hidden and subversive – this was right in my face, I couldn't avoid it! So the tactics that I had to use, to get over the resistance, was just about being honest and about being open and about saying, well actually I don't know.'

Reactions to organizational change are to be expected. Ford et al. (2008) view resistant behaviour as a form of engagement with the change and argue that resistant behaviour should be regarded as a critical factor in implementing change successfully. Listening to employees and trying to understand the reasons for their reactions may enable the change agent to adjust the scope and pace of the change, and thereby increase the success of the organizational change. When change agents know the concerns people have regarding an organizational change and the reasons why a change typically fails, they can employ a series of strategies and tactics to overcome obstacles.

Managing Resistance

Despite your best efforts to create organizational and individual change readiness, it is unfortunately not possible to avoid resistant employees. What is needed is a clear and succinct strategy to deal with resistant employees. Although the formulation of an organization-wide strategy to manage resistance is important, it is also important to devise a strategy that specifically addresses individual level resistance. A first step in formulating an individual level strategy is to understand the reasons why employees resist, understanding their core beliefs toward the change. Explore and try to understand the following:

Understand the reasons for resistance

- The evidence they use in framing their arguments
- The logic they use
- The language they use in articulating their objections

Many of the reasons why employees resist change can be attributed to poor leadership or inappropriate managerial behaviour. As a rule, managers love facts, figures and reasoning to build a case for change. While this is obviously important, it is not enough to inspire and enlist employees in organizational change. Employee commitment towards change is only possible if the leader is able to engage the hearts of employees, their emotions and feelings. Duck (1993, p. 113) argues in this regard that change is 'fundamentally about feelings, companies that want their workers to contribute with their heads and hearts have to accept that emotions are essential to the new management style'. Kotter and Cohen (2002) argue in this regard that people do not change because they are given the results of a comprehensive analysis but because they are shown a truth that influences their feelings. In practice it means the leader needs to make the change real (allowing employees to see and feel the change), permit employees to speak about their anxieties, and help employees to deal with their fears and feelings. Garvin and Roberto (2005) argue leaders must pay close attention to employees' emotions as this influences their receptiveness for change. The following can serve as guidelines in managing the emotions of employees:

How to manage the emotions and reactions of employees towards change?

- Accept the existence of emotions and feelings.
- Empathize with the feelings and emotions of employees.
- Provide opportunities for employees to share and discuss the feelings and emotions. Help them to

articulate the strengths and weaknesses of their logic.
- Help them to understand 'what is in it for them' when the change is successful.
- Provide training opportunities.
- Allow participation and involve employees in the change process.
- Act as a coach and provide support.

Chapter Summary

As indicated in the beginning of this chapter, this chapter builds on Chapter 3, and explores additional change variables that may impact on how employees react to change. More specifically, it demonstrates how elements of the change process, that is, *how* we implement the change, the *way* we manage it, the organizational context and individual variables, influence how employees respond to change. Having a clear understanding of the difference between *reacting* versus *resisting* change enables us to manage employee reactions more effectively. A key theme throughout the chapter is that, as a change leader, *you need to get people to understand what the change means and need to understand what does the change mean to the employee.* The change leader has different tools at his or her disposal in creating change readiness but the starting point is the leader. The change leader needs to act according to his or her value system, have high levels of self-awareness and act authentically. The ability to act authentic influences the ability of the leader to demonstrate appropriate leader behaviours and may influence employee acceptance of the change.

KEY INSIGHTS FROM PRACTICE

Reacting towards change is not the same thing as resisting change.

Experiencing change reactions from employees does not mean that they resist – it demonstrates that they still care about the organization.

Creating change readiness is a process and you need to invest time to create it.

Identify potential employee reactions before you implement the change and formulate strategies to manage it effectively.

Do not underestimate the power of the psychological contract that employees have.

Use the informal communication channel to your advantage.

The best method to create readiness is to create an organization that is built for change.

References

Amiot, C., Terry, D., Jimmieson, N., and Callan, V. (2006). A longitudinal investigation of coping processes during a merger: Implications for job satisfaction and organisational identification. *Journal of Management*, 32, 552–574.

Armenakis, A.A, Harris, S.G., and Mossholder, K.W. (1993). Creating readiness for organisational change. *Human Relations*, 46 (6), 681–703.

Avolio, B.J., Gardner, W.L., Walumbwa, F.O., and May, D. (2004). Unlocking the mask: a look at the process by which authentic leader's impact follower attitudes and behaviours. *The Leadership Quarterly*, 15 (6), 801–823.

Barsade, S.G. (2002). The ripple effect: emotional contagion and its influence on group behaviour. *Administrative Science Quarterly*, 47 (4), 644–675.

Bernerth, J.B., Armenakis, A.A., Field, H.S., and Walker, H.J. (2007). Justice, cynicism, and commitment: A study of important organizational change variables. *The Journal of Applied Behavioral Science*, 43, 303–326.

Bommer, W.H., Rich, G.A., and Rubin, R.S. (2005). Changing attitudes about change: Longitudinal effects of transformational leader behaviour on employee cynicism about organisational change. *Journal of Organizational Behavior*, 26, 733–753.

Bordia, P., Hunt, E., Paulsen, N., Tourish, D.J., and DiFonzo, N. (2004). Uncertainty during organizational change: Types, consequences, and management strategies. *Journal of Business and Psychology*, 18 (4), 507–532.

Carroll, S.J. and Flood, P.C. (2010) *Change Lessons from the CEO: Lessons from the Arts*, John Wiley & Sons, Ltd: Chichester.

Davidson, J.O. (1994). The sources and limits of resistance in a privatized utility, in Jermier, J.M, Knights, D., and Nord, W.R. (eds) *Resistance and Power in Organizations*. (pp. 69–101). New York, NY: Routledge.

De Ridder, J. (2004), Organisational communication and supportive employees, *Human Resource Management Journal*, 14 (3), 20–30.

Duck, J.D. (1993). Managing change: the art of balancing. *Harvard Business Review*, 71, 109–118.

Eby, L.T., Adams, D.M., Russel, J.E.A., and Gaby, S.H. (2000). Perceptions of organizational readiness for change: factors related to employees' reactions to the implementation of team-based selling. *Human Relations*, 53 (3), 419–442.

Ford, J.D., Ford, L.W., and D'Amelio, A. (2008). Resistance to change: The rest of the story. *Academy of Management Review*, 33 (2), 362–377.

Gardner, W.L., Avolio, B.J., Luthans, F., May, D., and Walumbwa, F.O. (2005b). 'Can you see the real me?' A self-based model of authentic leadership and follower development. *The Leadership Quarterly*, 16 (3), 343–372.

Garvin, D. and Roberto, M. (2005). Change through persuasion. *Harvard Business Review*, 83 (92) 104–112.

George, J. and Jones, G. (2001). Towards a process of model of individual change in organizations. *Human Relations*, 54, (4), 419–440.

Ghoshal, S. and Bartlett, C.A. (1994). Linking organizational context and managerial action: The dimensions of quality of management. *Strategic Management Journal*, 15 (95), 91–112.

Herold, D.M., Fedor, D.B., and Caldwell, S.D. (2007). *Journal of Applied Psychology*, 92 (4), 942–951.

Holt, D.T., Achilles, A., Armenikis, Feild, H.S., and Harris, S.G. (2007). Readiness for organizational change: The systematic development of a scale. *Journal of Applied Behavioural Science*, 43, 232–255.

Hornung, S. and Rousseau, D.M. (2007). Active on the job – proactive in change. How autonomy at work contributes to employee support for organizational change. *Journal of Applied Behavioral Science*, 43 (4), 401–426.

Isabella, L.A. (1990). Evolving interpretations as a change unfolds: How managers construe key organisational events. *The Academy of Management Journal*, 33 (1), 7–41.
Jick, T.D. and Peiperl, M.A. (2003). *Managing Change: Cases and Concepts*. New York: McGraw-Hill.
Johns, G. (2006). The essential impact of context on organizational behaviour. *Academy of Management Review*, 31 (2), 386–408.
Jones, R.A., Jimmieson, N.L., and Griffiths, A. (2005). The impact of organizational culture and the reshaping capabilities on change implementation success: The mediating role of readiness for change. *Journal of Management Studies*, 42 (2), 361–386.
Kotter, J.P. and. Cohen. D.S. (2002). *The Heart of Change: Real-Life Stories of how People Change their Organizations*. Cambridge, MA: Harvard Business School Press.
Lee, J. and Peccei, R. (2007). Perceived organizational support and affective commitment: the mediating role of organization-based self-esteem in the context of job insecurity. *Journal of Organizational Behavior*, 28 (6), 661–685.
Lewin, K. (1951). *Field Theory in Social Science: Selected Theoretical Papers*. New York: Harper.
Mabin, V.J., Forgeson, S., and Green, L. (2001), Harnessing resistance: using the theory of constraints to assist change management, *Journal of European Industrial Training*, 25 (2–4), 168–191.
Marshak, R.J. (2002). Changing the language of change: how new contexts and concepts are challenging the ways we think and talk about organizational change. *Strategic Change*, 11 (5), 279–286.
Nadler, D.A. and Tushman, M.L. (1989). Organisational frame bending: Principles for managing reorientation. *The Academy of Management Executives*, 3 (3), 194–204.
Oreg, S. (2003). Resistance to change: Developing an individual differences measure. *Journal of Applied Psychology*, 88 (4), 680–693.
Oreg, S. (2006). Personality, context and resistance to organizational change. *European Journal of Work and Organisational Psychology*, 15, 73–101.
Oreg, S., Vakola, A., and Armenakis, A. (2011). Change Recipients' Reactions to Organizational Change: A 60-Year Review of Quantitative Studies. *Journal of Applied Behavioral Science*, 47 (4), 461–524.
Peach, M., Jimmieson, N.L., and White, K.M. (2005). Beliefs underlying employee readiness to support a building relocation: A theory of planned behaviour perspective. *Organisation Development Journal*, 23 (3), 9–22.
Piderit, S.K. (2000). Rethinking resistance and recognising ambivalence: A multidimensional view of attitudes toward and organisational change. *Academy of Management Review*, 25, 783–794.
Porras, J. and Robertson, P. (1992). Organizational development; Theory, practice and research. In M.D. Dunnette and L.M. Hough (eds). *Handbook of Industrial and Organizational Psychology* (2nd edn), *Vol.* 3 (pp. 719–822). Palo Alto, CA: Consulting Psychologists Press.
Rafferty, A.E. and Griffin, M.A. (2006). Perceptions of organizational change: A stress and coping perspective. *Journal of Applied Psychology*, 91, 1154–1162.
Robinson, S.L. and Rousseau, D.M. (1994). Violating the psychological contract: Not the exception but the norm. *Journal of Organizational Behavior*, 15 (3), 245–259.
Rousseau, D.M., Sitkin, S.B., Burt, R.S., and Camerer, C. (1998). Not so different after all: a cross-discipline view of trust. *Academy of Management Review*, 23, 393–404.
Rousseau, D.M. and Tijoriwala, S.A. (1999). Assessing psychological contracts: issues, alternatives and measures. *Journal of Organizational Behavior*, 19 (1), 679–695.

Rubin, R.S., Dierdorff, E.C., Bommer, W.H., and Baldwin, T.T. (2009). Do leaders reap what they sow? Leader and employee outcomes of leader organizational cynicism about change. *Leadership Quarterly*, 20 (5), 680–688.

Schein, E. (2004). *Organizational Culture and Leadership* (3rd edn). San Francisco: Jossey-Bass.

Stanley, D.J., Meyer, J.P., and Topolnytsky, L. (2005). Employee cynicism and resistance to organisational change. *Journal of Business and Psychology*, 19, 429–459.

Weick, K.E. (1995). *Sense Making in Organisations*. Thousand Oaks, CA: Sage.

Weitz, R. (2001). Women and their hair: Seeking power through resistance and accommodation. *Gender and Society*, 15, 667–686.

Yukl, G., Gordon, A., and Taber, T. (2002). A hierarchical taxonomy of leadership behaviour: Integrating a half century of behaviour research. *Journal of Leadership and Organizational Studies*, 9, 15–32.

Yukl, G. and Mahsud, R. (2010). Why flexible and adaptive leadership is essential. *Consulting Psychology Journal: Practice and Research*, 62 (2), 81–93.

Zhao, H., Wayne, S.J., Glibkowski, B.C., and Bravo, J. (2007). The impact of psychological contract breach on work-related outcomes: a meta-analysis. *Personnel Psychology*, 60 (3), 647–680.

CHAPTER 5

Understanding How People Change

Chapter at a Glance

In this chapter you will learn the fundamentals of the processes people use to change and the specific phases they go through when they experience change. Employees experience change differently and it takes time for employees to make sense of the change and to fully commit towards the change. You can encourage individual level change if you are able to recognize the stages your employees are in and help them to move through the process of change. The chapter further aims to give insights into specific actions you can take to minimize barriers to individual level change and help your employees to move towards change acceptance.

Beginning Cases: Preparation

Despite the importance of recognizing emotions in the change process, managers often feel uncomfortable with the 'softer side' of leading change. Change interventions are managed on a project management basis without giving sufficient attention to the processes that employees go through in any change process. The following quotations provide further illustration:

Change creates strong emotions

Break change down in manageable and achievable steps

Empowerment leads to feelings of control

'In any organization, people have an anxiety around change even if it is to take an advantage of an opportunity. I tend to break change into manageable chunks. I used this mountain analogy of base camp one, base camp two, and so forth and try to make the change into biteable sizes. This enables people to know that by such a time we'll need to be there, and once they get a confidence around that, you tend to get more willingness to engage. People need to feel that you're asking them to take steps that are achievable – it is important they feel some sort of control over the process.'

Why do change efforts fail?

Changing too fast

Not having a clear end state

Lack of organizational engagement

Lack of senior management commitment

Unwilling to adapt your change strategy

Ignoring employee emotions

'Change was initiated by US head office – not evolutionary, but revolutionary change. They drove the change very quickly, they did not articulate the future and all of that stuff. Two years later the thing is grinding to a halt. So for me it was about that, they didn't have organizational engagement, the people that mattered were not capable of visualizing it, feeling a future that would be better than what we have now. There is a huge difference between agreeing and signing off on it and feeling it, because unless feeling it they not going to make it happen and it was very interesting to watch. I used to go to meetings and watch the way senior people just recoiled from active engagement, chose not to know and the devastating thing was that it took a long time and a lot of resource and a lot of money was still being spent. Consultants were paid a lot of money, contracts were entered into with outside providers. Have you ever seen that movie, The Field? *It was set in the turn of the century the early 1930s where this farmer, who is obsessed with land and getting this field and it takes over his whole life and it screws up his family and at one point he is getting mad and he was driving his cattle and they were running heedlessly toward the cliff and he just keeps driving them and everybody can see the only thing*

Escalating commitment to a failing course of action

Lack of line-management buy-in

Not listening to your people

Making the wrong assumptions around change support

You do not walk-the-talk

at the end is a cliff, and all the cattle are going to go down the cliff and that is all that is going to happen and that is what it felt like to an awful lot of people. They came to the conclusion that the only way this is going to stop is when there are a couple of dead cows in the ditch. Looking back it was apparent from the start that there was not line management engagement. The people had made the calls and the operating companies didn't buy this, they didn't understand it, they didn't feel it, it cut across everything they believed. There is a bunch of people who just don't get the need for change. You have to be open to change and getting two things right, i.e. the voice of people who say this change initiative is actually more fundamental than the way it has been articulated, the scope of the change was more broad organizationally than that which has been understood versus you just don't like change and are not prepared to move. Change will fail if you assume that people are on your side, do not communicate and if people don't understand the purpose of change in the first place. You need to ask yourself: does the change make sense to the people on the ground and have you prepared, have you researched, have you really understood what you are trying to achieve? You need to be prepared to demonstrate and display the conviction of the message that you are trying to deliver – if you do not do that, there is a poor chance of success.'

Chapter Introduction

In order to manage the change process effectively it is important to understand (1) 'how' people change and (2) experience change. Organizational change is always mediated through individual level change and having a clear understanding of the different phases people go through in the change process, will enable you to design effective change interventions. As indicated in the previous chapter, people experience different emotions during a change process. These emotions may be positive or negative, and individuals may cope with the change in different ways. The nature and scale of the change also influence how people experience change; some changes may be more substantive and may require major adjustments. People change in different ways, experience change differently and change at a different pace. Therefore, change agents and change recipients may also have different levels of change readiness. Change agents, who are responsible for planning and implementing the change, may view the proposed changes as necessary, may improve organizational effectiveness or provide new organizational opportunities. This means they already have the opportunity to make sense of the change and internalized the potential consequences of the change. In contrast, if the recipients of change are not involved in the preliminary analysis or part of the initial planning of the change, they may view organizational changes as unnecessary and disruptive. Change agents may therefore be more ready for the change comparing to the readiness levels of change recipients. As one change consultant explained 'if you look over your shoulder and no one is following, you are not leading anyone anywhere'. It is therefore important that change agents do not make assumptions about the readiness levels of employees but actively try to determine their levels of readiness. Similarly change agents need to *sense check* that other members of the management team are on-board also. This is achieved by understanding how individual level change comes about.

Understanding Individual Level Change

Understanding individual change processes enable us to devise effective strategies that are supportive of the needs of employees. In a change management context we are particularly interested in the influence of an individual's knowledge, attitudes and beliefs on behaviour. The following approaches explain how people change and how they experience change.

The Nature of Habits

Have you ever tried to lose weight, start a new fitness routine or stop smoking? If this is applicable to you then you will know that it is not easy to change. Webb et al. (2009, p. 597) state in this regard that 'many efforts to change behaviour are characterised by complete failure or by short-term success followed by relapse'. A key reason why we find it difficult to change our behaviour is a lack of understanding of our habits and how habits work (Duhig, 2012). Habits can be defined as learned dispositions to repeat past responses (Wood and Neal, 2007, p. 843) or putting it differently, much of our behaviour takes the form of repetitive actions. For example, when driving a bicycle, you may be conscious about performing the habit, but the actual performance may involve little thinking. This is because the key building block of a habit is a 'script' or a knowledge structure (Fiske and Taylor, 1984). The script or knowledge structure provides a rule which tells us that in a certain situation a specific response is adequate – it requires very little thinking on our part. Habits are acquired 'through incremental strengthening of the association between a situation (cue) and an action, i.e. repetition of a behaviour in a consistent context progressively increases the automaticity with which the behaviour is performed when the situation is encountered' (Lally et al., 2010, p. 998). Habits help us to free up some mental space and to use our cognitive functions efficiently. There is also a downside in the use of habits. Jager (2003) highlights aspects such as ignoring new information or actively seeking new information about a changing situation. This may be typical of what happens during organizational change. People are so used operating in a certain way that may ignore environmental cues and continue to operate on autopilot.

Habits have three components – there is a *cue* or a *trigger* for a specific behaviour, a *routine* which is the behaviour itself, and a *reward*, which is how your brain decides to remember a habit for the future (Duhig, 2012). People continue to perform in a certain way because they find outcomes of their behaviour enjoyable and rewarding. This is why it is so difficult to change bad habits! In order to be able to break habits, we need to understand the three components of a habit, that is, the *trigger*, the *behaviour* or routine itself and the *reward* you receive from executing the behaviour (Duhig, 2012). He argues that although changing habits are not easy, it can be done. Firstly, identify the cue that is triggering the behaviour; secondly, identify the reward that you receive from executing the behaviour and lastly come up with a plan to replace your current (old) routine with a new one. In practice it means that the only thing you need to change is the routine – the cue and reward you receive can stay the same. While this is true for individuals, it is also applicable to organizations – organizational habits determine employee behaviour. Organizational routines can be a source of inertia and inflexibility but it can also be a source of change. It is therefore important to consider the role and impact of organizational routines (especially culture) on employee behaviour when implementing organizational change.

Stages of Change

In the previous section the role of habits in shaping behaviour was discussed and a method for changing habit explored. The transtheoretical model of individual level change (DiClemente and Prochaska, 1998) provides us with a further and more comprehensive explanation of how individuals change. It demonstrates that when individuals change, they normally move through five phases of change (see Figure 1), that is, pre-contemplation, contemplation, preparation, action and maintenance. At each phase of the process, an individual makes decisions that either move the individual toward, or away from, behaviour change. Movement between the phases therefore depends on a set of forces that change an individual's thought processes. This means the individual weighs the pros and cons of changing or putting it differently, assessing the advantages and disadvantages of changing behaviour or accepting the change. This can be illustrated as follows:

Potential benefits	Potential disadvantages
• Will the change enable me to do my work better? • Will opportunities for advancement increase? • Will I be able to work more autonomously?	• I will have to work longer hours • I will have less time for my family • I do not have the skills to cope with the change • Things are working well, there is no need for change

Individuals will only change if the potential advantages outweigh the potential disadvantages. The model views behaviour change as (1) dynamic; (2) acknowledges that people change at different rates and (3) that behavioural change takes place in identifiable steps or stages. An important element of the model is recognizing that people not only move through different phases, but it is also possible to relapse, that is, revert to a previous phase. Relapse can take place at any stage and behavioural change often takes place after a process of progressing and relapsing. This means that a number of attempts through the different phases are needed before the change goal is achieved. From Figure 1 it is clear that individual level change is not a linear process and that employees are in different phases of the change process. However, organizational change is normally implemented using the following approach: (1) opportunity for change is identified; (2) comprehensive analysis is completed and a change plan formulated; (3) implementation team is formed (4) change is communicated and (5) change is implemented.

The assumption is that effective communication prepares the employees for the change and that when the change is to be implemented, employees are ready to take action. This has significant implications when change is implemented: our interventions and communication strategies should address *where* individuals are in the change process. The failure of many organizational change efforts can be ascribed to an inability of change agents to understand the basic psychological principles of change. Focussed change strategies will enable individuals to move through the different change phases more quickly and effectively. The five-step process (Levesque, et al., 1999) and managerial action that can be taken to assist individuals moving through the different phases can be explained as follows:

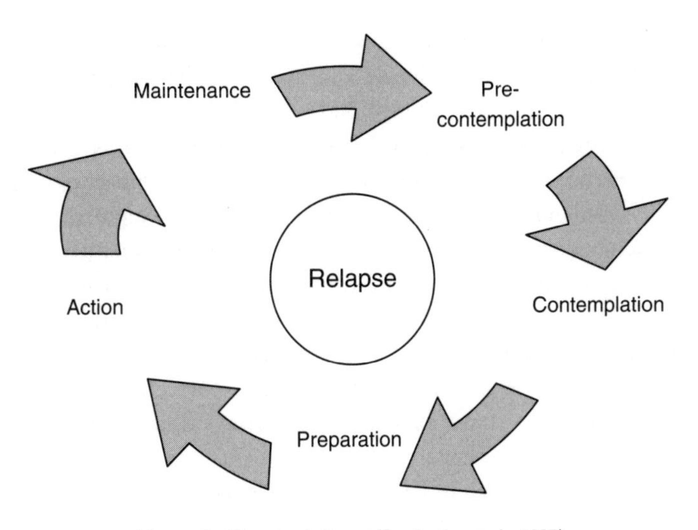

Figure 1 Phases of change (Prochaska et al., 1997)

Pre-contemplation (Not thinking about the change): In this phase the individual does not recognise that there is a problem or that there is a need for change and has no intention of changing their behaviour. Resistance is a key characteristic of this phase. By demonstrating appropriate behaviours, change leaders can help employees to become more aware and move towards the next phase: contemplation. The following behaviours may assist employees in this regard:

Managerial actions

Create a safe environment

- Have 'Town Hall' meetings and present the case for change. Create a safe environment where employees are willing to share their emotions.

Create further context for the change by effective communication

- Use storytelling to create further context for change. Share personal insights, giving facts about the change and own interpretations of the impact of change.
- Increase the level of change communication and help change recipients to make sense of the imminent change.

Allow employees to express and share their emotions

- Have sessions where employees can express their feelings and emotions about the change, discuss potential and foreseeable problems and create possible solutions to overcome change barriers.

Explain the negative consequences of not changing

- Discuss how not implementing the change will lead to negative consequences.

Contemplation (Aware and thinking of the change): Although the employee is aware and thinks about the change and may consider potential strategies to adapt to the organizational change, he/ she has yet make a commitment to change. Putting it differently, in this phase the employee is 'still sitting on the fence'. He or she is becoming aware of the negative impact of maintaining the *status quo* and benefits of changing, but is still weighing the pros and cons of changing. In this phase the employee is trying to identify the personal benefits of changing behaviour and the negative consequences if the change is accepted. The following behaviours may help employees to move from the contemplation phase to the next phase, preparation:

Managerial actions

Help employees to understand their own change philosophy

Explain change message and identify change barriers

Build the confidence levels of your employees

- Provide opportunities for employees to assess and express their feelings and emotions about the change.
- Help employees to identify and articulate their core beliefs about the change.
- Use logic, evidence and help employees to assess the advantages and disadvantages of the change.
- Explore potential barriers to change that may impact on the willingness of the employee to make the change.
- Discuss the individual benefits of the change as well as the potential disadvantages. Be open, honest and authentic about what is going to happen and how it is going to impact the employee.
- Explore employees' levels of confidence to be able to change successfully.

Preparation (Taking steps needed for changing): In this phase employees are preparing themselves mentally for the change and there is an intention to take action. They are willing to take small steps towards changing and take calculated risks. Discussions with colleagues about 'what the change is going to look like in practice' and probabilities of change success, are common in this phase. Helping employees to move from the preparation phase towards the action phase is important and the following behaviours can be considered:

Managerial actions

- Use brain storming sessions to identify employee concerns and formulate strategies to overcome the concerns.
- Assist employees to understand where they fit into the change and the impact of their contribution towards the change.

Use a variety of tools e.g. brain storming, goal setting, coaching, reflection and a learning journal to make the next step

Demonstrate your commitment towards the change

- Set goals and milestones that will help employees to understand the change path.
- Be specific in terms of expected new behaviours.
- Demonstrate visible commitment towards the change: walk-the-talk
- Use, coaching, small group discussions and training to raise the self-efficacy levels of employees.
- Use visualization techniques to explore future opportunities.
- Use role-play to explore what their new roles and work identities are going to look like.
- Allow time for individual reflection.
- Encourage employees to keep a learning journal in which they articulate their feelings, emotions and behaviours.
- Create peer support networks.

Action (Making the change): In this phase the individual has put the planning into action, is making the necessary changes in their behaviour and is an active participant in the change process. Employees in this phase may be more willing and open to accept help and seek assistance from others. Despite being willing to engage with the change process, this is also the phase where employees, after experimenting with new behaviours, may decide that the change is not working for them. They may revert to previous phases of change, for example; preparation, contemplation and so forth. It is therefore important that the change leader is conscious of potential relapse and the following behaviours may assist in this regard:

Managerial actions

Use a variety of tools e.g. consolidation of reflections; discussion sessions; experience sharing opportunities and Socratic dialogue to prevent relapse

- Allow employees to consolidate personal reflections in a learning journal. These reflections can be used as input for individual and group discussions.
- Let employees participate and identify change barriers that may impact on the change process.
- Develop joint action plans with employees to overcome barriers to change.
- Monitor the process.
- Have sessions where employees discuss 'how' their roles have changed and are changing.
- Allow employees to share change experiences and best practices.
- Build levels of self-efficacy of employees by demonstrating supportive behaviours, acknowledgement of small successes.

- Use guest speakers and case studies to create further context for the change.
- Use Socratic dialogue to enhance understanding. A group of six panellists assumes a role/position based on their understanding from change challenges and engages in dialogue. The moderator asks the panellists questions and direct questions from one panellist to another that results in the sharing of varied perspectives on the issue. Members of the audiences are invited at appropriate intervals.

Maintenance (successfully maintaining the change): The employee works to make the change effective and maintain the new behaviour. As with the previous phases, the employee may relapse or regress to previous stages. It is also important to note that many people may need to go through the stages several times before lasting change occur. The following behaviours may be helpful in institutionalizing change:

Managerial actions	
Create an environment that supports the change e.g. changes in culture structure and processes **Provide feedback** **Help employees to deal with stress and anxiety** **Reward appropriate behaviours**	• Provide progress reports on status of the change implementation process. • Allow employees to share the key insights from their learning journals. • Clarify and confirm organizational values. • Use social support mechanisms for example employee support groups to resolve change problems. • Adapt organizational systems, structures or processes to institutionalize the change. • Ensure that organizational culture support change efforts. • Implement support programmes that may help employees to cope with anxiety and stress. • Provide progress reports, demonstrate managerial commitment towards the change. • Celebrate successes and provide recognition. • Plan for potential relapse.

Relapse (Reverting to old behaviour): As already indicated, moving through the different phases is not a linear process. It is possible to move towards a phase and after some time, moving back to a previous phase. Relapse is a natural component of the learning process – it is through our mistakes and reflecting on these mistakes, that real learning takes place. The effective change leader will be able to anticipate relapse in employees and be able to learn from it. The following behaviours may be helpful in preventing relapse in your employees:

Managerial actions

Explore the reasons for relapse

Help employees to revisit their change philosophy

Build confidence levels of employees

Use coaching

- Explore reasons for relapse.
- Provide opportunities for employees to assess and express their feelings and emotions about the change.
- Help employees to identify and articulate their core beliefs about the change.
- Use logic, evidence and help employees to assess the pros and cons of the change.
- Discuss the individual benefits of the change.
- Explore employees' levels of confidence to be able to change successfully.
- Using coaching to help employees to move forward.

Endings and New Beginnings

Bridges (2003) provides us with a different perspective on individual level change. He argues that individuals move through three overlapping phases: *endings*, the *neutral zone* and *new beginnings* in the change process. There are no clear boundaries between the different phases and employees can be in more than one phase at any time. *Endings* refer to a separation from the past – in this phase the employee has to make for example sacrifices; break with well-known routines, may need to learn new knowledge and skills, lose friends and changes in social relationships, or is required to give up power and control. It is also in this phase where employees may resist the change and want to maintain the *status quo*.

Helping employees through the ending phase . . .

- Raise awareness of upcoming changes and clearly articulate the need for change.
- Help employees to make sense of the change.
- Plan for the skills and knowledge they may need.
- Provide clear milestones of the change journey – draw a change map so that everyone clearly understands the way forward.
- Be honest about the possible challenges expected but also emphasize the potential opportunities.
- Create peer support networks.
- Use rituals and ceremonies to help employees to break with the past.

- Communicate, communicate and communicate.
- Tell employees what is going to stay the same.
- Create forums where employees can voice their concerns.
- Change organizational cultural artefacts, for example, symbols used in the organization.
- Celebrate individual differences and acknowledge that not everyone is going to change at the same pace.

In the *neutral zone* the individual is not fully engaged with the future and is still trying to make sense of the change. This in-between state brings its own challenges but also creates new opportunities. In this phase employees are accepting that changes are going to take place but may experience emotions such as bewilderment, anxiety and anger. Bridges (2003, p. 38) explains the neutral zone as follows '. . . it is the journey from one identity to another, and this takes time'. This highlights three important elements: (1) change is about a personal experience, (2) it influences how people view themselves, that is, their identity and (3) it takes time for any successful change to occur.

Helping employees through the neutral zone . . .

- Provide development opportunities for employees to learn required the knowledge and skills.
- Continue to help employees to make sense of the change as well as their role in the change – use creative methods that will aid in the sense making process. Reflective exercises, role-plays and Socratic dialogue serve as examples in this regard.
- Allow employees to experiment with new behaviours and allow mistakes.
- Use development tools such as coaching and mentoring to assist employees in moving to the new beginnings phase.
- Understand that the process is going to take time.
- Use visualisation exercises to help the employees to visualize a clear picture of what the future will look like and how they fit into that future.
- Address the mind as well as the heart in all communications.
- Help employees to identify new opportunities.

The last phase, *new beginnings*, refers to acceptance of the change and a readiness to embrace the new. However, new beginnings not only relate to acceptance of the change for example the adaptation to new structures, systems and processes but also an acceptance of the self. It is also about internalizing new values, new behaviours and attitudes or putting it differently accepting a new identity.

Helping employees new beginnings phase . . .

- Build the self-confidence of employees.
- Use feedback to highlight change successes.
- Build trusting relationships between employees themselves and leaders.
- Expect that some employees may revert to old behaviours.
- Continue to use development tools such as coaching and mentoring to assist employees.
- Walk-the-talk – demonstrate through your own behaviours and attitudes that the change was needed.

Employees experience change in different ways and the role of the change leader is to move employees who are affected by change to move through the different phases of change. The change agent unfreezes forces (Lewin, 1951) that maintain the *status quo* and before any change is possible, employees must understand why changes are necessary. The change agent therefore needs to ensure that the driving forces, those, forces supporting change, exceed restraining forces, those forces resisting change. Change takes time and it is therefore important to allow sufficient time for employees to adapt to organizational change. If we want employees to change, they must not only understand it, but also see the potential benefits of the change. Allowing employees to participate, share their emotions and creating a climate in which employees feel safe may assist in the various transition phases. Therefore, the timing of the change is an important consideration. On the one hand you need to keep the momentum of the change and on the other hand you need to create space for employees to adjust to the change. This can be explained as follows by a CEO:

Change needs leadership and managerial behaviours

'People look towards the leadership of an organization to identify the direction of the organization. You need to talk to people on a level that they can understand, try to contextualize what is the change that you need, why you need it and why if you don't get to change you'll end up with consequences.

Engage employees in dialogue

You need to say that clearly enough in a way that people can comprehend. Dialogue is important and if your arguments are strong enough you will start to get commitment. Also important is to identify key people who may help to move thinking

Have a clear and robust change strategy

Understand the emotions of not only employees in the change process, but also the emotions of management

Ensure procedural fairness

Provide affected employees with choice

forward and to try to engage actively with them. I would certainly invest a lot of time in the planning side – you need a robust change plan – what is the rationale, the justification and how it will stand up to various arguments. Try to anticipate all the questions because when you get into the communication piece of it and people start to ask questions, you need to be able to answer it. The planning piece is really critical as it is an opportunity when the leadership are in most control of the situation and you get an opportunity to shape it, to test it, to get it as close to a shape that you can comfortably live with. In a lot of change the pressure comes on middle management and sometimes on senior management, mostly management supervisors. They are the people that actually bear the brunt of it and you do need to constantly stay close to them as a group. If you have redundancies or you've got selection processes, particularly in mergers, there is a big emotional piece around that. You have to constantly manage it and you have to (1) satisfy people that the selection process is fair, (2) your criteria is fair, and (3) explain to the people who don't get the roles. Provide them with a reasonable explanation as to why they didn't make it and offer them some kind of track, either they can accept redundancy or they can go into project work or whatever, but not closing the door for them.'

The Experience of Change

Psychologists have long recognized that people have a dislike to loss and are inclined to want to hold on to the known. Many changes represent loss. Kubler-Ross (1975), through her research on individual responses to imminent death, gives us some insight on how individuals experience loss. The study illustrates the different stages that people go through and include *shock* (numbness), *denial* (this can't be happening to me), *isolation* (leave me alone), *anger* (why me), *bargaining* (or an attempt to postpone the inevitable), *depression* (about what has been lost and for the loss to come) and *acceptance* (the struggle is over). Different variations of this model (based on the model of Kubler-Ross,

1975) are available in change literature (e.g. Adams, et al., 1976). The basic premise is that the emotional reactions experienced by employees during organizational change are comparable to the stages of grief associated with personal loss. Change leaders who are able to recognize the phases individuals move through can help employees by acknowledging their feelings, provide opportunities to ask questions, share emotions and by providing personal support. The next discussion explores the (1) transitions or journeys that change participants go through when confronted with organizational change, (2) managerial actions that may facilitate the movement through the different phases and (3) change actions that will definitely lead to a change disaster.

Awareness of imminent change: When employees become aware that change is going to happen, speculation starts. This phase is characterized by uncertainty and if information is not readily available, the grapevine will be used to gain clarity and obtain information about the change. The following leader behaviours may help your employees to cope with this phase:

Leader actions

- Ensure your employees belief in your ability to lead the change effectively. Do you have high levels of credibility in the organization?
- Communicate the change clearly and succinctly, keep the message simple.
- Be open and honest with employees.
- Allow time for feedback and reflection.
- Involve the employees in the design of the change implementation process.
- Actively manage the grapevine by using key people in departments, business units to communicate the change message.
  Use social media e.g., for example, Twitter and Facebook, discussion forums, change blogs, story cards and so on, to help you to disseminate and communicate your change message.
- Measure the change readiness levels of your employees.

By demonstrating behaviours that are supportive, by being authentic, open and honest, the change leader can assist employees in gaining a heightened sense of awareness of the change. Ignoring the stages people go through or paying superficial attention to the emotions employees experience may lead to high levels of resistance. Demonstrating the following behaviours is a sure recipe for creating a change disaster:

Change actions that will definitely lead to a change disaster

- Not having a clear change strategy/change roadmap or communication plan.
- Not willing to be flexible and adapt your change strategy if needed.
- Sending out an email to inform employees.
- Having one or two Town Hall meetings and tell employees what is going to happen.
- Ignoring the feelings and emotions of employees.
- Ignoring honest feedback from employees.
- A belief that all employees are going to embrace the change.
- Trying to implement the change in a toxic organization, that is, low levels of trust between management and employees, low managerial credibility and employee perceptions that management does not care about employees, are manipulative and narcissistic.

Shock/confusion: Change can create confusion in the organization and changes for example role clarity and the stability of relationships. Employees may experience emotions such as astonishment, immobilization and a feeling of disconnectedness. They find it difficult to understand and cannot believe the change is going to happen. Typical responses from employees are 'this is not happening to me . . .' and 'if I survive long enough the change will go away'. The following behaviours may help employees to move towards the next phase:

Leader actions

- Allow employees to share their feelings – use group discussions and reflection.
- Use coaches to help employees to work through emotions.
- Be visible and walk-the-talk.
- Use support groups to help employees to understand.
- Repeat the change message.

Experiencing these emotions can be regarded as a natural part of the change process. This may happen despite all the change preparations and actions you took in trying to minimize the impact of the change. Consistent and continuous communication is a key element of helping employees to understand the reasons for change as well as providing sufficient time for employees to assimilate the change. Demonstrating the following behaviour may impact negatively on your change efforts:

Change actions that will definitely lead to a change disaster

- A strong belief that 'they will get over it'.
- Announce the change but carry on with business as usual.
- Have a time-lapse between announcing the change and action/implementing the change.
- Telling employees that you understand how they feel but you are unable to express appropriate emotions and behaviours.

Resistance: After some time lapse, employees may react negatively to change. In this phase there is a realization that the change is not going away and may have negative consequences. This phase can also be regarded as a dangerous or risky moment in the change process. An inability of the change leader to move the change recipients forward may lead to a derailment of the change process. Employees may exhibit different types of behaviour, for example: *sabotage* (seem to go along, but only to demonstrate a lack of agreement later in the change process); *easy agreement* (agreeing with little resistance without really understanding what is being agreed to) and *silence* (provides no input). Demonstrating effective leader behaviours in this stage is of the utmost importance and the following behaviours can be considered:

Leader actions

1. Do not view employee reactions to the change as resistance but as an opportunity to improve your change process.
2. Help employees to understand the reason for change – formulate a compelling business case that addresses the 'head' as well as the 'heart'.
3. Involve employees in the change process.
4. Be visible and show that you care.
5. Tell stories, anecdotes and give examples of where similar changes worked in the past.
6. Provide emotional support.
7. Provide opportunities where employees can share emotions and experiences.
8. Use team coaching to address change barriers and assist employees to develop alternatives.
9. Clarify roles, expectations and help employees to understand what the organization is going to look like after the change.

At the heart of any resistance lies the fear of loss. It is therefore important to understand the reasons why employees react and as discussed in Chapter 4, you need to incorporate strategies in your change plan to address the possibility of resistance. The reasons for many failed change efforts can be found in resistance or the inability of employees to adapt to organizational changes. What is called for is change leadership action, implementing decisive strategies that will address change resistance. Demonstrating the following behaviour is a sure way to derail your own change process:

Change actions that will definitely lead to a change disaster

- Being arrogant and believing that you have all the answers.
- Believe you can implement the change on your own – around yourself with powerful individuals.
- Dictating change.
- Confusing change management with project management.
- Ignoring the fact that change takes time.
- Being defensive.
- Not communicating consistently and continuously.

Acceptance of reality and testing: In this phase employees accept the need to change and slowly let go of the past. They start to realize that the change is not going away and accept the reality of change in the organization. There is a growing sense of optimism and excitement and employees are willing to try out new behaviours. This may take the form of doing things differently, that is, experimenting with new behaviour, taking calculated risks and so forth. Demonstrating the following behaviour may impact positively on your change efforts:

Leader actions

- Help employees to explore the assumptions they have of the organization – what are the underlying thoughts and feelings that organizational members believe to be true?
- Clarify organizational values and the strategic direction of the organization.
- Change the cultural artefacts or symbols used in the organization. This may be expressed through logos, types of award, uniforms, art on the walls, and so on.
- What are the rites, ceremonies and taboos in the organization? What needs to be changed?
- Analyse and change the language used in the organization if necessary. What are the jargon, signals, signs humour, metaphors and slogans used in the organization? What are the unique stories, legends used that need changing?

- Set clear objectives and milestones, and communicate progress on a regular basis.
- Help people to understand that there is no going back – the only option is moving towards the future.
- Use recognition and praise to celebrate successes.
- Allow employees to experiment with new behaviours.
- Encourage employees to takes risks.
- Build self-efficacy levels of employees: demonstrate your belief that they have what it takes to change.
- Create opportunities for employees to provide feedback and share change experiences.
- Use a performance management system to clarify roles, expectations and standards and have regular review meetings.

From the previous discussion it is clear that change can be painful and employees may experience strong emotions in the change process. But, we also need to believe that our employees have the capacity and capability to change when needed – do not underestimate the resilience and tenacity of your employees. Demonstrating the following behaviours is a sure recipe for creating a change disaster:

Change actions that will definitely lead to a change disaster

1. Underestimating the power of organizational culture and values on change implementation effectiveness.
2. Not creating or ensuring alignment between systems, processes and structure with the change initiative.
3. A belief that employees need to be forced to change.
4. Underestimating the influence of your own change philosophy on the way you lead and implement change.
5. Not having realistic expectations of the change.
6. Underestimating the power of middle management and supervisory level to undermine the change process.
7. Underestimating the ability of employees to change and adapt to a new way of being and doing.

The art of leadership is to assist and guide employees through the change journey. The leader needs to reduce the disruptions brought on by the change and acknowledge that change is not about systems, structure or processes, but it is all about the people in the organization. Organizational change takes time and what is needed is patience and not being overly fixated on achieving results. Results will happen if you acknowledge the fact that people change at different rates, experience change in different ways and your role is to assist employees in the change process. Build relationships, align expectations, seek feedback and allow employees to work through the change, making sense of it. Caring, demonstrating empathy and relational behaviours is also a function of your ability to understand yourself – your values, motives and levels of self-awareness and the impact of these on your own behaviour.

It is important to remember that the experience of change is not always negative and people do not experience only negative emotions. Change can also evoke positive emotions; for example, hope or the anticipation of a better future. Antonacopoulou and Gabriel (2001) link the experience of positive emotions to the amount of control we allow the change participants to have. They put it as follows:

> . . . in our lives together and in our organizations we must account for the fact that everyone there requires, as a condition of their being, the freedom to author their own life. Every person, overtly or covertly, struggles to preserve this freedom to self-create. (p. 7)

Allowing people to be in control can take many forms and participation and involvement in the change process serve as examples in this regard.

The following exercise may be helpful

Reflect on your lifeline (Chapter 1) and identify a major transition point or crucible as described in your lifeline and answer the following questions:

1. What happened?
2. Describe the change using the classification of Bridges (2003). What happened in each phase (i.e. endings, neutral zone and new beginnings)?
3. What emotions did you experience? How did you deal with those emotions?
4. What are the key insights you can extract from your own experience with change?

Principles of Individual Level Change

Whereas the previous discussion highlighted the importance of understanding individual level change processes and experiences of change, it is also useful to have an understanding of the conditions needed for people to change. Fishbein et al. (2001) argue that the following factors are necessary for individual change:

- The individual makes a commitment to perform the behaviour.
- There are no organizational barriers that make it impossible to carry out the behaviour.
- The individual has the skills to perform the behaviour.
- The individual believes that the advantages of the new behaviour to be more important than the disadvantages of the behaviour.
- The individual experiences more pressure to perform the behaviour than not to perform it.
- The individual perceives that performance of the behaviour is consistent with his or her self-image or values.
- The individual's emotional reaction to performing the behaviour is more positive and negative.
- The individual perceives that he/she has the capability to perform the behaviour under different circumstances.

Organizations do not change until individuals within it change. Therefore, change leaders need to create organizational conditions that are supportive of individual level change. Organizational change should be regarded as a process and not an event and this implies that sufficient time should be made available for employees to adjust to organizational change. Change agents need to focus their interventions and use appropriate tools to assist employees in the change process.

The Relationship Between Individual Level and Organizational Level Change

It is also important to understand the influence of organizational level change on employees. The Burke–Litwin (1992, p. 528) model of organizational performance (Figure 2) provides us with a roadmap which demonstrates the interrelationship between different organizational elements. Putting it differently, it explains the functioning of an organization from a systemic perspective (i.e. a change in one element may lead to changes in another) and describes the relationships between the different elements, its context and effectiveness (Cummings and Worley, 2005). The model highlights 12 key change points with the external environment as main input and individual and organizational performance as output (Burke and Litwin, 1992). The model distinguishes between *transformational* and *transactional* components and this can be explained as follows:

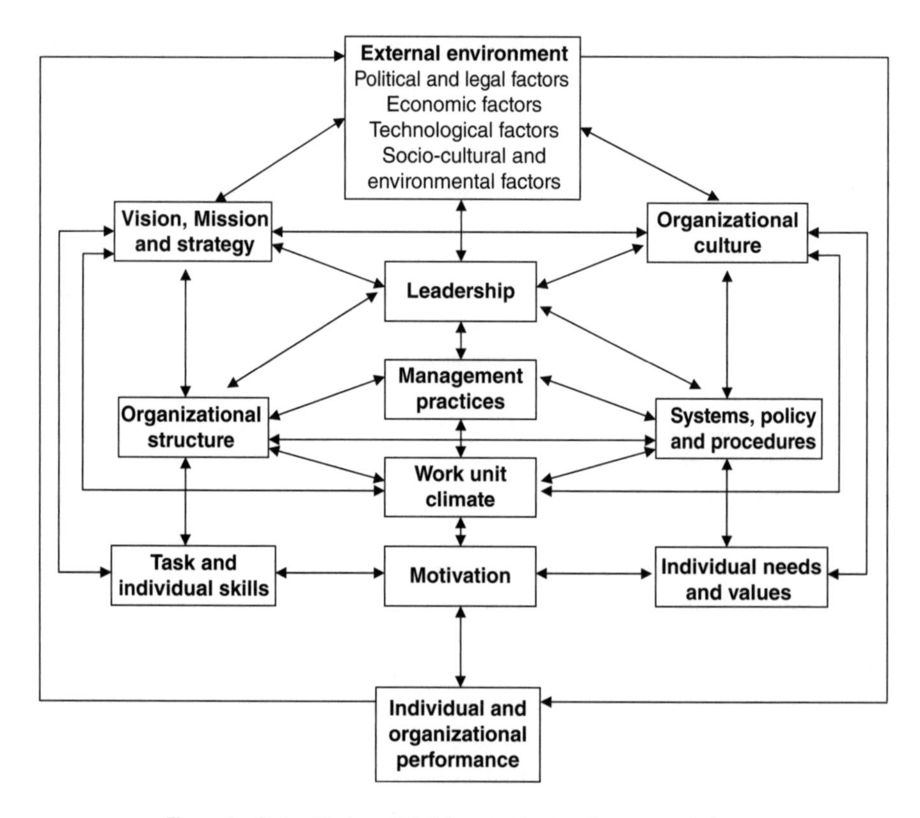

Figure 2 Burke–Litwin model of Organizational performance and change

- The top part of the model highlights the transformational factors of change. Transformational variables such as culture, leadership as well as mission and strategy interact with environmental forces. It is changes in the external environment that causes an organization to change its mission, culture, leadership and its operating strategies. Changes in these elements have broad systemic impact, creating revolutionary change for the organization (Burke, 2002) and for the individual. In contrast, the lower half of the model represents the transactional factors of change.
- Transactional variables include elements such as management practices, structure, systems and processes, work unit climate, motivation, individual needs and values, task requirements, task and individual skills (Burke and Litwin, 1992). The internal factors relate to the 'inner workings' of the organization that stimulate an organization to change.

Changes in the transformational factors affect the transactional factors and the transformational and transactional factors impact on individual and organizational performance. Organizations are usually concerned with increasing operating efficiencies and decreasing costs and this sometimes motivate or necessitate organizational change. Internal changes for example changes in top management or the leadership of an organization may lead to changes in the leadership style and may lead to changes in the vision of the organization, structure of the organization, culture and management practices. This in turn may lead to changes on an individual level, that is, change in tasks, motivational levels and so forth. This is why is it important to understand an organization and change from a systemic perspective. Therefore, when we implement change in an organization we also need to anticipate not only the impact on other elements of the organization but also unintended consequences of the change. Changes in the bottom half of the model (transactional factors) refer to first-order changes and represent actions which are focused on continuous improvement, are normally developmental in nature and take evolutionary or incremental steps toward the change. In contrast, second-order change refers to radical change and takes on a revolutionary nature (Burke and Litwin, 1992). The model as depicted in Figure 1 helps us to understand the type of change (i.e. transformational or transactional) required and to align our interventions toward factors in the organization that may produce the required change (French and Bell, 1999).

Chapter Summary

This chapter highlights the processes employees use and the phases they go through when organizational change is implemented. The importance of understanding these phases is highlighted and it is emphasized that the change leader, by using appropriate behaviours, can assist employees to move more effectively through these phases. These behaviours create a context in which employees feel safe and provide opportunities where employees can participate, share emotions and be supportive of the change. The role of emotions is highlighted and it should be clear from this chapter that employees experience different emotions and adapt to change at different tempos. This has specific implications for the way we implement, manage and lead organizational change. In practical terms it means that the change plan should be flexible enough to accommodate the different levels of change readiness (as reflected by the different change phases). It also implies that the change leader needs to use some form of measurement to determine the phases of individual level change and create appropriate phase-specific interventions. Effective change leaders not only need to be able to use behaviours that are appropriate for the situation, but also have a clear understanding of the impact of their own change cycle. This also relates to aspects already addressed in the previous chapters of this book. It is not possible to assist employees effectively through the different changes phases if you are not able to lead change authentically (Chapter 1); an understanding of your own levels of change readiness (Chapter 2); winning the hearts and minds of employees when leading change (Chapter 3); or have a clear understanding of the variables that may influence employee reactions towards change (Chapter 4).

KEY INSIGHTS FROM PRACTICE

Individuals experience change differently and change at a different pace.
The different levels of employee readiness for change has important implications for implementing and leading change.
Change leaders need to create specific conditions that will enable change participants to embrace and accept the change.
Be aware of the different tools that are available that may help you in moving individuals through the different change phases.
Be patient when implementing change – change is a journey, it is not an event.
Provide time and space for employees to adapt to organizational changes.
Expect challenges but do not give up.

References

Adams, J., Hayes, J., and Hopson, B. (1976). *Transition – Understanding and Managing Personal Change.* London: Martin Robertson.
Antonacopoulou, E.P. and Gabriel, Y. (2001) Emotion, learning and organisational change – towards an integration of psychoanalytic and other perspectives. *Journal of Organizational Change Management*, 14 (5), 43–51.
Bridges, W. (2003). *Managing Transitions: Making the Most of Change* (2nd edn). Cambridge, MA: Da Capo Press.
Burke, W.W. and Litwin, G.H. (1992). A causal model of organizational performance and change. *Journal of Management*, 8 (3), 523–546.
Burke, W. (2002). *Organisational Change: Theory and Practice.* Thousand Oaks, CA: Sage.
Cummings, T.G. and Worley, C.G. (2005). *Organizational Development and Change.* Mason, OH: South-Western.
DiClemente, C.C. and Prochaska, J.O. (1998). Toward a comprehensive, transtheoretical model of change: Stages of change and addictive behaviors. In W.R. Miller, and N. Heather, (eds) *Treating Addictive Behaviors*: (2nd edn) *Applied Clinical Psychology*. (pp. 3–24). New York, NY: Plenum Press.
Duhig, C. (2012). *The Power of Habit: Why We Do what We Do.* New York: Random House.
Fishbein, M., Triandis, H.C., Kanfer, F.H., Becker, M., Middlestadt, S.E., and Eichler, A. (2001). Factors influencing behaviour and behaviour change. In A. Baum, T.A. Revenson and J.E. Singer (eds), *Handbook of Health Psychology* (pp. 3–17). Mahwah, NJ: Lawrence Erlbaum Associates.
Fiske, S.T. and Taylor, S.E. (1984). *Social Cognition.* Reading MA: Addison-Wesley.

French, W.L. and Bell, C.H., Jr. (1999). *Organization Development: Behavioral Science Interventions for Organization Improvement* (6th edn). Upper Saddle River, NJ: Prentice-Hall.

Jager, W. (2003). Breaking bad habits: a dynamical perspective on habit formation and change. In L. Hendrik, W. Jager and L. Steg (eds). *Human Decision Making and Environmental Perception. Understanding and Assisting Human Decision Making in Real-Life Settings*. Liber Amicorum for Charles Vlek. Groningen; University of Groningen.

Kubler-Ross, E. (1975). *Death: The Final Stage of Growth*. Englewood Cliffs, NJ: Prentice-Hall.

Lally, P., van Jaarsveld, C.H.M., Potts, H.W.W., and Wardle, J. (2010). How are habits formed: Modelling habit formation in the real world. *European Journal of Social Psychology*, 40 (6), 998–1009.

Levesque, D.A., Prochaska, J.M., and Prochaska, J.O. (1999). Stages of change and integrated service delivery. *Consulting Psychology Journal*, 4, 226–241.

Lewin, K. (1951). *Field Theory in Social Science: Selected Theoretical Papers*. New York: Harper.

Prochaska, J.O., Redding. C.A., and Evers, K. (1997). The transtheoretical model of change. In Glanz, K., Lewis E.M. and Rimer B.K. (eds), *Health Behavior and Health Education: Theory, Research, and Practice* (pp. 60–84). Jossey-Bass: San Francisco, CA.

Webb, T.L., Sheeran, P., and Luszczynska, A. (2009). Planning to break unwanted habits: habit strength moderates implementation intention effects on behaviour change. *Journal of Social Psychology, British Psychological Society*, 48, 507–523.

Wood, W. and Neal, D.T. (2007). A new look at habits and the habit-goal interface. *Psychological Review*, 114 (4), 843–863.

CHAPTER 6

Coaching for Change Success

Chapter at a Glance

In the previous chapters it was highlighted that employees react differently to change and that negative reactions towards organizational change may derail the change process. Coaching is an important tool that leaders can use in the change management process, not only to help individuals to adapt to change but also to help managers to understand and implement the organizational change plan. Effective coaching provides a platform where individuals and groups can give their opinions, obtain feedback and share their emotions. Coaching your managers will empower them to use the same techniques with their subordinates and thereby create energy for the change. This chapter is a skills building chapter, highlighting specific principles to keep in mind when coaching your employees. Furthermore, it provides you with a structure to follow when coaching individuals and teams.

Beginning Cases: Preparation

Coaching should be integrated in the change management process and ensures that the change plan is implemented in a structured way. It also emphasizes the human element in the change process, keeps your change programme on track and helps to achieve the desired change results. Take a look at the following quotes:

Coaching is a powerful conversation
Coaching has a specific purpose

Prepare for the discussion

Acknowledge things that went well

'Just taking time to regularly sit down with people. So, you want to have a conversation about a behaviour that you want to get from an individual. You try to project it into a situation and say – "if I was seeing their behaviour this is what it would look like in that scenario." So, you set it out as – "here is what I've seen, here's what I need to see, how can we move you up the stage where you are doing more of what I want to see". If you're not seeing the behaviour you want then you need to say "well, you've done fine on these things, you're not doing fine on these things so you need to do more on this". It's almost like a sports coaching activity – the view that a lot of sports people would have that really it's about that focus sometimes on that extra 2–3% that makes the difference. It creates a genuine conversation, around the person moving up the competency chain rather than, three out of five or a two out of five, out of context, the approach is to say "on this competency – this is what someone scoring eight out of ten would be doing – these are the behaviours we would see. Can you try to show that more?" If I ask for x behaviour and I get it, and, if I acknowledge it and say that's great, you're more likely to repeat that behaviour as a discretionary behaviour in future, it's just human nature.'

Coaching is an important tool in the leader's toolbox

'But beyond that, as a leader, your job is to communicate, to counsel, to support, to coach, to listen, to observe, to inspire – that's the job of a leader and if you've got the vision, the objectives and the framework of behaviours, then actually, change is fine, because you've always got to shift your way towards that elusive vision that you have.'

Coaching should have a clearly defined target population

'I'm heavily dependent on the people I've identified as change agents in the organization. I'm investing time and energy in them, building their confidence, keeping them on track, giving the guidance and the

Be willing to invest time
Use appropriate relational building techniques

Coaching helps to clarify the change plan

direction and I just keep on giving the positive pats on the back saying "yeah, absolutely, this is great, this is exactly what we need to do". Some of them are coming every now and again, having got the wobbles, saying "ooh, don't know if we're doing the right thing, don't know if this is the right time, don't know if we're letting the right people go, what if we get into legal challenges about x, y and z?" So that time and investment in a relatively small number, but, in very key people, in very key positions, in the organization is paying off and that's how I'm dealing with it organizationally.'

Chapter Introduction

Guiding employees through change and individual transitions is a key task of the leader. Bridges (2003, p. 3) states in this regard,

> . . . it isn't the changes that do you in, it's the transitions. They aren't the same thing. Change is situational: the move to a new site, the retirement of the founder, the reorganisation of the roles on the team, the revisions to the pension plan. Transition, on the other hand, is psychological, it is a three-phase process that people go through as they internalise and come to terms with the details of the new situation that change brings about.

Coaching individuals and teams can be regarded as a powerful tool the leader can use to accelerate organizational change and help employees to move through the transitions. Kouzes and Posner (2002, p. 296) describe the role of leaders as coaches as follows:

> Leaders actively seek out ways to increase choice, providing greater decision-making and responsibility for their constituents. They also develop the capabilities of their team and foster self-confidence through the faith they demonstrate in letting other people lead. In taking these actions, leaders act as coaches, helping others to use their skills and talents, as well as learn from experiences.

Applying coaching principles during organizational transformation can be an empowering experience for employees. The leader helps the employee to find their own answers, understanding their current reality, developing options and taking action. For coaching to be used as an effective tool during organizational change, the organizational culture needs to be supportive of coaching as an intervention. The organization needs to clarify (1) what the purpose of coaching is going to be in the change process, (2) how is it going to take place, (3) what is involved, (4) who is it for and (5) what contextual considerations need to be taken into account (Bachkirova and Kaufmann, 2008). This should be communicated to everyone in the organization and failing to do so may undermine the power of coaching as a change intervention. Somers (2007, p. 244) also highlights the importance of communication and training managers to be coaches and argues that 'managers must be trained in how to coach and not left to work it out for themselves simply because they are managers'. Similarly, coachees need some training or at least quality information on what coaching is and what it isn't, what to expect from coaching and how to access it if they need it.

What is Coaching and What it is Not

Coaching has been described in many ways and an agreed definition does not exist. Despite this lack of a unifying definition it seems there is agreement that coaching can be regarded as a helping, collaborative relationship with the purpose of guiding the employee in finding his or her own solutions to a problem (Grant, 2005a,b). Coaching can help employees to explore their emotions and feelings about the organizational change, explore their own mental models about the change and develop coping strategies. The term 'coach' refers to the person who provides the coaching and 'coachee' refers to the one who receives the coaching. The role of the coach is therefore to help employees or teams to gain insight into their thinking and behaviours – not to provide answers but helping them to find their own insights and solutions. Shaw and Linnecar (2007, p. 177) summarize the role of the coach by stating that

> . . . it is the art of creating an environment, through conversation and a way of being, that facilitates the process by which a person can move toward desired goals in a fulfilling manner. It requires one essential ingredient that cannot be taught: caring not only for external results but for the person being coached.

Effective coaching is about creating a supportive climate, asking the right questions to help the employee to clarify his or her thinking. It is a conversation with a specific purpose and the purpose is to assist employees to make sense of the organizational change, interrogating their own beliefs, attitudes and behaviours towards the change and developing effective strategies coping with the change. Gallwey (2001, p. 182) argues that effective coaching in the workplace holds a mirror up for clients, so they can see their own thinking process. The use of ineffective coaching processes will lead to dysfunctional outcomes. Having good intentions to assist employees is not enough; take a look at the following scenario:

A missed opportunity for coaching . . .

'Well in one case, I was consultant to the board of an organization that had gone through particular difficulties and had a difficult past in a very public kind of way, and was in transition back to where they were trying to normalize the operations of the business and a CEO had been brought in, who was operationally effective and understood the business and understood what had to be done, but struggled with the relationship, in particular. There was a history with a particular, very senior, individual in one region of the organization and this had been an issue for a number or years, prior to the CEO coming in. There was a chairman then came in who was guiding the CEO in dealing with this issue. It became apparent that the resolution of the issue wasn't going to be what the CEO felt should happen which was to get this person out of the organization. That just wasn't legally possible. So, the chairman who was guiding was a very astute politician and was guiding the CEO through a process that would have resolved the matter, in a way that allowed the organization to function as it needed to, but it would have kept both the CEO and this other individual in the organization. The process seemed to be going along just fine until the CEO just couldn't handle it and he took, he departed entirely from all our agreed processes, and launched what was an unprecedent, personal attack in writing, on this individual, and thereby self-destructed. He had to be, in fact, dismissed from his own position so he derailed not only his position in the organization, he ended up having to sue for a settlement and derailed his career completely. He never worked again in any context. So, his inability to exercise power effectively completely derailed his career. He didn't have the political skills to be effective at the next level and this was not because of the scale of the organization, but because of the complexity of the politics involved. He simply

> *didn't have the skills and particularly he didn't have the patience. He had been successful in the past by imposing his will really on others and being very effective at operational work, and that model no longer worked and he didn't have the ability to flex. So he lost. . .'*

Coaching should not be confused with mentoring or therapy. Although coaching shares similarities with other disciplines such as mentoring and therapy, it is important to distinguish between coaching and related concepts. Bluckert (2005) argues in this regard that mentoring is characterized by an expert novice relationship versus coaching emphasizes an equal partnership between the coach and coachee. Bluckert (2005, p. 93) gives a further explanation of the differences between coaching and therapy and states that coaching focusses on the present and future and therapy deals with the past; the focus of coaching is not to rectify emotional pathology or to create emotional healing. The focus of coaching is to improve an individual's effectiveness in the work context. Coaching is also more action and results orientated, when compared to therapy.

Principles to Keep in Mind When Coaching Adults

From the previous section it is clear that 'coaching is fundamentally about helping people fulfil their potential by allowing them to recognise the things that hold them back and by helping them discover ways around them' (Somers, 2007, p. 10). Any change process involves learning; it may be the acquisition of new knowledge, skills or changing attitudes and behaviours. Ross-Ashby (1958, p. 86) for example, states that for any organism or system to survive, the rate of learning (L) must be equal or greater ($L \geq C$) than the rate of change (C) in the external environment. Learning enables employees to adapt to changes in the external environment and it can be argued that 'to learn is to change' and 'that learning involves change'. Coaching is also about helping employees to change and this involves or requires a process of learning. The way adults learn provides us with a number of principles that form the foundation of any coaching or change process. The following principles (from Knowles et al., 2010) provide guidance for coaching and helping your employees to learn;

Adults need to know why they need to learn something: Adults need to know why they need to learn something before undertaking to learn it. They need to know *why* they need to learn something, understand *what* are they going to learn and *how* the learning is going to be conducted. Adults may resist learning when they feel others are imposing ideas, information or actions on them. Not knowing why learning something is important may lead to low levels of motivation. In practical terms it means you need to view employees as partners in the coaching process and assist them in formulating their own goals and help them to understand the value of internalizing new behaviours and learning. This implies that as a change coach you need to provide some structure for the coaching session, for example, articulating the purpose; collaboratively determine the coaching agenda, that is, 'what do we need to discuss and why' and help the employee to determine what outcomes need to be reached. Viewing the employee as a partner in the coaching process provides the employee with some control over the process that may reduce feelings of anxiety and stress.

Adults have a self-concept of being responsible for their own lives and making decisions: The adult learner is therefore self-directed in the learning process and willing to take responsibility for his or her own learning. Adults develop a psychological need to be treated by others as being capable and self-directed. Adults are also internally motivated to learn and are motivated by factors such as a desire for increased job satisfaction, quality of life, increase in self-esteem, and so on. The starting point is that as a change coach, you need to demonstrate authentic behaviour, be trustworthy and show respect for the employee. Demonstrating a philosophy 'I accept you as who you are' is a sure way to develop or build a trusting relationship. Your role is not to judge or ridicule, but to provide guidance, help and support. You actively need to build the self-confidence of your coachee, and providing honest feedback, recognition and so forth all serve as examples in this regard.

Adults have experience and this experience provides a rich resource for learning: Adults want the opportunity to use their exciting knowledge and experience gained from life experiences. This means they want to use their experience in the learning process. As leaders we are used to and good at providing advice and solving business problems, strive to achieve results and are action orientated. While these characteristics are useful in a business context, they are less helpful in a coaching situation. The purpose of coaching is to guide the coachee to find answers to their problems and *not* to provide them with answers. The change coach needs to draw on the life experiences and knowledge of the coachee and help them to explore options and potential solutions.

Adults become ready to learn those things they need to know or be able to do to cope with their real life situations: Learning must have relevance and they need to see the linkage between the learning and the usefulness in practice.

Coaching is a dynamic process and the end result of any coaching session should enable the coachee to leave the coaching session with a clear understanding and action plan of 'how to move forward' or 'what the next steps in the process are'. Provide opportunities for participation, encourage active reflection and help them to apply their solutions in their work environment.

Adults are life-centred (i.e. task- or problem-centred) *in their orientation towards learning:* Adults learn best through practical experiences and prefer hands-on problem solving activities. This implies adults want to be actively involved in the coaching process and coaching solutions should focus on the here and now.

Implications of Using Adult Learning Principles for Coaching

An integral part of building and maintaining the coaching relationship and coaching process, is the integration and application of adult learning principles in the coaching process. From the previous discussion it is clear that adults are internally motivated and self-directed; they bring life-experiences, knowledge and learning to any learning experience; they are goal and problem orientated; they are practical and want to be respected. These principles have the following implications for the manager as a coach:

Implications for coaching . . .

- Do not be judgemental and accept the employee for who they are.
- Demonstrate authenticity, empathy, openness and honesty.
- Accept the fact that you are not in control of the coaching process.
- Build the self-concept of the employee but at the same time being aware of the impact of 'self' on the relationship.
- Guide employees towards an understanding of 'why they need to learn or need to change something'.
- Belief that the employee is able to (through support and interaction) to find an answer to their own problems.
- Use a non-directive approach: ask – do not tell.
- Do not impose your expertise or solutions on the employees.

- Listen: ask questions and guide employees to form their own insights, conclusions and action plans.

Adult learning principles provide us with a useful framework when we engage in coaching with adults. They provide us with useful information we can use in our coaching: for example, adults have experience we can draw on; they are willing to take responsibility for their own actions and most importantly, they have the answers to their problems. This means you can be non-directive in a coaching conversation. In a change context we can draw on their experiences and guide them to find solutions to their problems. This can be explained as follows:

Be aware of your impact on others

Success in one context does not guarantee success in another

Demonstrate interest in your employees

'I accepted a job as a senior manager in a company about 15 years ago. The culture of the organization was quite different compared to my previous organization – it was a real touchy and feeling type of culture. You know – a high emphasis was placed on relationships, being nice – the average tenure of employees was 10 years and more. I was used working in a high performance culture – in my previous organization it was all about results, outputs and if you were not able to make the grade, they got rid of you. The leadership style was fairly directive, performance driven and the people side was not that important. I was highly successful in this organization and got promoted a few times, so it is no surprise that I used the same leadership style in the new organization. In the beginning it was a disaster – I was highly task-focussed and output driven. People started to complain about my style – I was too hard, too focussed etc. I worked long hours and expected of my subordinates to do the same – it was all about reaching our objectives, making process improvements and changing stuff – implementing new policies, procedures – you know the saying "new brooms sweep clean"! Anyway – I was getting results but the people were stressed, I think I was a shock to their system. My boss at that time was a lot older than me and I am sure he heard about all the complaints. So he called me to his office one day to discuss how I am doing – I suppose you could classify that as a

Create a discussion climate by asking questions

Build the self-esteem of the employee

Allow the coachee to find his or her own solutions

Provide support – don't judge

coaching conversation – although in those days it was called a discussion. He asked me a lot of questions of how I was getting on, talked about my family, how I was feeling about the new job and what problems did I experience. I was quite happy – objectives were met, we were moving forward. Thinking back to that conversation, he handled it quite skilfully. He steered the conversation towards my subordinates – how were they getting on, any problems – and then made some observations – he could see I was driven, work was important to me and praised the fact that we reached all our objectives. He asked my opinion on how they experienced the changes and I gave him a balanced view point – some were happy but some may find it difficult. To cut a long story short – he guided me to understand that my behaviour may impact negatively on some of them. Through discussion he helped me to understand that I need to look after the emotional side of my employees as well. So I think through discussion he created awareness. He didn't give me his solutions but helped me to develop my own – that was powerful. I think the conversation could have easily gone the other way – he telling me to change. I got the distinct impression that he really wanted to help me – he was never critical and really supportive.'

Your role is to create a safe climate where employees are willing to share their experiences, emotions and problems. By being open, honest and authentic in your interaction will allow the building of trust and increase your own level of credibility. Coaching is an integrated part of the change role and by using coaching techniques appropriately will enable you to implement organizational change successfully.

Skills Needed to Coach

Being able to coach employees require a number of different skill sets for example being ethical, the ability to create a relationship with an employee, applying communication skills, that is, listening and questioning techniques effectively, creating awareness and insight, planning and goal setting and managing progress and accountability (ICF, 2012). To coach somebody also implies that you need to be willing to take personal risks, prepare thoroughly and invest your time. This can be illustrated as follows:

Do not be afraid to engage in a coaching conversation
Coaching is a skilled conversation

'Leaders don't engage in those conversations because they lack the ability or the skill or even the motivation to do it. It's rare enough for leaders to find leaders on any level are really willing to have those conversations as often as they should, and just to have them and say it and be comfortable in their ability to do that without causing a breakdown in the relationship. And the key factor there is, do you have the skill to have that conversation and not damage that relationship or that person's motivation? So, those are constant, even at a supervisor level, from supervisor to chief executive, those are some of the most difficult skills to exercise, effectively, I think.'

Have a clear understanding of what you want to achieve
Take time to prepare for the conversation

'An effective conversation is really about having a clear understanding of what you want to achieve. You need to invest time in preparing for the conversation – play it out in your mind – what do you see as the end result of the conversation?'

However, the starting point in being an effective coach is to have self-insight and awareness about the impact of your own behaviour on the employee, being non-directive in exploring problems and unconditionally accepting the employee. Flaherty (2005, p. 41) believes effective coaching can be achieved through really listening to the employee's responses and creating a relationship that is built on openness, appreciation, fairness and shared commitment. The following quote provides further clarity:

Creating the coaching relationship
Be yourself

Ask appropriate questions

'I don't think I have a magical approach – In any conversation I am myself, it is a little bit of what you see is what you get. I really don't try to impress people – some will like me and some won't – and for me that is OK. People like to talk about themselves – they just need the opportunity to do so. So I think I use questions – trying to understand the other person and to know him or her a little bit better. I had a professor at university and he always

Be relaxed

Demonstrate real interest in the other person

Control your emotions

Build trust

said "the key to finding a good answer is the ability to formulate good questions". This is obvious but you need to ask the "'right" question before you will get a good answer. I read somewhere if you really want to build rapport you need to mirror the posture of the other person, simulate their gestures – as this will make them feel more comfortable. I do not do that, it feels a bit phony to me. I try to relax during a conversation because if you are stressed and in a hurry it will definitely show in your behaviour. So I guess the way I try to build a relationship is to ask questions and focus my attention on the other person. You really need to demonstrate that you find the other person interesting. This is a skill – normally my emotions are fairly visible – so I try not to show negative emotions – what works well for me is to try to identify the key points of the conversation, this keeps you focussed on the conversation. Building a relationship with somebody doesn't happen overnight, it takes time. You need to be consistent – you need to be the same person in every conversation and I am sure that if you are the same in each conversation, show interest, ask good questions over time you will build trust and trust is key in any relationship.'

The ability to ask well-defined and powerful questions can be regarded as a fundamental building block of the coaching process. The technique of questioning may sound simple – we all know how to ask a question. Unfortunately it is not so easy. The ability to formulate and ask questions that will elicit the answer you are seeking is a skill that needs to be developed. Your job as a coach is, through conversation and dialogue, to guide the employee in finding his or her own solutions to a problem. Questions are used to gather information, building rapport and initiating action. It is obvious: the use of poorly formulated questions will lead to low quality answers and is not helpful to an employee. Before asking a question, make sure you understand *what do you want to achieve with the question?* A question should only be asked if the answer is going to help the employee to gain insight and understanding. The use of well-formulated questions can be compared to a key that is able to unlock the mind of the employee. This means you need to develop the ability to ask the right question, in a precise way and at the right time. Questions can be classified as open-ended, clarifying and probing questions. Look at the following examples of questions relating to these categories:

Type of questions	Examples of questions
Open-ended questions	• Tell me how you feel • What was that like for you? • How does it feel to hear that? • What is different now for you?
Clarifying questions	• What does that mean? • Could you be more specific? • What are your concerns?
Probing questions	• Why do you think this is the case? • What are your options for solving the problem? • Is there an option that you have not yet considered?

On the one hand you need to be able to frame the questions appropriately and on the other you need to be able to listen carefully, hear and understand what the coachee is saying. This is also known as reflective skills, paraphrase what the employee is saying and repeating the statement in question form. Using this technique allows you to verify that what you are hearing is accurate – it is about testing your own understanding. It is important to listen not only to the words but also trying to understand the underlying emotions which are expressed. This is achieved by observing verbal and non-verbal cues of the coachee. The use of reflective skills also allows the coachee to hear what he or she has said, and it gives him/her an opportunity to explain more about what is meant. Examples of typical questions you can ask to clarify your own understanding are as follows:

- It sounds like . . .
- It seems as if . . .
- It feels like . . .
- What I hear you saying . . .
- Example of reflecting meaning: You feel. . . (feeling word) because (content). . .

Putting it differently, reflecting skills can be regarded as a 'checking out and making certain' process. You can reflect the *content of the message* (reflecting the content of the other person in your own words); *reflect feelings* (i.e. reflecting the feeling component in your own words) or *reflect meaning* (i.e. reflect both the content and the feelings of the conversation). Summarizing the conversation is also a technique that can be used (i.e. condense a section of the conversation into three or four sentences). When engaging in a coaching conversation we need to

(1) listen for information (e.g. what are the major issues); (2) listen for emotions (e.g. how is the employee feeling); and (3) listen for value expression (e.g. what values are articulated) and how this may influence behaviour. It may be useful to have an understanding of your current level of coaching skill competence. Assess your coaching skills by completing the following questionnaire:

As a coach I am able to . . .	Scale				
	Low				High
Demonstrate respect	1	2	3	4	5
Refrain from giving solutions	1	2	3	4	5
Ask questions that reflect active listening	1	2	3	4	5
Ask powerful questions	1	2	3	4	5
Be open minded	1	2	3	4	5
Challenge perspectives	1	2	3	4	5
Establish rapport	1	2	3	4	5
Listen not only for words but also for emotions	1	2	3	4	5
Maintain standards of honesty and integrity	1	2	3	4	5
Recognise my own emotions	1	2	3	4	5
Sense others feelings	1	2	3	4	5
Display appropriate emotions	1	2	3	4	5
Clarify priorities	1	2	3	4	5
Provide constructive feedback	1	2	3	4	5
Summarize a conversation succinctly	1	2	3	4	5
Reflect on information and synthesize	1	2	3	4	5

Take a look at your self-assessment scores: are there any behaviours (e.g. items measured as a 1, 2 or 3) you need to practise? How are you going to do it?

The Coaching Process

Coaching is an effective method for helping employees to cope with change. The success of coaching is dependent on a number of factors and these factors are illustrated in Figure 1. Passmore (2007) highlights in this regard important elements of effective coaching, that is, developing and maintaining the coaching partnership and the processes used in the coaching process. From Figure 1 it is clear that the coach needs to create specific conditions and needs to continue to work on (1) creating and (2) building the relationship (Passmore, 2007).

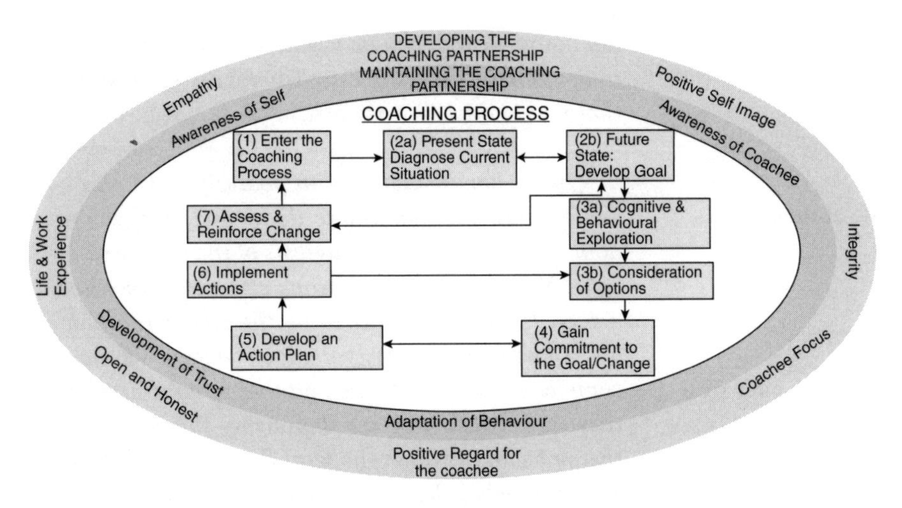

Figure 1 Integrated coaching model (Adapted from Passmore, 2007, p. 69)

Developing and maintaining the coaching partnership: The coaching relationship can best be described as a partnership between you (as coach) and the employee and is also the starting point of a successful coaching conversation. It is important to set the ground rules from the outset for example: clarifying expectations, what are the responsibilities of the coach/coachee, how often will you meet, confidentiality, how progress is going to be measured and so on. This is a two-way conversation and the output of this conversation is that both parties have a clear understanding of the purpose, approach and roles of everyone in the coaching process. A key success factor of the process is your ability to develop trust between you and the coachee. This is achieved by projecting openness, honesty and acting according to your own values. This can be illustrated as follows:

Be willing to share information about yourself

'I started to focus on creating personal relationships with people. So I started to let my guard down a bit, I suppose, and talked more about myself. I suppose it made me realize that people respond incredibly well when they genuinely had a relationship with me – a relationship that was real and comfortable and not scary.'

Exposing vulnerability helps to build trust

'I'm conscious of my impact on other people as a leader, so being emotional because something is amazing, is unlikely to be an inappropriate thing. But being emotional because something is bad or

Control your emotions

Demonstrate empathy	*did not work well can be negative. I think you need to demonstrate empathy, let employees understand that you know how they feel.'*
Be authentic	*'It's being honest and true to yourself and being – having faith in what you're doing and why you're doing it, having the best interests of the employee at heart Not trying to be someone else who looks like a good leader but trying to be the leader that you are.*
Develop your own style	*I know some very, very good leaders who are completely different to me and they're good at what they do because they are thoroughly themselves in their jobs, rather quiet thoughtful types for instance. So I genuinely believe it's about understanding when you perform best and using those things in order to inspire others.'*

This is only possible if you have a clear understanding of who you are, or putting it differently, if you are *authentic*. This means that you need to have a positive image of yourself, operate with integrity and demonstrate real interest in the coachee. In Chapter 1 the role of authentic leadership in change management was discussed in detail. You need to be willing to unconditionally accept the coachee – nobody is perfect – and be non-judgemental. Solomon and Flores (2001, p. 5) are of the opinion that 'trusting is something we individually do, it is something we make, create, build, maintain and sustain with our promises, our commitments, our emotions and our sense of our own integrity'. The coach needs to build the self-concept of the coachee but at the same time be aware of the impact of self on the coaching relationship. It can, therefore, be argued that the authenticity of the coach, 'the unobstructed operation of one's true, or core self in one's daily enterprise' which consists of four components: awareness, unbiased processing, authentic action and relational authenticity (Kernis, 2003, p. 13), may have a positive impact on the coaching process. Furthermore, adults need to understand why they need to learn or need to change something and are motivated to learn if they perceive that learning will help them to perform better (Knowles et al., 2010). On a practical level it means the coach needs to believe that the coachee is able to (through support and interaction) to find an answer to their own problems and also be able to demonstrate openness and empathy (Passmore, 2007). The role of the coach is therefore helping adults to learn or to change their behaviour by drawing and reflecting on past experiences. This is achieved by listening, asking questions and guiding coachees to form their own insights and action plans. However, irrespective of the coaching approach – behavioural, person-centred or cognitive – the coach needs to be flexible and willing to adapt to the coachee's agenda or, putting it differently, helping coachees to reach their own conclusions and set their own action plans (Hooijberg and Lane, 2009).

The GROW model (Whitmore, 2003) is the most probably the best-known and most used coaching model used in organizations today. The GROW model breaks the coaching session into four, interrelated phases: **G**oals, **R**eality, **O**ptions and **W**ill. The process provides structure and allows novice coaches to follow a tried and tested process. The coaching process is not a linear one and you might find yourself moving between the different elements at various stages in the coaching conversation. An important building block of the process is the ability to ask powerful questions. More specifically, this approach explores the following:

Goals: After establishing rapport, the coach asks the coachee or proposes what the topic of the coaching conversation should be or asks what the coachee wants to achieve? In this phase the coach and the coachee sets specific goals for the session. It may be helpful to set SMART goals, so:

- be *Specific* (what exactly do you want?);
- *Measurable* (how will you know when you have achieved it?);
- *Achievable* (where are you right now on this?);
- *Relevant* (how important is this to you?);
- *Timely* (by when do you want to achieve this goal?).

The identification of goals provides a roadmap of where to move next in the coaching process.

***R**eality:* what is the current position or what is happening now? Before you can move a situation forward you need to get very clear picture of what 'is happening now?'. It is a bit like taking stock – trying to understand the assumptions and perceptions of the coachee and examining how the current situation is impacting on the coachee's goals. As the discussion progresses, you may also want to challenge these assumptions and perceptions as appropriate. It is also an opportunity to help the coachee to understand his or her reality by providing feedback, specific examples or the use of self-assessment. Aim to get a comprehensive understanding from the coachee in areas such as strengths, shortfalls, motivations and approaches to overcoming challenges. This means you need to increase the level of self-awareness of the coachee, stimulate reflection and an understanding of behaviours that may impact on performance

***O**ptions:* What alternatives are available? You need to assist the coachee in coming up with alternatives. Invite ideas, suggestions from the coachee and make sure that relevant alternatives are developed and allow the coachee to make choices about the most appropriate alternative. Encourage solution-focussed thinking and use brainstorming to develop alternatives. Offer your own suggestions with care – the purpose is for the coachee to develop options. Help the coachee to develop resilience, leveraging strengths and overcoming weaknesses.

***W**ill or Way forward:* What will you do and what is the next step? In this phase you need to assist the coachee to develop a clear plan of action. This needs to be specific and you also need to (1) identify potential barriers and (2) possible solutions to overcome these barriers. The coachee needs to commit him or herself to action and determine how progress is going to be measured. The formulation of a clear action plan will assist in the attainment of goals. Also assure the coachee of your continuing support and commitment to the process.

As already indicated, coaching is not a linear process. It is a non-linear process. For example, a session usually starts with defining the goal of session but after discussing the current reality you may move back to the goal setting phase and redefine the initially stated goals. The key of being an effective coach is to be flexible and adaptable – the GROW model only provides a map or a broad framework. It is not prescriptive and as you gain more experience you will be able to develop your own coaching model and approach. Coaching is a journey and key to improve as a coach is to reflect after each coaching session. In every coaching session, remember to do the following:

- Build rapport – demonstrate interest – try to understand what is important to the employee.
- Match your body language (e.g. posture, gestures) and maintain eye contact.
- Try to understand the employee's 'model of the world'.
- Do not lecture.
- Build the self-efficacy levels of the employee.
- Use reflective listening.
- Be open, honest and authentic.
- Ask open-ended questions.

The following structure: *phases of coaching for change* and *possible questions* may help you to get the coaching process off the ground.

Coaching for change	Example questions to ask
Developing a relationship and understanding the current situation	• How are you feeling about your current situation? • What makes you think you need to change? • What will happen if you don't change? • What is happening at the moment?

- What would be the good things about changing your behaviour/what is the worst thing that may happen if you do not change?
- What have you tried so far?
- On a scale from 1–10, how confident do you feel that you are able to change?
- What might you do to increase your level of confidence? What is holding you back?

Setting goals

- What outcome would you like from this session or what would you want to achieve by the end of this session?
- How can I help you get past some of the difficulties you are experiencing?
- If you were to decide to change, what would you have to do to make this happen?
- What is holding you back from finding a way forward?
- What support do you need to make this happen?

Development of options

- What would you like to see different about your current situation?
- What is your ideal outcome?
- What options have you considered?
- Imagine yourself in five years when everything is exactly as you wish. How have you changed from what you are today?
- Would you like suggestions from me?
- Which option do you like most
- What are the pros and cons of your selected options?

Future steps

- What are the next steps? What approach do you intend to use?
- What are the barriers that you foresee?
- What do you need from me or other people to help you achieve your goal?
- How will you know when you achieved it? How will you measure success?
- Is there anything else you would like to talk about?

The following conversation between a CEO and coachee captures the essence of a coaching conversation relating to the leadership of change. The GROW model (Whitmore, 2003) is used to facilitate a discussion about organizational change. The context of the conversation is as follows: *Christine (CEO), whose organization has recently acquired a competitor business as a wholly owned subsidiary and is now operating a wider range of services. She is concerned that the merger of the two companies is a major challenge as there seems to be a mismatch in cultures and she is uncertain how far to try to integrate the two sides of the business. She decided to make use of the services of a professional coach to help her to gain clarity on the major change issues.* Read the following coaching conversation:

Coach	*'So, Christine, it sounds like you have been really busy since we last met, do you want to tell me what has been going on for you?'*
Christine	*'We officially merged with Servenow on March 1st and the past three months has been about getting the basics right. We have not attempted any kind of integration beyond those legal, financial and operational things that had to be put in place. Plus we have been expanding and have started operating in two new localities since March, so my time has very much been focussed on supporting the operations director and the guys on the ground through all of that.'*
Coach	*'It sounds like you have had your work cut out. How are you feeling about where you are at right now?'*
Christine	*'Good. I think we have achieved a lot in a short time and I'm impressed with the Servenow staff. They are really focussed on the clients and I relate to that, there is a can do attitude that is really positive. But there is still a lot to do, still a lot that needs to change. When I think about what needs to happen it can get overwhelming. I know people are already really stretched so I am concerned that adding in additional change project is tough but I am not convinced we should go on too long the way we are. Maybe its not realistic to think about this right now.'*
Coach	*'I understand your concerns for staff, their buy-in and energy would be important going forwards. I wonder, would it be helpful to outline some of those changes you feel are important. Perhaps getting the end goals clear would help to tease out the scope of what you are thinking about.'*

Christine *'Yes it would, actually I have been doing a lot of thinking about this. I know I want to change to standard back office procedures where we can. And I think we can draw from both sides of the business to get best practice here. Then there is standard HR stuff such as recruitment and skill development, I think we can bring some of these areas together. We have already been forced to bring together some of the reporting processes but I know we have more to do on that one. I think the biggest question is on integrating cultures. We come from different backgrounds and disciplines originally. I don't know. Is it possible or desirable to try to bring people together under one set of values and behaviours or are the specific services just too diverse?'*

Coach *'OK so you sound like you have some clarity on getting common best practice procedures on operational, HR and reporting procedures. Are you in a position to articulate what that looks like in terms of success criteria before we move on to look at the culture question?'*

Christine *'Not yet, no, but I have a plan to do that and I'm meeting with my lead team next week to map those goals more precisely. People are pushing for some of this where they are supporting disparate operations in particular.'*

Coach *'So you feel OK you can get clarity on where you are going in this area?'*

Christine *'Yes, I think so. I think once we have met to discuss the goals and the scope of each project I may be able to understand the scale of what we have to tackle. I trust my team to tell me what is achievable and by when, so I guess at the end of that we can make some clearer plans about the priorities and the way forward there.'*

Coach *'OK so tell me a little more about the question about bringing together two cultures. What is important to you about this?'*

Christine	*'I think working to a common set of values enables an organization to operate from a firm foundation. Our parent company, Service Fast, has operated to a common set of values particularly relating to clients and how we want to do business. I'm not sure we have ever really made a big deal of it but the common understanding about really caring for clients amongst those of us who were here at the start permeates through the major decisions we make, Actually I felt coming together with Servenow was right because of their innovative client focus. Actually the innovative elements I think we can learn from. As I said earlier there is a real can do attitude with the new staff I would like to build on with all staff.'*
Coach	*'Hmm. . . so if I play back what I am hearing – you see benefits to the organization to have values that guide decisions and your approach. There is at least one core value around client focus that you share and there is mileage in building greater emphasis with all staff around the can do attitude, perhaps linked to creativity or innovation. Is that it?'*
Christine	*'Yes, partly but more than this, now I say it out loud I think this moment in our company history seems instinctively to be the right time to review and strengthen our values based approach and use it as an opportunity to be the best we can be by building on the strengths from both organizations. Servenow use more technical language as their focus is IT and infrastructure and Serve Fast has been more on the softer people services. Historically, our people come from different disciplines and use a different language. I'm wondering if it's possible to bring the core ideas together so both sides of the business feel their expertise is valued.'*
Coach	*'Wow. It feels as if you are building a sense of this being really important to you. Say a bit more about the motivation for this and what an end point might look like.'*

Christine *'Yes I am. Articulating the reasons behind it is making me feel that I have to put a priority on this. I think it can make the difference and maximize the strengths of two organizations coming together. In fact I'm starting to think that* not *doing this work is not an option. An end point would be bringing two organizations together as one using the same language which they can then apply to their own service models. This would build an appreciation of what each side is doing and raise opportunities for synergies and learning from each other. I think it could build engagement and motivation too. Perhaps it might even raise career opportunities for some in areas they had not considered.'*

Coach *'So where are we? Earlier I heard you say people are stretched, and I'm also hearing that this work is important along with the best practice projects we outlined earlier.'*

Christine *'Yes that is right. But I think we are always going to be busy, we cannot let that stop us from working on the more strategic stuff.'*

Coach *'OK great, so what options do you see for moving forwards?'*

Christine *'Well, I think I would like to start with my lead team. I want to get their input on describing and integrating values along with the practical projects. In fact, there might be an influence on what we do in terms of practical work so perhaps I should start with this. I also want to dig around a little and see what is written or implied in the values held by the two sides of the business; maybe I am making some assumptions about how far apart we really are. Or if there is a significant discrepancy I need to know about it now.'*

Coach *'What else?'*

Christine *'I'm going to sound out a couple of the Board, see what thoughts they have and how much appetite* *there is to invest in this work. And I'm wondering about resources, if we take this forward do I need some expert help to support us? I'm not sure at this point, maybe I need to talk to my HR business partner about that.'*

Coach *'OK, so would it help to recap what you have taken from the discussion so far?'*

Christine *'Yes, I have totally convinced myself I have to work on this culture change and to make it a priority. The people already say they see some benefits in practical sharing and integration so this work could provide a framework for that. I need to talk to my lead team, my board and my HR partner about taking the work forwards but after this conversation it will be about when and how, not if.'*

Coach *'Great, so when do you think you can get this moving?'*

Christine *'Right away. I will see Jane in HR this afternoon if I can or at least book a meeting for this week. And I will catch Norman from the Board; he is calling me about something else tomorrow anyway so I will add this to my agenda. I want to get some soundings in this week before I meet with the Lead Team next week. The full Board is in three weeks' time so I can follow up with some of the others informally then too. I have a couple of hours on Friday put aside for desk work, I am going to look in to getting some company documents pulled together for then. In fact I can ask Louise my PA to help with that.'*

Coach *'So is there anything else we need to cover before we finish for today?'*

Christine *'No I don't think so, I am going to take 10 minutes now to write up some of the ideas we have covered. It was useful to articulate the end point and the motives behind the work. I can use that when I'm enrolling others.'*

Coach *'How are you feeling?'*

Christine *'Great thanks, I can see a way forward now, and the emotional energy I was putting towards mulling over this I feel I can now put in to getting it moving. I feel as if I have changed my perspective. I'm more confident about why this is the right thing to do. I'm quite excited about getting started.'*

The importance of the ability to reflect is highlighted by Gosling and Mintzberg (2003, p. 56) and they put it as follows:

> . . . everything that every effective manager does is sandwiched between action on the ground and refection in the abstract. Action without reflection is thoughtless; reflection without action is passive. Every manager has to find a way to combine these two mindsets – to function at the point where reflective thinking meets practical doing.

As a change coach you need to do some *reflection-on-action*, meaning you are thinking about what you and coachee did, judging your own success and what you can do differently in future. Reflect on the conversation between Christine (CEO) and the coachee and do the following exercise:

A useful exercise. . . Analyse the coaching story and identify the following:

- Stages of the coaching conversation.
- Types of questions asked.
- Is it possible to infer behaviours used?
- Was the conversation successful?
- What will you do differently?

Critical Success Factors for Using Coaching During a Change Programme

Coaching is a powerful approach that may help employees to move forward in the change process. For coaching to be effective the organizational context need to be prepared and certain activities be put in place. The following actions may assist in this regard;

- Link the coaching programme specifically to the organizational change initiative. Be clear in terms of objectives, that is, what do you want to achieve,

who is going to be coached, who are the coaches and how are you going to measure success?
- Train the managers in coaching practices and communicate the purpose and expectations of the coaching programme.
- Design the coaching programme as an integral part of the change process, it should not be added as an additional afterthought.
- Monitor and evaluate progress of the coaching programme and make adaptations if necessary.
- Eliminate cultural barriers that may impact negatively on the success of your coaching programme.
- Coaching is not a quick fix – allow time for change.
- Create an open, trusting, non-judgemental and supportive environment for effective coaching.
- Demonstrate objectivity and empathy.

Coaching provides you with the opportunity to keep your change process on track, obtain feedback and help employees to accept the change. Coaching is a useful tool and all leaders should invest time to develop their coaching skills. Unfortunately, many leaders confuse coaching with a performance management discussion or believe they are excellent coaches. To be an effective change coach needs a willingness to invest time and effort in developing your coaching skills. It is not sufficient to have coaching practice sessions, what is needed is to reflect after each coaching session and analyse the content of the discussion, the processes used to coach and to determine the effectiveness of your coaching session. Reflecting on and learning from you own coaching experiences will enable you to improve your coaching practice. Finding answers to the following questions may be helpful in this regard.

- What did the coachee say?
- What did I say?
- Why did I respond in that way?
- How did each of us feel?
- What if I had framed and asked my questions differently?
- Would that have made any difference to the outcome?
- What can I do next – where can I go from here?

Chapter Summary

The chapter focusses on coaching as a leadership tool that can be used in implementing and leading organizational change. It emphasizes the integration of adult learning principles in the coaching process as this defines (1) how to approach adults in the coaching process; (2) the importance of building the self-concept and empowering employees to find their own solutions to problems. The use of specific techniques, for example, questioning and reflective listening were highlighted and the coaching process described. We emphasize the importance of using an integrated approach in coaching, that is, developing and maintaining a coaching partnership and the processes you follow when coaching. To become an expert coach needs time, a willingness to invest energy and to continuously practice your coaching skills.

KEY INSIGHTS FROM PRACTICE

Coaching is a process and takes an investment in time.

Coaching enables the change leader to keep the change plan and change process on track.

Applying coaching principles correctly and appropriately, can accelerate organizational change.

Coaching forms an integral part of the leader role and every leader should be an expert coach.

A coaching programme should be designed as an integrated part of any change process.

Develop a coaching plan which clearly states the purpose, stakeholders involved and implementation strategy.

Develop the coaching skills of middle managers and first line supervisors before you implement organizational change.

Develop a measurement system that will enable you to track the effectiveness of the coaching programme.

References

Bachkirova, T. and Kaufmann, C. (2008). Many ways of knowing: how to make sense of different research perspectives in studies of coaching. *Coaching: An International Journal of Theory, Research and Practice*, 1 (2), 107–113.

Bluckert, P. (2005). The similarities and differences between coaching and therapy. *Industrial and Commercial Training*, 37 (2), 91–96.

Bridges, W. (2003). *Managing Transitions: Making the Most of Change* (2nd edn). Cambridge, MA: Da Capo Press.

Flaherty, J. (2005). *Coaching: Evoking Excellence in Others* (2nd edn). Burlington, MA: Elsevier Butterworth-Heinemann.

Gallwey, W.T. (2001). *The Inner Game of Work: Focus, Learning, Pleasure and Mobility in the Workplace*. Toronto, ON, Canada: Random House.

Gosling, J. and Mintzberg, H. (2003). The five minds of a manager. *Harvard Business Review*, November, 54–63.

Grant, A.M. (2005a). A personal perspective on professional coaching and the development of coaching psychology. *International Coaching Psychology Review*, 1 (1), 12–22.

Grant, A.M. (2005b). What is evidence-based executive, workplace and life coaching? In M. Cavanagh, A.M. Grant and T. Kemp (eds). *Evidenced Based Coaching, Vol. 1* (pp. 1–12), Bowen Hills: Australian Academic Press.

Hooijberg, R. and Lane, N. (2009). Using multisource feedback coaching effectively in executive education. *Academy of Management Learning and Education*, 8 (4), 483–493.

ICF (International Coaching Federation) (2012) website, available online at: www.coachfederation.org/ (accessed 1 July, 2013).

Kernis, M.H. (2003). Toward a conceptualization of optimal self-esteem. *Psychological Inquiry*, 14 (1), 1–26.

Knowles, M.S., Holton, E.F., and Swanson, R. (2010). *The Adult Learner: The Definitive Classic in Adult Education and Human Resource Development*, MA: Butterworth-Heinemann

Kouzes, J.M. and Posner, B.Z. (2002). *The Leadership Challenge* (3rd edn). San Francisco: Jossey-Bass.

Passmore, J. (2007). An integrative model for executive coaching. *Consulting Psychology Journal: Practice and Research*, 59 (1), 68–78.

Ross-Ashby, W. (1958). Requisite variety and its implications for the control of complex systems. *Cybernetica*, 1, 83–99.

Shaw, P. and Linnecar, R. (2007). *Business Coaching: Achieving Practical Results through Effective Engagement*. Chichester: Capstone Publishing.

Solomon, R.C. and Flores, F. (2001). *Building Trust in Business, Politics, Relationships, and Life*. New York: Oxford University Press.

Somers, M. (2007). *Coaching at Work: Powering your Team with Awareness, Responsibility and Trust*. San Francisco: Jossey-Bass.

Whitmore, J. (2003). *Coaching for Performance, Growing People, Performance and Purpose*. Boston, MA: Little, Brown.

CHAPTER 7

Change Politics and Change Levers

Chapter at a Glance

In previous chapters the importance of leading change authentically, personal preparation for the change and winning the hearts and minds of employees were highlighted. Furthermore, the importance of having an understanding of what change truly means to employees as well as strategies the change agent can use to enhance change engagement, were explored. In this chapter the role of power and politics, the formulation of an own-change strategy and the use of context specific change levers are discussed. These components form additional building blocks and provide you with strategies and tactics that can be used to implement and lead change effectively.

Beginning Cases: Preparation

How do we use power and politics in leading and implementing change in such a way that it acts as an enabler? What are change levers and why is it dangerous not to develop your own change model to enact and implement change? Answers to these questions are reflected below and in the rest of the chapter.

Understand the reasons for change

Use appropriate levers to enact and implement change

Develop you own change model that reflects the uniqueness of your context

'I suppose change leadership shouldn't be undertaken simply for the sake of change. So reading a book and saying change will be built into your organization is not a good reason to change. The reason you change your organization is that by changing you will achieve business objectives more efficiently and more effectively. Change is not an easy process, it takes a lot of effort and it is a continual process. Change is also about the three "c's"' – communication, celebration and competency. If you use all the change models and change books to stimulate your thinking in terms of how to implement change your organization, then that is fine. Inevitably you will find that in the process of change you have moved a long way away from that model and I think that is part of the process. Every business or organization is a unique entity because of the people it has, the unique challenges it faces and there isn't a one size fits all.'

Understand how power is used in organizational change

Not all types of power are appropriate when implementing change

Real power exalts from leadership

Power should be distributed throughout the organization

'Power is endemic to the whole organizational system, and, it is so because, if you really think about power, what is power? Power is the capacity to get what you want, out of a system, out of an organization, out of a group of people or whatever. There are different forms of power and it could be coercive power by which you can force your power onto others for whatever reason, and I think that's a very weak form of power. You can have a form of secretive power, a secret cult type of power game, and that is equally weak, and it exploits people and perhaps exploits yourself as well in the process, but the strongest form of power, this is where it's relevant to all organizations everywhere, I think, it's power which exalts from leadership, from the capacity to persuade and to influence. And if you think of any organization, you have that requirement, within the organization, for somebody, some group, some individuals, to take leadership, to persuade and to influence and that doesn't mean that if the person at the top is giving leadership or persuasion and influence, that nobody else can do so. It's a

layered form of thing that even at the lowest levels, you can, you should I think in a healthy organization, experience leadership, persuasion, influence and none of those layers, of those three things are in conflict with each and the other. It is also possible that you can have too much politics in an organization and is it unhealthy or damaging to an organization. I believe, yes, you can have too much, very often you have it, and when you have too much politics in an organization whatever type of politics, it deflects the organization from perhaps its core mission, it's ethical values at the time, and it becomes corrosive and that I think is a very major, negative feature when politics enters into organizations too much.'

Dysfunctional politics may derail your change initiative

Chapter Introduction

In Chapter 3, the role of leadership was discussed and explored. It was highlighted that the leader needs to frame the change; shape behaviour and build capacity for change. Implicit to these discussions was the role of power and politics and change levers that we use to enact change and elements of an effective change strategy. Building on Chapter 3, we explore and operationalize specific strategies you can use to enhance your own level of influence during organizational change as well as strategies to implement and effect change. Reliance on mechanistic change models and steps is not sufficient to enact change. Power and politics are key elements of organizational life and having an understanding of how power is distributed in the organization will help you to move the change process forward. A key challenge for change agents is the ability to use power in such a way that employees who feel powerless are empowered. Despite the importance of power and politics in organizational change, negative connotations are attributed to the use of power and politics as a change technique. The perceptions or mental models we have about power and politics will influence how we use it practice. The next part of the chapter discusses and summarizes further lessons we can learn from real change practices and how we can use these lessons in building our own change models. The chapter concludes with a discussion on change levers and highlights the fact that the effective use of change levers is not only dependent on timing and sequencing but also on having an understanding of the context in which you want to implement the change.

Power and Politics

The concept 'power' has been defined and viewed in many different ways. It can be regarded as the capacity of a person, team or organization to influence others (French and Raven, 1959) or the ability to shape reality in such a way that employees do what is expected without the use of explicit power (Clegg, 1989). In organizational change, power is used to implement change and influence employee's behaviours and attitudes. It is, therefore, important to have an understanding of the power bases available to you. There are a number of sources of power and Beer and Walton (1987) and Hill and Judge (2010) propose a number of power bases a change agent can use to influence the change process:

- *Competence, expertise and reputation.* The higher your own level of competence and expertise, the more important it will be as a source of power that you can use to influence people. Furthermore, your reputation is probably the most important asset that you may have in an organization and building it takes a long time and it is easy to lose it fairly quickly. A strong and positive reputation contributes towards personal credibility and having high levels of credibility are important in any change process. Formulate strategies that will enable you to build your reputation: for example; actively seeking opportunities to become more visible, being trustworthy, dependable and walking-the-talk, may all help you in this regard.
- *Relevant experience and track record.* Having relevant experience and a track record of leading change successfully will increase your source of personal power.
- *The ability to develop relationships with key individuals.* You can increase your level of power by developing relationships with powerful individuals in the organization. Building relationships needs a focused strategy. Key questions you need to find answers to are: What do you want to achieve? What are you offering that will be attractive to them? What role do you want them to play?
- *Position in social and organizational networks.* Your position in a network, whether central or peripheral, as well as the number of people you are connected to, will determine not only your level of prestige and status, but also your level of power in the organization. The more interpersonal connections you have and the higher your level of social capital (i.e. number of relationships built on trust and trustworthiness), the more influence you will have. This may allow you to get access to information, resources and advice from the members in your social network.
- *Group support.* Highly cohesive groups, those where members are aligned towards a common goal and where high levels of trust exist between members, are powerful mechanisms to enact change.

- *Control over resources, knowledge and information.* If the change agent is highly skilled and is able to provide resources or knowledge that is highly sought after, he/she can increase their level of influence. This is also true if you control the flow of information, deciding what is communicated, whom will receive the information. However, the use of dialogue, trying to understand the interest and perspectives of the change recipients and exploring possible options, may be more effective than using manipulative behaviour.
- *Demonstrating charismatic behaviour.* Demonstrating behaviours such as being inspirational, involving people in decision-making, being sensitive to employee needs and effective communication may influence how employees perceive you. The use of verbal and nonverbal behaviours (e.g. the use of metaphors, body gestures and anecdotes) may further influence employee perceptions, emotions and mental models about the change.
- *Formal position in the organization.* This refers to your position on the organizational chart and refers to power allocated to your position in the organization. All managers have legitimate power and reward power (ability to allocate appropriate rewards) and coercive power (punishment and sanctions) serve as examples in this regard.

Given the changes in the external environment and consequent impact on the way organizations operate, it is important to revisit the way we use power in organizations. Power derived from your hierarchical position may not be sufficient anymore to enact and implement change. In order to cope with the complexities in the external environment, organizations moved to less formal and decentralized structures and team-based working. This influences the ability of a manager to use formal power sources and increases the need for the (1) use of personal power bases and (2) sharing power with employees. Conger and Kanungo (1988, p. 474) argue that managers should, 'through the identification of conditions that foster powerlessness and through their removal by both formal and organizational practices and informal techniques of providing efficacy information', empower employees. By creating an environment where employees experience choice, meaningfulness and impact (Thomas and Velthouse, 1990), and the willingness to share power, managers become more powerful. This can be explained as follows:

What is your real level of power in the organization?

'I think power is, it's about status and I think those are interesting terms, you know, a person's perception or their own power, may have very little to do with their actual power in the organization but then they feel powerful because of their title, or their role, or their control over certain key decisions processes

or be it that they may not be in any way affected by exercising that power, how they feel will come to affect their behaviour. The level of power they feel they should have because of their position is often quite at odds with what it should be the case or what is useful, but is really sure to try to influence how you manage change.'

How do you use your power in practice?

'They may feel quite powerful by virtue of imposing those rules and therefore whether they start out feeling powerless and therefore do that in order to acquire power or the feeling of power, I think, it depends on the personality. They may do it because they feel quite powerful and they may want to feel even more powerful so I'm not sure it always starts with powerless feelings, but in a lot of cases it's certainly a power play in that people use these roles and rules and key decision points in a variety of ways to exercise power.'

Do not underestimate the power of low level employees

'There is also power in sitting in the key point in the process, even though a relatively low level of people, for instance, the people who control the registration of students, maybe quite low level people, but in terms of getting things through the organization here and getting a program up and running, they are powerful. They can also make things happen for you that people at a much higher level would tell you are impossible, and they can suddenly make it all go away, if they choose to. But that's power. And so bringing them with you, that ability to understand that process, know who the key players are, often not the senior people at all, but also to build and do simple things like courtesy and being nice to people whenever you bump into them and just being pleasant and friendly and positive in your demeanour, I find goes a long way with people who don't really know you. They say, "oh, there you are" and they're kind of happy to see you, and you can use that as a lever to get them to help you. Because you can't really offer them anything, so that's a good test of, I think, of a learned skill over time.'

Politics is part of organizational life and (1) it is not possible to ignore the role politics play in any change process and (2) it can be used to the change agent's advantage. Politics is an essential skill in managers who wish to get things done. A widely cited definition of politics is the perspective provided by Pettigrew (1977, p. 85) and he defines politics as follows:

> . . . politics concerns the creation of legitimacy for certain ideas, values and demands – not just actions performed as a result of previously acquired legitimacy. The management of meaning refers to a process of symbol construction and value use designed both to create legitimacy for one's own demands and to delegitimize the demands of opponents.

The use of political behaviour can be regarded as power in action i.e. deliberate actions by employees to influence strategies and to serve personal interests. In terms of organizational change where the levels of uncertainty are high, political behaviour is to be expected. The use of political behaviour is not necessarily bad, that is, achievement of personal goals, but may 'be a means for managers to serve organizational goals when they have diverse opinions and beliefs about change objectives (Hope, 2010, p. 199)'. Irrespective of the reason of why politics manifests itself in the organization, the change agent needs to be able to recognize and deal with it in an effective manner. In practical terms it means that you need to understand the existing power structure, relationships between people and identify the key players in the change process. Take a look at the following quotation:

Power and politics are integrated in organizational life

It may serve as a motivational tool

Understand the impact of power and politics on behaviour

'I think power and politics are everywhere. As long as there are two people or more in the room there's got to be power and politics. You can wish it was different but it is not. It's a critical part of the human condition, it's what drives people, it's what makes them successful, you manage it by making it work to your advantage, at the end of the day you have to understand what makes people tick and what motivates them. You will have some people that definitely want to lead in the front, banging their chest, and want recognition. I would use this to my own advantage – if that is what lights a fire and what makes them effective, that's what I would play. If they are a different type of manager or different type of leader then I would do it differently. As I said before all change has to be effected, made happen by people. So to deny that, you know peoples'

definition of self-worth and how this makes me look. To deny that that's not a big part of how they internalize future state or changes – is just naïve – so you really have got to think about what it is going to mean for the individual, how is he or she going to look against his or her peers? I think you do have to have clear rules about protocol, what is acceptable and what is not acceptable, to make sure comments are constructive and not destructive. Simple things, meeting rules when you are having these open sessions, let you enforce rules such as respect and language and listening so that you do not line up opportunity for the board room bullying. Unless you believe you can effect change without people managing the politics and the egos out of it is actually a big enabler because it is the most base of human motivation there is and in many cases much more powerful than your bonus. At the end of it, it is about organizational hierarchy and status and all that stuff.'

You can use power and politics to your own advantage without disempowering individuals

To be able to influence, the change agent not only needs to understand the influence of power and politics on behaviour, but also have a clear understanding of what he or she wants to achieve. Putting it differently, you need to determine (1) what you want to achieve that needs the use of power and (2) who are the key players, (3) how successful will you be in influencing their behaviour and (4) what are the influencing tactics that you are going to use. Table 1 provides an overview of possible power tactics that you can use in a change context.

The successful use of influencing tactics is to large extent dependent on an understanding of the context, the stakeholders involved and their levels of organizational power. It is therefore important to develop an influencing plan, that is, having a clear understanding of *how* and *when* you are going to use a tactic or a combination of influencing tactics. An important step in the process is the identification of key stakeholders; the assessment of their relative importance and ways to involve key stakeholders in the change process. Drawing a 'power map' may useful to understand stakeholder patterns of dependence and interdependence. Table 2 provides the structure of a typical power or stakeholder map.

Compiling a stakeholder map will enable you to have a clear understanding of their level of power, their attitude towards the change programme, their

Table 1 Influencing tactics in a change context (Adapted from Flood et al., 2000)

Tactic	Description
Reasoning	Provide facts and details of for example the reason why it is necessary to change, that is, build a business case for the change.
Forming of coalitions	Getting support of, or influencing powerful or like-minded people to back up your idea or to support you arguments. The forming of alliances with powerful people will also increase your own level of power.
Delaying the process of execution	Actions are initiated but execution is deliberately slow or delayed. Asking for more time, information, more resources are examples of typical tactics used.
Bargaining	Use negotiation through the exchange of resources, favours, and so on.
Control of information	Controlling the flow of information puts you in a powerful position.
Use of pressure	The use of warnings, sanctions and threats.
Use of networks	Joining or forming interest groups that have a common objective. The group operates on the basis of friendships and personal contacts.
Impression management	This refers to influence the impression others have of you. Different techniques can be used, for example: • Conformity – agreeing with someone to get their approval. • Flattery – complimenting others in an effort to appear likeable.

Table 2 Stakeholder map

Name of stakeholder	Role of stakeholder in the change process	Level of power	Attitude towards change programme	Importance to success of the change programme	Influencing tactics/strategy to involve key stakeholders
Stakeholder 1		High	Positive	High	
		Medium	Neutral	Medium	
		Low	Negative	Low	

importance to the change programme and lastly, how are you going to win them over. It is obvious that if a stakeholder has a *high level of power*, has a *negative attitude* towards the change programme and is *important* to the success of the change, you need to invest a lot of energy to win them over. The use of reasoning, forming of a coalition and the use of social networks maybe used in combination to increase their level of acceptance. This can be explained as follows:

Ensure that you include all relevant stakeholders

'We have put a lot of effort into influencing the trade union representatives. By involving them in discussions, by opening up the books, supporting them to

attend conferences – we have tried to show them the changes that are coming. So they were very familiar with the reasons why we need to change. It was really about education and influence. The relationship between the senior management and the trade union representatives was very strong there was a lot of informal private conversations that happened between the CEO, directors and trade unions' officials. Well there are two levels on which the politics works that you need to take account of. When I kicked off this process it was very important that I got the support of the Board, the executive leadership team. It was to get the board to accept and support what we are trying to do and why we are doing it. The employees reacted very negatively and there were a lot of rumours – it was important that they understood why this was happening and what the ultimate aims of the organization were in making these changes. So that's one level of power and distraction and politics that you need to deal with. If you don't have a board understanding and supporting you are never going to make the change in the organization. Within the organization you have got an even more destructive force which operates at all levels in the organization. A very big challenge was trying to convince people of the personal opportunity in the change process – but not everyone was convinced. There are still individuals who are less open to change because they feel a personal threat to the change that's coming. So the challenge is to try and help people to understand the change. I have resistance but I think we are beginning to turn it over – you can't afford to shy away from the difficult conversation from explaining to someone that, yes, I know your title says that you are director of X and this new organization structure will not have you as director of X but it doesn't lessen how you're viewed in the organization or the influence on how your career will develop. So it is important to take that head on and be very open and honest and then to help the person understand. Positive re-enforcement is critical but

Determine contextual relevant strategies to influence stakeholders

Be willing to have difficult conversations

also you can't afford to ignore the resistance, the politics and the existing networks that you are breaking into and push that aside.'

The question then arises – what do I do, after trying every available tactic and they are still not on-board? The answer to this is dependent on your own role, position and status in the organization. Negative attitudes may kill your change initiative. A CEO explains his view and approach as follows:

Be willing to make difficult decisions

Empower employees by allocating sufficient resources for the change

'So how do you make sure that people actually go into change with the right attitude? By the way that's not to say that everybody has to agree with everything that you're doing because you do want people that will challenge but if somebody's going in absolutely adamant that it's the wrong thing then having had the debates, and if you're still sure that the change that you're making is right, if people still have the wrong attitude, especially leaders, there may come a point where you have to say this obviously isn't the company for you anymore because you don't agree with the changes that we're making but we've heard your view but we're absolutely sure this is still the right change. Because otherwise people could become blockers to change or worse, they could de-rail the change and harm the whole organization. And then the third one for me is whether we allow people to make the change and that can be about giving them the right resources, the right equipment, the right tools, the right funding or time, you know, are we allowing people to make the changes that we set out to?'

During any change process you need to be willing to make difficult choices and take personal risks in an attempt to influence key stakeholders. In order to do this you need to have an understanding of how to use power strategies effectively. It is all about understanding your own level of power, drawing on sources that may increase your powerbase and ultimately, the timing and use of power strategies. Managing power and politics in an organizational setting is not easy as there is no recipe that you can follow. The following story illustrates how power and politics were managed in a work context:

How to manage power and politics in the workplace

Be aware of the games people play

Be willing to speak out

Do not be afraid of conflict

'When I was working in the United States I was in a senior management role and a part of that role involved being part of a credit committee. Now there's a credit side of the bank, I was on the treasury side of the bank, so it was only because of my rank that I was allocated to this credit committee. So I was assigned to this, but I didn't have a background in credit, and the group, the rest of the other seven members of the committee was led by a person who was also my senior in the geographic location – were all credit specialists, had a career in credit and lending. So I joined this committee and very early on became concerned about what they were doing, they were making loans, that appeared to make no sense to me from the point of view of capital at risk and the return available which was what I was trying to do and there were transactions that I wouldn't have dreamed of doing in the side of the house I was in, but they weren't bonds, they were loans, so they kept explaining to me that this is a completely different type of business and you build up a portfolio over time and it'll all come right in the end, and it's all about relationships, but I just couldn't see the return ever happening. I mean, it was a purely financial issue, so I kind of sat through a couple of these meetings and read the documents and I couldn't make sense of it, so I brought it up off line with my general manager, who was the head of the credit committee as well, and he was kind of oh, he would kind of patronize me and say you know, for somebody with no credit background, I could understand how they wouldn't understand this, so anyway I said, well, look I'm very uncomfortable with the transactions you're doing so, you know, I've noted that we don't actually vote at the credit committee and everybody kind of says yay, or nay and a kind of a nod. I said I think it should be put to a vote, so he was most reluctant to do that but in the end conceded that and said, well I want it documented in some way that I have some issues with some of these loans, and so he eventually agreed that we could vote each week and so on, but

our relationship deteriorated very rapidly around this time. That wasn't something that troubled me greatly at that time in my life because I didn't find conflict to be anything that I wasn't well used to and so, anyway he agreed to vote and on a weekly basis he took the transactions we took forward and these were corporate kind of loans, participations, so they were multimillion dollar deals, which I was well used to, but not bad ones being done all the time. So it would go to the vote at the end of the meeting and I would vote against it and the other seven people would vote for it, so then there had been a tradition of, you know, after this monthly meeting of the committee we all go out for a drink and I became excluded from the drink afterwards. There would be mutterings of oh no, I'm going straight home and then I'd see the group hurrying down the street to the pub and they changed pubs to avoid me. I was living in New York, it was quite isolating, because these were my management colleagues, but I stuck to it because I felt it was completely wrong and I kept saying what I had to say. I could see, you know, they were property based loans, we were getting such a small return, we would never make money out of even one of them and if any loans we were doing went wrong we were already in a loss situation. If several went wrong, there was a very significant risk and it was a huge risk, so this went on for a couple of years. Towards the time I was leaving anyway the whole thing came home to roost and they started having to make loan loss provision against these loans. An audit group came from head office to investigate and the general manager was dismissed after an extended career in the bank and the loan committee members, all of them really lost their careers as a result. So, what happened to me, I was leaving anyway, but I was never mentioned in the audit reports, in the reviews it was never brought up with me that there was a document on record there that I had said, the only voice dissenting, and so, what did I learn from that? It was a values-based decision –on a personal interest basis, they would

Do not succumb to group pressure and sanctions

Be like a broken record – repeat your message consistently

Do not be naive and then surprised by the outcome . . . understand the endgame

> *have obliged me to shut up and just not vote or not go to the committee. That would have been more politics I suppose, because my career, if I had stayed in the bank, and it hadn't gone wrong, would have been seriously damaged by that.'*

Managers are not always willing to engage in power games or political behaviours believing that 'they are different and will not stoop so low'. This negative view of power and politics is a naïve perspective as it is not possible to escape power and politics in an organization – especially when you are implementing change. Surviving in a highly politicized environment takes mental agility, tenacity and the ability to strategize. The first step to survival is to acknowledge that it exists in your organization, do not ignore it or be unwilling to engage in playing the game. The next step in the process is taking 'a CT scan' of your organization – it is a bit like putting the organization through a machine and trying to understand the following:

- Existing power relationships in the organization – who do you depend on/what is the nature of that dependency?
- Typical games people play.
- The endgame of the political players.
- The strategies you can use to neutralize power bases.
- What power and influence do you still need to develop?

Surviving and implementing change in a highly politicized environment needs an extraordinary amount of skill. Being authentic and acting according to your own values provide a solid foundation for managing power and politics in any organizational context.

Change Management Practices Revisited: Designing Your Own Change Strategy

Managing change is complex and there is no formula or recipe that we can use to implement and manage change effectively. It seems there is agreement that the application of available change management models, recipes and approaches are not always helpful in ensuring change success. Conversely, organizations implement major change without having a clear understanding of contextual challenges that may impact negatively on their change efforts. Their change strategy is made up as they go along! Despite this awareness, we consistently use these models or continue having unclear strategies without an

Table 3 Best practices from the literature

Practice	Author
System and environmental diagnosis, identification of the need for change and the development of a change vision	Buchanan et al. (2005)
Development of a detailed change implementation plan, i.e. setting of objectives, determination of stages and milestones	Whelan-Berry et al. (2003)
Understanding and anticipating employees reactions to change and creating change readiness	Holt et al. (2007)
Creating a sense of urgency	Kotter (2012)
Building a case for change and effective change communication	Lewis et al. (2006)
Demonstrate leadership and leadership commitment	Kotter (1996)
Alignment of systems, processes and practices with the change initiative	Kanter et al. (1992)
Change practices need to be aligned to organizational context	Mayer and Stensaker (2006)

understanding of their influence on change success. It seems the way ahead is to formulate your own strategy, which integrates best practice and is built on an understanding of the operating context of the organization. From the literature perspective it seems we can think about integrating the practices from Table 3 in our change plan:

It is clear that the starting point is to have an understanding of forces for change, building a case for change and designing a blue print that will enable you to reach your change objectives. This blueprint should be detailed, dividing the change process into manageable chunks with clear milestones and communicated to change recipients. The communication must be clear, specific and enable employees to have an understanding of why it is necessary to change. A key success factor when implementing change is the demonstration of appropriate leadership behaviours and visible commitment towards the change process. Effective communication and leadership practices contribute towards making employees ready for the change. The change strategy should be contextualized, taking into account the unique characteristics of organizational life, strategy and culture of the organization. It is also possible to extract specific guidelines as articulated by the CEOs we interviewed. Take a look at the following narratives:

Visualize what change do you want to achieve

'You must know what change you want, you must visualize it, and you must have a very clear strategy and plan for yourself. Passion is a huge part of it. You can convince people if you are really, really

Be passionate about the change

passionate about something, and if you really believe it will work you have a better chance.'

Have confidence in your own ability

Do not be afraid to take risks

Inspire employees

Understand the emotions of employees

'But I would start probably by talking about that – it's about courage to always do what you believe is right for the long term good of the business and not just the short term. I think my advice again would be never underestimate if you think times are tough, how much your people will be feeling the same and therefore your responsibility is to live in their shoes more on a day to day basis rather than your own, to try and always – every time you're with somebody in your organization, try and leave them feeling a little more optimistic, a little better, a little more motivated about the future than they were before you started speaking to them.'

Identify powerful individuals that are going to help you to drive the change

'I'd do the change quicker, I'd cut deeper, faster. I took too much time, So some of it was around my own level of confidence so I moved much more slowly. I've got a good understanding now on how to identify the resistors, but also how to identify the people who are your change agents who are going to drive the change.'

Form a guiding coalition

'You should start with a very small group, four or five people, just a sufficient critical mass of people who have a shared view about where they want to take the organization.'

Make change a normal part of organizational life

Create change capacity

'I would certainly say make change a normal part of corporate life; encourage, train and educate your people to understand that change is a good thing, that they need not be frightened of it, that change brings with it opportunity and progress.'

Visualize what change do you want to achieve

Be passionate about the change

'You must know what change you want, you must visualize it, and you must have a very clear strategy and plan for yourself. Passion is a huge part of it. You can convince people if you are really, really passionate about something, and if you really believe it will work, you have a better chance.'

Be a bridge builder between the 'old' and the 'new'

'I think one of the things is that, don't make the change be about yourself, it is about getting the people who are in the organization to understand the change that is needed and then become the helper of the bridge building, as opposed it all being about you having the right answer, there never is fully one answer to the problem.'

Understanding networks

Change interactions patterns if necessary

'I think you do have to use that. I think it is important to recognize that that's what an organization comprises of. It comprises of a whole lot of informal networks very often. It's important to understand the networks that are there, who are the key players, how they are connected with to a network and if you do, and you will never know them all. If you do you can use it very positively by getting the message across and out and listen to other messages coming back in. So, you can use those networks in a very positive way. If those networks start to become destructive you have got to address it. You just got to go in and change it. You can offer them different types of networking opportunities by getting them into work groups by making them work in work groups.'

Engage employees

Demonstrate commitment

'Engaging people to get their inputs and to hear their issues and problems and then allocate resources, invest energy and a continued presence of senior management and leadership of the CEO.'

Building on the perspective of Buchanan et al. (2005) who highlight the importance of system and environmental diagnosis and Hailey and Bolagun (2002) who argue that a change approach should be context sensitive, finding answers to the following questions may be helpful in devising your own change strategy;

- Understand the implications of your own philosophy about change, your assumptions about people and organizations on how you may frame, design and implement change in the organization.
- As the change agent: what is your current level of power in the organization? How will you rate your level of credibility? What skills do you need to develop in order to lead the change effectively? What support do you need – who is the sponsor of the change? Are you willing to take risks?

- Develop an 'elevator speech' of the anticipated change – what is the change about? What is the business case for the change? What is the scale of the change? How much time do you have to implement the change? Who is being affected and how many?
- Visualize your change: what is going to change? What does it look like when implemented? What is going to stay the same? How will you define success? What does success look like? Describe how employees feel and behave after implementation. What did you do to implement the change? What barriers did you experience and how did you overcome these barriers? How did you evaluate the success? What are the linkages between the change intervention and organizational strategy?
- Understanding the people component: How might people react to the change and how ready are they for the change? What reactions can be anticipated? How are their reactions going to be managed? What emotions are they likely to display? How is your change programme going to address the phases people went through to change? What are their current skill levels and what new skills do they need? What actions do you need to take to create change acceptance? What are the social networks you need to be aware of?
- Understanding the organizational component: what cultural elements are supportive of the change? What cultural elements need to be addressed? What are the systems and processes that may hinder or support the change? What new processes, procedures and practices need to be developed? How competent is the leadership in the organization in managing change? What skills do they need to implement the change? Do they need coaches to assist them in the change process?
- Designing the change plan: what are the components of the change? Are there identifiable phases in the change process? Is it possible to break the change into manageable chunks? What are the contextual factors that may influence your plan? Who is needed to implement the change? What are their levels of influence? Who do you need to win over to support the change? What are the implementation milestones? Who is responsible for what? What are the resources that you need? What are the unintended consequences of the change? How are the sponsors of the change going to demonstrate their commitment? What is their role in the change process?
- Designing a communication strategy: what is the key change message? Who needs to hear it? What mediums are you going to use to communicate the change message? What is the frequency of communication? Who is going to communicate it? What feedback mechanisms are available? How is feedback going to be used to improve the change process?
- Implementing the change: what change levers are you going to use to implement the change? The following discussion explains the use of change levers in more detail.

Understanding Change Levers

As already discussed, change agents have a number of tools available that can be used to implement organizational change: for example; communication, social networks, rewards, training and development and so forth. Given the importance of using appropriate change levers in implementing change, this will be explored in more depth. Hill and Judge (2010) argue that the effectiveness of the use of change levers is dependent on (1) the timing (i.e. when you actually use a specific lever) and (2) sequencing of the levers (i.e. the order you use the levers). Having a clear understanding of how you are going to implement your change plan is crucial for change success. Using Lewin's (1951) model, that is unfreeze, move and refreeze as a frame of reference, logic tells us that the use of some levers will be more effective when used in specific phases of the change process. For example, changing the structure before employees understand the reasons for change (the *Unfreezing phase*), may be highly unsuccessful. In contrast, using communication as change lever during the unfreezing phase will lead to a better understanding of why the change is needed, what is going to happen and how is it going to impact on employees. The following discussion provides examples of typical change levers, their purpose and when to use the levers. An adapted version of change levers as propagated by Hill and Judge (2010) serve as examples of change levers that can be used to enact change.

Communication: Communication needs to be used consistently and continuously during all the phases of the change process: unfreeze, move and refreezing. Design a comprehensive communication plan in which elements such as key message you want to communicate, when do you need to communicate, so the timing of the message and who is the audience or recipients of your change message. Communication channels such as face-to-face meetings and the use of electronic and print media, serve as examples in this regard.

Building credibility: It is not possible to implement change or influencing others if you are not credible and trustworthy. This does not happen overnight and a conscious effort is needed throughout the change process to build and maintain credibility. There are various strategies that you can consider in this regard, for example, walk-the-talk; follow through with promises; build relationships; maintain confidentiality and show respect. The following story provides some insights of how personal behaviour, being authentic and forgetting about your own ego, can help to build credibility:

An example of how to build your credibility in practice . . .

'Let me tell you of a friend of mine. He joined a new organization as CEO and he was coming in as a completely unknown CEO into a very traditional, established, organization. He described his arrival

on the first morning when the company secretary was waiting on the steps to greet him, and brought him in. As they were entering the building, the company Secretary referred to the fact that a number of the senior management weren't actually in the building this morning, because they had to have a meeting about something and they were actually renting a room in a hotel nearby. However, they would be in for lunch to meet him and all that and to give him a chance to settle in. So anyway, they moved on down the corridor and the Secretary, with great ceremony, swung open a big oak door and said and this is your office. He described himself as astonished at the scale and the luxury of the office which he beheld, which involved oak panelling and a gigantic oak desk, a kind of a mini library and another office off it and a shower and bathroom for himself and then another office off it which was bigger than any office he ever had before. This turned out to be his assistant's office and which was equally palatial. So, he was kind of completely taken aback and said, well you know, this is extraordinary and he said this seems, you know, far too much for what I would need. He said, you know, in my previous role as CEO, I operated off a help desk. I didn't even have a desk, nobody was there – I didn't even have a place to sit. So he asked the Secretary to go back down the hallway and they had passed a kind of an alcove which had cleaning materials. He said to the secretary – "Can we talk about this basin?' and the secretary was most apologetic and said "I'm sorry you shouldn't have to see the cleaning materials." and at which point he said "no, that's not the issue, if we can get those materials moved somewhere else and put a desk in there, that's where I'm going to work". This caused absolute consternation, the secretary was almost apoplectic! He said, "well look, this solves the problem because the team that are in the hotel, can now have their meetings in that office that you were going to give me, because I don't need it, and would save a lot of money". This caused other consternation and the secretary was reduced

Be authentic and stick to your values

Forget about your ego, status and importance

Being willing to say no can take you a long way

> *to offering him his own office and offering to work in the alcove himself, and very funny I thought, that during the course of the next two days, each member of the senior management team individually, approached him and asked him, could they work in the alcove and give him their office, to which he refused. This was only nine o'clock on his first day at the job, so he had laid down a marker and I thought it was a great example of symbolic action really and a sure degree of wisdom about the kind of thing he needed to do to make change happen and he's still battling it, there's several thousand staff, there's a hundred years of tradition, there's unions, there's other matters, but he's still doing it and I thought that was a great example of how to get things said without having to say a word.'*

Visibility of top management: Visible support and demonstrating commitment from senior managers are key success factors in all the phases of the change process. Senior managers sometimes underestimate their role and visibility in the change process. Given the perceived differences in power and prestige between management and employees, employees scrutinize the behaviour of senior management for evidence that management is not committed towards the change. Top management should be visible through all stages of the change process. They can demonstrate their visibility by attending meetings, sharing information openly and honestly and walk-the-talk.

Training and development: Building the knowledge and skills base of employees is a crucial step in any change process. The key to obtaining any *return on investment* from your training is to do a comprehensive needs analysis in order to have a clear understanding of the objective of the training programme. In periods of uncertainty, such as when change is implemented employees may lack motivation to improve their skills base and it is, therefore, important to create mechanisms that will facilitate learning transfer. Preparing employees for the training: for example, conversations on purpose of the training, clarification of expectations of training application and the identification of learning transfer barriers, serve as examples in this regard. Mentorship programmes, internal and external training programmes also serve as examples.

Coaching: Having coaching conversations with your employees is a powerful tool to create change alignment, addressing emotions and fears employees may have about the change. Effective coaching can assist employees in the 'unfreezing and movement' phase of the change process.

Social networks: Understanding the power of social networks, the structure of social relationships: for example, identifying informal leaders, cliques, isolated people and so on, will help you to improve communication and the inclusion of opinion makers in the implementation process. Understanding the interaction patterns of group members may be especially helpful before the change is implemented as well as during the movement phase of the change process. Strategies such as the designing of a sociogram, doing a stakeholder analysis and observation of team member behaviours during interaction may help you to understand the social networks in your organization.

Clarification of organizational strategy and values: Aligning employees to the strategy and values of the organization provides a compass to employees that guide their behaviour. The designing of behavioural norms: for example, *what behaviours are supportive of the values?* will help employees to understand what behaviours are acceptable and should be demonstrated. The development of behavioural norms; value clarification exercises and reflection can be used during the movement and re-freezing phases of the change project.

Clarification of an organization's strategy and values help employees to understand the endgame of the change process. 'Standing in the Future' is an exercise that allows your employees to participate, build commitment and gain insights into the change process. Take a look at how the exercise can be applied in practice as described by one CEO:

Standing in the Future: a useful team exercise

'We use this approach called "standing in the future", to try to get the leadership, more than anything, initially, to place themselves in the future and try to articulate for themselves and actually see and feel how the organization might be if it was going to be 50% more effective than it is today or it has turned around and/or survived. It enables the leaders to identify what the organization would look like under a range of headings (McKinsey 7s are good to use. Taking the McKinsey 7s model (strategy, systems, structure, shared values, skills, style and staff) you would actually write these up in what we call middle level of abstractions (i.e. short enough to be understood but not War and Peace*), our systems would be x or y. Clear enough, so people can*

understand but not so much detail that it is boring. You then go back to where you are today, under the same headings, and that helps you to identify a road map that you can say – ok the end game is here, in three years, this is where we are now. Here is what we have to do in the first 3, 6, 12 months of the plan that would put us on a good platform, to be sure we're going in the right direction and then add the other two years probably in less detail. And what it gives the leadership is a framework for them, in which to have this conversation. It also helps you to decide on priorities, what are you going to do, in what order? What are the milestones, how can we measure delivery – all critical in shaping a variable plan for change. Their issue about change is, I want to make change, but I want as high a level of predictability about the outcome as I can have, because they're often terrified that the change process wanders out of control and fails – and they have to take the consequences of failure. What these approaches do is give leaders a framework, that they can speak intelligently about to other people, that they can start to own. A way in which they can give people a vision of why things are being done, and changes implemented. So it gives them context, within which people at all levels can be engaged in issues of substance.'

Cultural levers: Organizational culture is often cited as the primary reason for the failure of implementing organizational change interventions. Change failure occurs because the fundamental culture of the organization remains the same. The use of effective cultural change strategies is therefore crucial in any transformational change process. Strategies such as doing a cultural audit; changing of rites, rituals and organizational stories may enable you to create an organization that is built for change.

Feedback: Feedback provides change recipients with a clear understanding of *how are we doing?* and *what else do we need to do to get there?* Effective feedback provides an opportunity for change recipients to measure their own contribution towards and effectiveness of the change process. Use feedback during all three phases of the change process; unfreeze, move and refreeze. Strategies such as the setting and communication of goals and milestones;

the use of dashboards to demonstrate the status of the change project and the creation of learning forums, serve as examples in this regard.

Systems and processes: Effective change management depends on an understanding of the interaction and interrelationship among systems and processes. It is therefore important to determine (1) how the systems and processes are interrelated and (2) what needs to change that will support the change interventions. The involvement of key stakeholders, mapping and changing of key processes and changes in reward and control systems, may help you to institutionalize the change.

Structure: To achieve change success, individual work needs to be coordinated and questions need to be answered around the following aspects:

- Who has decision-making authority?
- What policies, procedures, rules and job descriptions do we need that will support the change?
- How many management levels do we need in the hierarchy and what type of organizational collaboration do we need to support the change intervention?

The changing of an organization's structure is a powerful mechanism to use when you want to institutionalise organizational change. It is also important to be cognisant of the down-side of restructuring your organization. Disengagement, lower job satisfaction and employee morale may be negative consequences of your restricting process. Ensure you anticipate potential reactions and devise strategies to minimize the impact of restructuring.

The effective use of change levers is not only dependent on timing and sequencing but also on having an understanding of the context in which you want to implement the change. While the levers discussed serve as examples of typical change levers, your challenge is to identify and use levers that (1) are appropriate for the change and organizational context and (2) will move your change process forward. Keep the following principles in mind when you design levers that you are going to use when implementing the change:

- Applying levers in the change process is not a mechanistic and fixed process. Be flexible and adaptable when using them.
- Having a clear change plan and strategy is helpful as it provides a roadmap of where you are going.
- Don't think of the change process as a linear process but view it as a cyclical, iterative type of process.

- Levers work best when used in combinations, don't view the use and implementation of levers as a linear and sequential process.
- Evaluate the effectiveness of lever deployment on a consistent basis. Make adaptations as necessary the chunks need to be achievable.
- You need people to see and understand the change.
- Celebrate successes.

The levers should not be used in isolation or in a linear fashion. Use the levers in combination as this may be more effective. It is important to critically evaluate the appropriateness of the levers used – this means you need to reflect on the effectiveness of the levers used. Learn from mistakes, be flexible and adapt your lever strategy. Some managers explain the use of levers in the change management process as follows:

Importance of power and credibility

Be flexible and adapt your approach

Be patient

'For successful change you need to have both power (in the form of information/resources) and credibility. It is also important that you can establish a sense of urgency. Having a planned approach is best and being able to use a variety of approaches (or tools) to managing change is a good approach as you need to be able to adapt your approach to your organizations unique environment and culture. It is also important not to be impatient or underestimate the power or relationships/coalitions within your organization. Most importantly you need to be able to sustain the change for it really to be considered successful.'

Obtain managerial support

Understand the power of social networks and relationships

Have a clear and well-defined strategy

'In order to achieve effective change in an organization a strategy must be adopted and must be executed very carefully. It is important to obtain support from managers who hold key positions in the organization and who also are in the position to influence as many people as possible towards the change. Therefore it is very important in order to bring about change in an organization to recognize and use the social and professional network. After obtaining awareness from the persons involved it is crucial that in order to maintain or increase support in the notion of change the success and progress of the change at hand is quickly exhibited or else people will lose interest quickly. Having a well-planned

strategy as well as the careful execution of that strategy is crucial for the effectiveness of change management.'

Culture

Communication

Incentives

'For me the key pieces you got to create: you have got to create a culture of change, a culture that embraces change. This sounds nice but the step you have to do before that is layout the need for change – you got to create dissatisfaction with the status quo. *That is really, really easy to say but hard to do. You need people to really understand and internalize and think about the degree to which the* status quo *will change. There is a huge difference between people saying it and people feeling it and at some point you have to make a decision about those people who are just saying it. That's my biggest challenge personally and ultimately how we weather that curve and which leads me to the next point which is: you got to create an incentive, a vision of what the future could look like. A vision of how change creates opportunities.'*

The successful application of levers in the change process requires skill and experience. Reflect on previous change efforts and change levers used in the past and answer the following questions:

A useful exercise

1. Describe the type of organizational change?
2. What levers did you use to implement the change?
3. What levers worked well and which levers didn't?
4. If you have to do this all over again, what will you do differently?

Chapter Summary

This chapter highlights the importance of specific strategies you can use to enhance your own level of influence during organizational change as well as strategies to implement and affect change. The importance of understanding the role of power and politics in any change process is highlighted and it indicates that there is no escape from organizational politics. The change agent should use power and politics in such a way as to be supportive of the change process. This is achieved by understanding the power relationships in the organization, the typical political games people play and devising strategies to overcome potential power and political barriers. It is further explained that the key to any change success is the ability to build a change strategy that is context specific. In this regard change implementation practices from the literature and practice are provided as examples that may be included in the development of a change strategy. Furthermore, different change levers are discussed and it is indicated that the effective use of change levers is dependent on timing, sequencing and an understanding of the context in which you want to use it.

KEY INSIGHTS FROM PRACTICE

It is not possible to ignore power and politics.
Power and politics can be used as a force to implement change.
Use a variety of powerbases to build your influence.
It is not possible to implement change without high levels of personal credibility.
Take the different phases of change, that is unfreeze, move and refreeze into account when implementing change levers.
Always evaluate the effectiveness of change levers used, be flexible and adapt your strategy.

References

Beer, M. and Walton, A.E. (1987). Organisation change and development. *Annual Review of Psychology*, 38 (1), 339–367.
Buchanan, D., Fitzgerald, L., Ketley, D., Gollop, R., Jones, J.L., Saint Lamont, S., Neath, A., and Whitby, E. (2005). No going back: A review of the literature on sustaining organizational change. *International Journal of Management Reviews*, 7 (3), 189–205.
Clegg, S. (1989). *Frameworks of Power*. Sage: London.
Conger, J. and Kanungo, R. (1988). The empowerment process: Integrating theory and practice. *Academy of Management Review*, 13 (3), 471–482.
Flood, P. C., MacCurtain, S., and West, M.A. (2000). *Effective Top Management Teams*. Dublin: Blackhall Publishing.
French, J.R.P. and Raven B.H. (1959). The bases of social power. In D. Cartwright (ed.). *Studies in Social Power* (pp. 150–167). Ann Arbor, MI: Institute for Social Research.
Hailey, V.H. and Balogun, J. (2002). Devising context sensitive approaches to change: The example of Glaxo Wellcome. *Long Range Planning*, 35 (2), 153–178.
Hill, L.A. and Judge W.Q. (2010). *Change Management Simulation: Power and Influence*. Simulation and Teaching Notes. Boston, MA: Harvard Business Publishing.
Holt, D.T., Achilles, A., Armenikis, Feild, H.S., and Harris, S.G. (2007). Readiness for organizational change: The systematic development of a scale. *Journal of Applied Behavioural Science*, 43, 232–255.
Hope 2010

Kanter, R.M., Stein, B.A., and Jick, T. (1992). *The Challenge of Organizational Change*. New York: Free Press.

Kotter, J.P. (1996). *Leading Change*. Boston: Harvard Business Press.

Kotter, J.P. (2012). Accelerate. *Harvard Business Review*, 90 (11), 43–58.

Lewin, K. (1951). *Field Theory in Social Science: Selected Theoretical Papers*. New York: Harper.

Lewis, L.K., Schmisseur, A.M., Stephans, K.K., and Weir, K.E. (2006). Advice on communicating during organisational change. *Journal of Business Communications*, 43, 113–137.

Mayer, C. and Stensaker, I.G. (2006). Developing capacity for change. *Journal of Change Management*, 6 (2), 217–231.

Pettigrew, A.M. (1977). Strategy formulation as a political process. *International Studies of Management and Organisation*, 7 (2), 78–87.

Thomas, K.W. and Velthouse, B.A. (1990). Cognitive elements of empowerment: An interpretive model of intrinsic task motivation. *Academy of Management Review*, 15 (4), 666–681.

Whelan-Berry, K.S., Gordon, J.R., and Hinings, C.R. (2003). Strengthening organizational change processes: recommendations and implications from a multilevel analysis. *The Journal of Applied Behavioral Science*, 39, 186–207.

Conclusions

This practitioner-friendly guide highlights the latest approaches, issues and pitfalls of change management in a contemporary managerial environment. It aims to address the most fundamental questions such as, *how do I manage and implement change in the workplace?* A unique feature of each chapter is that it is based on real CEOs' experiences, the 'lived experience of change'. This approach not only contextualizes change but empowers the change leader to build his/her own model or approach. Linking and integrating real-world experiences with current theoretical perspectives on managing change facilitates theoretical depth and insight into the complexities of managing it. The importance of leading change in an authentic manner is highlighted and the mantra, *be true to yourself* and *understand who you are* emphasized. For us, this is the starting point of any change initiative; that is you, the change leader. Leading change in an authentic manner is important and this can be explained as follows:

Why is leading change in an authentic manner important?

- *Authentic behaviour creates trust*
- *Authentic behaviour leads to identification with the leader*
- *You cannot declare yourself as authentic – it is ascribed to you by your followers*
- *Do not underestimate your employees' ability to recognize inauthentic behaviour*

A successful change leader requires moral character, a strong concern for self and others and ethical values. Why is this important? As change leader you need to influence employees and they will only follow you if they trust you. We argue that a clear understanding of your own values, motives and emotions and demonstrating this in practice will enable you to create a context supportive of change: a context that is characterized by compassion, trust and openness. This is made possible by demonstrating the following behaviours:

What does it look like in practice?

- *Congruence between actions and words is crucial*
- *Being authentic means also a willingness to share your emotions*
- *Be willing to be open and honest about the 'self'*
- *Being authentic is being consistently genuine and true to yourself*
- *Authentic leaders do not hide behind masks*
- *Able to create meaningful relationships*
- *Act with passion*
- *Behaviour is value-driven*
- *Be results oriented*
- *Walk-the-talk*

The question then becomes, *how do I become an authentic leader?* Acting in an authentic manner is a choice you need to make. The starting point is to become introspective, looking 'inside' yourself and reflecting on your current behaviour and leadership practices. The following actions may facilitate and assist you in becoming more authentic in your leadership practices:

How do I become authentic?

- *Making a choice to become authentic is the first step on the authentic journey*
- *You have the power to make the choice*
- *Are you willing to take personal risk?*
- *Be willing to experiment with behaviours*
- *Draw your life-line and make sense of your life story*
- *Becoming authentic is a journey*
- *Have confidence in your own ability*
- *Create and make use of support structures*
- *Use your values as a guiding compass*
- *Invest in your own development*
- *Create work-life balance*
- *Create space for reflection*
- *Accept yourself with your strengths and weaknesses*
- *Engage in dialogue about your strengths and weaknesses*
- *Be open and honest in receiving feedback*
- *Be human: humans are allowed to make mistakes, feel uncertain and inadequate*

Being authentic in leading change is beneficial as it influences followers in a positive way. If the change leader establishes alignment between values and actions, he/she will 'say what they mean and mean what they say'. Trustworthiness is therefore inferred by displaying characteristics such as fairness, dependability, integrity and honesty and this can affect work attitudes and behaviours. Authentic change leaders also exhibit patterns of openness and clarity in their behaviour toward others by (1) sharing information needed to make decisions, (2) accept others' input and provide constructive feedback to their followers. Further advantages of leading change in an authentic manner can be explained as follows:

Why is authenticity important in leading change?

- *Mental models influence how we lead change*
- *Need to understand one's own impact on others*
- *Open and honest feedback helps to keep the change process on track*
- *Change recipients need leaders who are consistent, trustworthy and leading by example.*
- *Being transparent creates trust between the leader and follower, fostering teamwork*
- *Articulating your values, goals and motives provides certainty*
- *Before you are able to address change recipient's emotions, you need to understand and make sense of your own emotions*
- *Being optimistic and hopeful about the change process creates energy and provides impetus for the change*
- *Having personal integrity will enable you to build lasting relationships with your followers*
- *Need to act as a role model for change recipients*
- *Need to develop authentic characteristics in followers*

However, being able to lead change in an authentic manner is only one part of the story. Successful change leaders prepare themselves before they embark on any change journey. They are able to make sense of their own change philosophy, interrogate their own motives and view change as a learning process. They are willing to forget about their own egos, take personal risks, identify their own strengths and weaknesses in leading change and make a conscious effort to develop themselves. They are aware of their own dysfunctional behaviours and have a clear understanding of the personal characteristics needed to implement and lead change. More specifically, they give attention to the following:

How do I prepare myself for change?

- *Be willing to change yourself as the starting point of any change process is YOU*
- *Identify what you want to change and implement small and incremental changes*
- *Be willing to take personal risks*
- *Reflect on the new experiences and identify key personal learning and insights*
- *Have a clear understanding of your own philosophy about change*
- *Develop your skills as a coach*
- *Create balance in your life*
- *Identify your thinking traps*
- *Use significant others to help you to make sense of the change*
- *Embracing change is influenced by your personal mindset*
- *Use not only work colleagues as sources of information but also friends and family*
- *Do regular reality checks*
- *Avoid sycophants who tell you only what you want to hear*
- *Don't shoot the messenger who tells you the truth*
- *Reflect on your own style of leadership and the impact it may have on followers*
- *Be merciless when managing time: create opportunities for reflection*

Effective change leaders are also highly aware of their 'dark side'. This refers to the part of our personality that we don't know or don't want to know about. So what has the dark side got to do with leading change? While the leadership of change is about having a vision, changing systems, structures and processes, it is more about leading people; that is, creating commitment, engagement and support for the change. Key to successfully leading change is the ability to form relationships, act on feedback, listen to people, not being overly sensitive to criticism and demonstrating empathy. Furthermore, you need to commit to telling the truth, reward those who disagree with you, admit when you are wrong and create support for being open and authentic. Great leaders inspire people to move beyond personal, egoistic motives. This is only possible if you are willing to avoid the following behaviour:

What do I need to be careful of?

- *Being narcissistic*
- *Your own ego, status and importance*

- *Not tolerating dissent*
- *Demonstrating paranoid behaviour*
- *Grandiose thinking*
- *Status and prestige*
- *Enforcing change*

What is also needed is the ability to understand and control your own emotions or putting it differently, having high levels of emotional intelligence. Emotionally intelligent leaders are able to create enthusiasm, confidence and optimism in their employees. The following may assist you in this regard:

How do I manage my own emotions?

- *Express emotions in an authentic manner*
- *Understand the impact of your emotions on others*
- *Interpret your own emotions and decide when is it appropriate to display your emotions*
- *Ask yourself what will be gained by showing your emotions*
- *Your own resilience is critical if you are to display emotion in a useful way*
- *Some emotions have to be managed privately*

To lead change effectively, you need to believe in your own abilities, be able to recover from setbacks, have a strong desire to succeed, focus on the change task despite environmental distractions, be able to cope with pressure and manage your own uncertainties and anxieties. In short, you need to be mentally tough to manage and lead change effectively. Having the confidence that you have what it takes to manage change will also allow you to take risks. Taking risks means making a conscious decision to accept uncertain outcomes when change is introduced. Change is inherently uncertain and making a mistake is not the worst thing that may happen to you. It is only through our mistakes that we are able to identify problem areas and learn from it. Experiment with new behaviour and create a climate for your subordinates that is supportive of trying out new things. This can be summarized as follows:

What are the personal characteristics I need to lead change?

- *Being authentic*
- *A strong self-belief*
- *Desire to succeed*
- *Being able to cope with pressure*
- *Not be affected by setbacks*
- *Believe in what is possible*
- *Be willing to act as a servant*

- *Make time to discuss what is important to employees*
- *Be open and honest*
- *Compassion can take you a long way when you implement and lead change*
- *Do not be afraid to take risks*

Change leaders are open to feedback and encourage employees to share their own emotions and feelings. They are not afraid to deal with the emotional side of change and actively guide employees through personal transitions. They encourage employees to share their own emotions and feelings. They understand that change management is not only about changing systems, processes and structures, but it is also about creating hope, optimism and resilience in their change recipients. In order to lead change effectively, change leaders need to demonstrate task-oriented, relational-orientated and change-oriented behaviours. Their leadership style can be characterized as adaptable and flexible: the context determines what leader behaviours need to be demonstrated. Effective change leaders also demonstrate the following behaviours:

What behaviours do I need to demonstrate when leading change?

- *Obtain feedback*
- *Ask challenging questions*
- *Be willing to hear the 'good and bad' news*
- *Create an environment where people are willing to experiment and take risks*
- *Be accessible to your employees*
- *Walk the talk and model the change*
- *Be willing to speak out*
- *Do not be afraid of conflict*
- *Do not succumb to group pressure and sanctions*
- *Be passionate about the change*
- *Have confidence in your own ability*
- *Be authentic and stick to your values*
- *Inspire employees*
- *Understand the emotions of employees*
- *Asking the 'right questions' will help in raising the bar and stretching your employees*
- *Take personal ownership for the change*
- *Demonstrate behaviours such as communication, coaching, counselling and listening*

When implementing and leading change, it is important to (1) allow employee participation, (2) communicate effectively and (3) engage employees in the change process. Managing change is complex and there is no formula or recipe that we can use to implement and manage change effectively. It seems there is agreement that the application of available change management models, recipes and approaches are not always helpful in ensuring change success. Effective change leaders do not use change recipes. They design their own change process and implementation strategy that considers the organizational context. This is achieved by involving key stakeholders in the design process, that is, not only managers but also employees. This context- specific change strategy is flexible and takes into account the influence of variables such as organizational strategy, culture, values, networks and power when devising the strategy. Change is viewed as a continuous and non-linear process and is achieved by creating an organization that is built for change. When implementing and leading change, the following can also be considered:

What are important considerations when leading change

- *Authenticity is a key attribute in leading and managing change*
- *Successful change needs thinking out of the box*
- *Successful change integrates the 'hard' as well as the 'soft' side of leading change, that is, head + heart = change acceptance*
- *The top management team needs to demonstrate their commitment*
- *Identify and use appropriate change levers*
- *Build trust by being open, communication and provide honest feedback*
- *What does the change history of your organization tell your employees of the probability of future change success?*
- *Invest time to prepare your employees for change*
- *Understand the role of middle managers in implementing change*
- *Promise only what you can deliver*
- *Give recognition of things that are working well*
- *Recognize the contribution of past successes*
- *Tell the employees what is going to stay the same*
- *Organizational values is a powerful mechanism to create an organization that is built for change*
- *Understanding your culture: identify cultural variables that may impact on change implementation success*
- *Ensure processes, systems and procedures support the change*

- *An awareness and understanding of the external environment facilitates change*
- *It is easy to understand the need for change on a cognitive level; it is much more difficult to accept it on an emotional level.*
- *Any change should be linked to strategy*
- *Organizational change is always mediated through individual level change*
- *Creating change readiness should be a continuous activity*
- *Change should not be an add-on, it should be integrated in organizational life*
- *Create alignment on all organizational levels*
- *Break change down into manageable and achievable steps*
- *Create an environment that supports the change, for example, changes in culture, structure and processes*
- *Change needs both leadership and managerial behaviours to be aligned*
- *Understand the emotions of not only employees in the change process, but also the emotions of management*
- *Be willing to have difficult conversations*
- *Be a bridge builder between the 'old' and the 'new'*

A key success factor when implementing change is the demonstration of appropriate leadership behaviours and visible commitment towards the change process. Effective communication and leadership practices contribute towards making employees ready for the change. The change strategy should be contextualized, taking into account the unique characteristics of life, strategy and culture of the organization. Important to any change process is having a clear understanding of the end goal of the change as well as communicating it in an effective manner. The following guidelines may assist you in this regard:

Where do you want to go?

- *Make sense of the external environment*
- *Visualize what change do you want to achieve*
- *Have a clear understanding of the end goal*
- *Translate the change vision into an inspiring message*
- *Implementing a change vision needs passion, resilience and optimism*
- *Understand the 'here and now' but take a long-term perspective*

- *Have a clear roadmap of how to reach the end state by formulating specific objectives*
- *Revisit your change vision regularly*
- *Test your change vision for clarity and acceptance*
- *Does the reason for change grasp their hearts and minds?*

Tell your employees about it . . .

- *Use stories and analogies to bring the message to life*
- *Ask well formulated questions to help employees to think and reflect on an issue*
- *Inspire employees and help them to feel good about themselves*
- *Empower employees and hold them accountable*
- *Explain the negative consequences of not changing*
- *Explain change message and identify change barriers*
- *Structure and communicate the message that it is relevant for the target audience*
- *You cannot communicate enough*
- *Personalize the change for your employees – what does the change mean for them?*
- *Frame change in a positive manner*
- *Be like a broken record – repeat your message consistently*
- *Be visible and communicate face-to-face*
- *Share own personal experiences*
- *Use different communication symbols to facilitate understanding of the change*
- *Communication should create hope and optimism*
- *Build the self-esteem of your employees*
- *Be open and honest in your communication with employees*

Organizational change is always mediated through individual level change and therefore successful change leaders emphasize the importance of creating individual change readiness. Change recipients are provided with opportunities and resources to become ready and embrace change. Importantly, employee feedback is not viewed as resistance but as a mechanism to improve the change process. The following may be helpful in understanding and managing employees' reactions towards the change:

What about the people component?

- *Get the right team on-board*
- *Recruit for attitude and organizational 'fit'*

- *Capability can be developed through interventions*
- *Employees with the wrong attitude kill change*
- *Empower employees by allocating sufficient resources for the change*
- *Anticipate potential resisters and formulate resistor management strategies*
- *Experiencing strong reactions from your employees does not mean they are resisting change – it shows they still care*
- *Build their levels of self-efficacy*
- *Engage employees in dialogue*
- *Participating in any change process is a choice*
- *Reward value aligned behaviour*
- *Be aware of psychological contract breach*
- *Provide recognition*
- *Create and develop employee capacity to change*
- *Understand the reasons for resistance*
- *Empowerment leads to feelings of personal control*
- *Create a safe environment to speak up*
- *Allow employees to express and share their emotions*
- *Help employees to understand their own change philosophy*
- *Build the confidence levels of your employees*
- *Help employees to deal with stress and anxiety*
- *Help employees to re-visit their change philosophy*
- *Ensure procedural fairness*
- *Empower employees by allocating sufficient resources for the change*
- *If the urgency for change is low, it may be more difficult to convince employees of the need for change*
- *Provide affected employees with choice*
- *Build confidence levels of employees*

To be able to influence, the change leader not only needs to understand the influence of power and politics on behaviour, but also have a clear understanding of what he or she wants to achieve. Putting it differently, you need to determine (1) what you want to achieve that needs the use of power and (2) who are the key players, (3) how successful you will be in influencing their behaviour and (4) what are the influencing tactics that you are going to use. During any change process you need to be willing to make difficult choices and take personal risks in an attempt to influence key stakeholders. In order to do this you need to have an understanding of how to use power strategies effectively. It is all about understanding your own level of power, drawing on sources that may increase your powerbase and ultimately, the timing and use of power strategies. Managing power and politics in an organizational setting is not easy as there is no recipe that you can follow. Reflect on the following:

What about the role of power and politics?

- *Understand how power is used in organizational change*
- *Not all types of power are appropriate when implementing change*
- *Real power exalts from leadership*
- *Understanding networks and change interactions patterns if necessary*
- *Power should be distributed throughout the organization*
- *Dysfunctional politics may derail your change initiative*
- *What is your real level of power in the organization?*
- *Do not be naive and then surprised by the outcome . . . understand the endgame*
- *How do you use your power in practice?*
- *Do not underestimate the power of low level employees*
- *Understand the impact of power and politics on behaviour*
- *You can use power and politics to your own advantage without disempowering individuals*
- *Determine contextual relevant strategies to influence stakeholders*
- *Be aware of the games people play*

Finally, if we don't care about our employees, moving beyond the rhetoric of 'employees are our biggest asset', why are we surprised when our change efforts fail? Despite all our models, theories and approaches we use in managing people and change, we are still not able to get it right. Maybe the problem it is not 'them', the employees, but 'us' or putting it differently, our inability to lead change in an authentic manner. Leading change in an authentic manner is a choice and it is in your power to make it happen.

Index